Mathematical Tasks

The Bridge Between Teaching and Learning

Chris McGrane and Mark McCourt

First published 2020

by John Catt Educational Ltd,
15 Riduna Park, Station Road,
Melton, Woodbridge IP12 1QT

Tel: +44 (0) 1394 389850
Fax: +44 (0) 1394 386893
Email: enquiries@johncatt.com
Website: www.johncatt.com

ISBN: 978 1 913622 06 0

Set and designed by John Catt Educational Limited

Table of Contents

Foreword

Abandoned cars strewn the roads as I made my way painfully slowly through the Lake District National Park in torrential rain and gale-force winds on a dark Sunday morning in November 2015. I was driving to a secret spot I know at the foot of the mountain, Helvellyn, where I would park my battered Land Rover and head off up the hill on foot. Visibility was low and the wind strong enough to have brought down multiple trees. But I loved it.

That evening, sitting in a hotel room in Kendal, I listened as the news informed me that the storms were set to worsen, and that all travel should be avoided. In the bar later, locals talked in worried tones about the river bursting its banks and the bridge collapsing. The hotel receptionist advised me to head for home. But I hadn't come to Cumbria just to climb mountains, the next day I was set to meet mathematics teachers from the north of England to talk about teaching for mastery and all that it entails. There was no way I missing the chance to meet teachers.

The weather on Monday 16 November 2015 was indeed worse than the day before and I found myself in an empty meeting room without a single delegate and several messages from our office to say that teacher after teacher had decided not to make the journey or had attempted to get to Kendal but failed. It looked as though the event would not go ahead, but three teachers had not been in touch to cancel, so there was hope.

They arrived eventually. Battered by the winds and drenched by the rain, but cheery and with the expectation of an interesting day discussing mathematics teaching. One of those teachers had come all the way from Glasgow. That teacher was Chris McGrane and we spent the day talking about and doing mathematics together. It is always nice to meet a kindred spirit in life. I adore mathematics and teaching mathematics, I adore mathematical problems, getting under the skin of something *prima facie* impenetrable, going through the emotions of bafflement, beginning, struggle and enlightenment. I adore designing mathematical tasks, role playing in my mind what some unknown person would do with the task. How will it be attacked? How might I change elements of the task to bring about different thinking? What will the unknown person take from the task? How might they be different afterwards?

It was clear, from the very first time I met Chris that day, that he shared that love of mathematics and mathematical tasks. By mid-afternoon, the hotel staff were regularly popping into our meeting room to encourage us to leave before the town bridge was closed, but we were having too much fun.

In the following years, I have had the pleasure of getting to know Chris. I have visited him in his classroom several times and spoken to him at length about mathematics education. I have also been able to enjoy working with him as a colleague when he joined La Salle Education to lead all of our work in Scotland. It was a great appointment to make, the guy is a really smart cookie.

When Chris and I started working together, I suggested to him that we should write a new book, which would capture many of the shared interests we have; task and curriculum design were the obvious targets and this book is the result.

This book is Chris's story. You will notice the first person is used throughout – this is Chris's voice and very much his book. My role was in suggesting the book and that it might emerge from discussions with educators. The idea of a series of interviews with a wide variety of thinkers involved in teaching mathematics and in mathematics education more broadly led to invitations being sent to the wonderful contributors you will encounter in the pages that follow.

We were determined at the outset to ensure that this book did not fall into the trap of education fundamentalism. Too often today, educators seem determined to place themselves in a tribe at the expense of considering nuance and the possibility that genuine enlightenment might lie in conversations with those with whom they disagree.

We were absolutely delighted that so many wonderful mathematics educators agreed to be interviewed for this book. Their voices, their contributions, their tasks serve to animate the conversation throughout. And we do hope that it is a conversation with you, the reader. We hope that you will take the words contained here in the good faith with which they are intended – it is not our intent to tell you a correct way to design a mathematical task, but rather to give you access to a range of approaches that a range of educators have found to be impactful in a range of settings.

General themes emerge, of course. Perhaps these themes will prove useful to you in your own task design.

As the interviews came together and Chris arranged them into a narrative, my role was then to help structure the book, check and advise on research and citations and contribute some of my own writing here and there (I challenge you to spot any of it).

We believe that it is through doing mathematics that pupils learn mathematics. And what is it they do? Well, they work on tasks. The task is the medium. It acts as the bridge from what a teacher knows to what a pupil can learn, and just like the bridge in Kendal that wet, grey day, it is a bridge that is strong and true.

Working on this book with Chris has been great fun and genuinely interesting. We don't always agree and that is at the heart of why I enjoy working with him – one thing we both subscribe to, I think, is Cromwell's Rule. That is, the use of prior probabilities of 1 or 0 should be avoided. We are both sincerely interested in continuing to learn and both understand that mathematics and mathematics education are not static disciplines – they are in motion, still evolving, still being added to. We are both very open to the idea that we could be mistaken. This is why it was so important to us to include contributors from across the full spectrum of beliefs about mathematics education and we invite you to think carefully about what is proposed, particularly when it is a stated position with which you disagree.

As the statistician, Dennis Lindley, put it, assigning a probability should 'leave a little probability for the moon being made of green cheese; it can be as small as 1 in a million, but have it there since otherwise an army of astronauts returning with samples of the said cheese will leave you unmoved'.

In reading the contributions within this book, I have changed my mind about several things I previously held to be true. Chris has expertly brought together the thoughts and ideas of some of the most interesting mathematics education researchers and practitioners around today, whilst at all times shining a light on these insights from the perspective of a real mathematics classroom and the practical challenges faced there.

Mark McCourt
London
August 2020

Biographies

In conducting research for this book, I had the privilege of speaking to and corresponding with a variety of outstanding mathematics educators. This book contains extracts from many of these conversations. A number of educators also kindly contributed tasks for this book. Below are brief biographies of all those who generously gave their time and ideas.

Mike Askew

Mike has been a teacher since 1978. He started his career in primary schools and although most of his work is now in teacher professional development, he still thinks of himself as a teacher. Mike has taught all around the world and wherever he goes is always delighted by the joy that learners, young and old, can find in mathematical activity. As well as being a speaker and writer, Mike is Adjunct Professor of Education at Monash University, Melbourne. He has also been Professor of Mathematics Education at King's College, London and was a Director of BEAM Education, specialising in the publication of support materials and professional development for primary mathematics.

Andrew Blair

Dr Andrew Blair has been a teacher of mathematics for 30 years in inner-city comprehensive schools. He has been the head of department in four schools over 20 of those years and is currently Head of Mathematics at Haverstock School in Camden (London). Andrew devised the Inquiry Maths model to harness and develop students' creativity, initiative and agency. Students learn to reason mathematically by following lines of inquiry and to regulate and direct the course of their inquiries. Andrew set up the influential website www.inquirymaths.org to share classroom experiences of mathematical inquiry. Teachers from around the world have contributed to the site. Andrew has a PhD in maths education from King's College, London. His thesis focuses on the relationship between inductive and deductive reasoning in Inquiry Maths lessons.

Sam Blatherwick

Sam Blatherwick is Head of Maths at Ashby School in North West Leicestershire. He has been teaching maths for 10 years and has been Head of Maths for two years. Sam's particular interests at the moment, as a Head of Faculty, are the development of reasoning and problem solving with lower attainers at GCSE level, and the development of conceptual understanding of higher GCSE content to prepare students for A level maths. He shares ideas and activities on his blog, www.logsandroots.wordpress.com.

Laurinda Brown

Laurinda Brown is a retired Honorary Reader in Mathematics Teacher Education at the University of Bristol, School of Education. She is enjoying supervising doctoral students, writing and editing as always, but missing teaching on the PGCE mathematics course that was the central part of her professional life. For more information and a publications listing, see www. bristol.ac.uk/education/people/laurinda-c-brown/index.html.

Hugh Burkhardt

Hugh Burkhardt is Emeritus Professor of Education at the University of Nottingham. He has been at the Shell Centre for Mathematical Education at the University of Nottingham since 1976, as Director until 1992. Since then he has led a series of international projects including, in the US, Balanced Assessment, the Math Assessment Resource Service (MARS), and its development of a Toolkit for Change Agents. He is the Project Director of MARS with particular responsibility for project processes and progress; he is also a Visiting Professor at Michigan State University.

Hugh takes an 'engineering' view of educational research and development – that it is about systematic design and development to make a complex system work better, with theory as a guide and empirical evidence the ultimate arbiter. His core interest is in the dynamics of curriculum change. He sees assessment as one important 'tool for change' among the many that are needed to achieve some resemblance between goals of policy and outcomes in practice. His other interests include making mathematics more functional for everyone, through teaching real problem-solving and mathematical modelling, computer-aided maths education, software interface design and human–computer interaction.

Hugh, along with his colleague at the Shell Centre Malcolm Swan, was the first recipient of the Emma Castelnuovo Award for Excellence in the Practice of Mathematics Education, awarded by the International Commission on Mathematical Instruction (ICMI). In 2013, he won the ISDDE Prize for Excellence in Educational Design for 'his leadership of the Shell Centre for

Mathematical Education, his contributions to a large number of its influential products, and the development of its engineering research methodology'.

Tom Carson

Tom Carson has taught mathematics in secondary schools in Glasgow and is currently the Principal Teacher at Hillhead High School. He is currently working on a doctorate investigating the link between thinking philosophically and thinking mathematically. He is particularly interested in how this might help prepare for shifts in attention as students work on problems. Tom can be found on Twitter as @offpistemaths

Jonathan Dunning

Jonathan has been teaching maths for 10 years, after an earlier career working for NGOs and the NHS. He spent nine years at Leventhorpe School, where he ended up as Head of Maths and ran the subject knowledge course for the local School Centred Initial Teacher Training (SCITT); for many years, he was also involved with the PGCE at Cambridge University. Jonathan is currently settled at Saffron Walden County High School, where his main interest is working with colleagues to embed effective tasks into schemes of work. He can be found on Twitter as @WaysWithMaths.

Colin Foster

Colin Foster is a Reader in Mathematics Education at Loughborough University's Mathematics Education Centre. His research interests focus on the learning and teaching of mathematics in ways that support students' conceptual understanding. He is particularly interested in the design and use of rich tasks in the mathematics classroom, and in finding ways to enable students to develop the necessary fluency in mathematical processes to support them in solving mathematical problems. His website is www.foster77.co.uk and he is on Twitter as @colinfoster77.

Tom Francome

Tom is a Senior Fellow in the Centre for Mathematical Cognition at Loughborough University's Mathematics Education Centre. He taught mathematics in schools and worked for many years as a Head of Mathematics and Head of Faculty. Tom established an innovative approach with his department, built on the philosophy that every pupil can develop as a mathematician through sensitive teaching, collective effort and rich mathematical experiences; this approach was recognised nationally when his department won the TES Award for 'Maths Team of the Year 2015'. Tom also contributed lesson materials for the EEFfunded project on Best Practice in Mixed-Attainment Teaching, and this work was awarded the 2016 BCF-BERA Routledge Curriculum Journal Prize.

Tom was previously a lecturer in secondary mathematics education at the University of Birmingham. He now teaches on Loughborough University's outstanding mathematics PGCE and, in his wider role at the Centre, works to integrate basic research, academic scholarship and practical experience. Tom is interested in all aspects of educational research, particularly equitable approaches to teaching mathematics and the development of expertise. He is currently conducting PhD research into the nature of practising in mathematics.

Tony Gardiner

Until recently, Tony held the position of Reader in Mathematics and Mathematics Education at the University of Birmingham. He was responsible for the foundation of the United Kingdom Mathematics Trust (one of the UK's largest mathematics enrichment programs) in 1996; he also initiated the Intermediate and Junior Mathematical Challenges, created the Problem Solving Journal for secondary school students and organised numerous masterclasses, summer schools and educational conferences. Tony has contributed to many educational articles and internationally-circulated educational pamphlets. He has also made contributions to the areas of infinite groups, finite groups, graph theory and algebraic combinatorics.

In 1994–1995, Tony received the Paul Erdős Award for his contributions to UK and international mathematical challenges and olympiads. In 2011, he was elected Education Secretary of the London Mathematical Society. In 2016, he received the Excellence in Mathematics Education Award from Texas A&M University.

Dave Hewitt

Dave Hewitt taught in secondary schools for 11 years, including five as a Head of Faculty. He gained a national reputation as a mathematics teacher before moving into teacher education. He worked as a Lecturer in Mathematics Education at the University of Birmingham, becoming a Senior Lecturer in 2000; in 1994, he gained his PhD based on the idea of the economic use of time and effort in the teaching and learning of mathematics. In 2014, Dave moved to Loughborough University to start a new mathematics teacher training course. In addition to initial teacher education, he has worked with Masters and PhD students at both universities.

Dave's research has focused on several areas including theoretical frameworks – such as dividing the mathematics curriculum into two classifications (*arbitrary* and *necessary*) – and empirical studies involving students' learning of algebra. He is also interested in the ways technology can be used to help students develop mathematical awareness and gain fluency. To this end, he has developed computer software including *Developing Number* and *Grid Algebra*. He has given talks and run sessions at many national and international conferences over the last 30 or more years.

Dave has always felt it important to have one foot firmly placed in the mathematics classroom, through his work with trainee teachers in particular, and one foot within the mathematics education research community. He has a strong sense of one informing the other.

Helen Konstantine

Helen has worked at the same Barking and Dagenham school for 14 years and became a lead practitioner several years ago; her role is focused on whole school CPD. Helen loves being in the classroom so she is not interested in positions that would reduce her time there. She particularly loves discussing maths with pupils: it is in these moments that she finds ideas for questions, activities or resources. She usually sketches something on the visualiser for the class at that moment, then creates something more permanent on her laptop later. Helen shares many of her tasks on her blog, mathshko.com

Gary Lamb

Gary has taught for fourteen years in four different schools and was Principal Teacher of Mathematics at St Andrew's Academy for almost five years. Now, Gary works as a Mathematics Educator with the La Salle Education team, leading CPD in Scotland.

Gary's main areas of interest are mastery learning, didactics and the science of learning. He is also focused on system-level improvement in mathematics education and is dedicated to narrowing the current attainment gap. With a lived experience of working with pupils who have lost faith in mathematics, Gary has spent much of his career researching and experimenting with ways in which we can rapidly improve learning opportunities and progress of low attaining pupils.

Dan Lewis

Dan has taught maths at comprehensive schools in and around London for 12 years, following a fairly unfulfilling stint on a graduate training scheme at an investment bank. For the past several years, his role has been as a senior teacher helping to develop maths teaching in his own school as well as supporting teachers from other local schools. He has also been involved in improving parental engagement with their children's maths work, which remains a passion of his.

In terms of curriculum, Dan's primary interest is in teaching and developing approaches to support classes working within a mixed-attainment structure. He is also interested in emerging algebraic thinking and, more recently, the role of proportional reasoning throughout the secondary school curriculum (greater than we might think, he would argue!).

Examples of Dan's resources, general thoughts on maths and maths teaching can be found on Twitter @4301maths.

John Mason

John is a retired Professor of Mathematics Education at the Open University. He takes an experiential approach to teaching and is interested in mathematical problem-solving, structure of attention, and the role and use of mental imagery. He now builds applets for his own interest and for use by others. Publications, presentations and animations can be found at pmtheta.com

Gerry McNally

Gerry has been teaching mathematics in secondary schools since 2007. Before that, he spent over 20 years working in the betting industry after graduating in Chemistry; he gained a second degree, in Psychology from the Open University, during this time. Gerry sees mathematics as one of the many expressions of the human mind's ability to seek, perceive, explore and exploit patterns and connections, with a view to making sense of the world and seeking coherence. To his mind, it is a creative and constructive world of ideas and he tries to reflect this view as far as possible in his teaching. Other interests include the natural environment and music; his blog can be found at germinalmaths.com

Dan Meyer

Dan Meyer taught high school math to students who didn't like high school math. He has advocated for better math instruction on *CNN*, *Good Morning America*, *Everyday With Rachel Ray*, and http://TED.com. He earned his doctorate from Stanford University in math education and is the Chief Academic Officer at Desmos where he explores the future of math, technology, and learning. He has worked with teachers internationally and in all fifty United States. He was named one of Tech & Learning's 30 Leaders of the Future. He lives in Oakland, CA

Jo Morgan

Jo Morgan is a maths teacher and Assistant Principal at a secondary school in South London. She wrote the book *A Compendium of Mathematical Methods* and she also runs the award-winning website http://resourceaholic.com where she shares teaching ideas and resource recommendations. Jo is very active in online maths teacher communities, tweeting as @mathsjem. She is an enthusiastic collector of antique maths textbooks and has a keen interest in how maths education has changed over the centuries.

Fawn Nguyen

Fawn is a first-year Teacher on Special Assignment (TOSA) with Rio School District in Oxnard, California. Before this, she was a middle school teacher for 30 years. Fawn was the 2014 Ventura County Teacher of the Year, and in 2009 she was recognised as a 'Math Hero' by Raytheon. In 2005, she was awarded the Sarah D. Barder Fellowship from the Johns Hopkins Center for Talented Youth.

Fawn blogs about her lessons and classroom teaching at fawnnguyen.com. She authors three websites for teachers – visualpatterns.org, between2numbers. com and mathtalks.net – and she is one of the editors for mathblogging.org.

Fawn has been a keynote speaker and workshop facilitator at maths conferences throughout the country. She is also part of the UCSB Mathematics Project leadership team since 2005. In 2012, she co-founded the Math Teachers' Circle in Thousand Oaks, California. She also served a three-year term as a committee member of NCTM's Professional Development Services Committee (PDSC) from 2015 to 2018.

Mike Ollerton

Mike spent two years in primary schools, 22 years in secondary maths and 10 years in Initial Teacher Education. He still loves teaching and is passionate about problem-solving, inquiry and mixed attainment groups. Mike is the author of many articles and several books. Mike's website is https://mikeollerton.com. Mike can be found on Twitter as @MichaelOllerton

Luke Pearce

Luke studied maths at Cambridge, then taught at Highgate School in London (where he was assistant Head of Department) and at Magdalen College School in Oxford. He is currently Head of Department and Head of Assessment at Geneva English School. He shares resources and blog articles on his website http://lukepearce.eu

Richard Perring

Richard has been working in maths education for over twenty years. In 2005, he joined the Devon Learning and Development Partnership, working as a consultant to help develop the Secondary National Strategies for Maths. Since then, he has worked in a number of roles, including some time as Associate

Director for Secondary at the NCETM. At the same time, he has worked on several textbooks and other publications and projects.

Now freelance, Richard leads Work Groups for his local maths hub and contributes to projects for NCETM, including the Secondary Teaching for Mastery programme. He is particularly interested in the use of pictures and representations to challenge students to think mathematically.

Richard can be found on Twitter as @LearningMaths!

Chris Smith

Chris Smith teaches Maths in East Ayrshire. He was Scottish Teacher of the Year in 2018 and is a member of the Scottish Mathematical Council, TES Maths Panel and Enterprising Maths in Scotland team. Chris is heavily involved in Maths Week Scotland, creating and running the national 'Maths wi nae Borders' competition since 2017.

Chris tweets as @aap03102, is married to Elaine, has three young Mathematicians called Daisy, Heidi and Logan and, carried along by the rest of #TeamSmith, he won the 2019 series of "Family Brain Games", a BBC programme hosted by Dara O Briain. Chris is passionate about puzzles and committed to inspiring young people with the undeniable relevance and unashamedly geeky beauty of Mathematics. His annual PiDay antics are legendary and the subject of his 2015 TEDx talk. Chris is well known for his Mathematical songs too- the piano is often out in his classroom as he leads his students in singing classics like "the PI-MCA", "Use a Ruler" and "Quadratic Formula Song". Since 2007, Chris has written a free weekly Maths newsletter with lesson ideas, Maths trivia, puzzles and a milk rota. The newsletter now has thousands of subscribers- just email aap03102@gmail.com if you'd like to sign up.

Dave Taylor

Dave has taught in inner city schools in Leeds for 12 years; he has spent the last 10 years in his current school, seven of them as a TLR (Teaching and Learning Responsibility) holder. He has a desire to teach children the correct maths at the correct time, and to build children's confidence in their mathematical abilities. You can find some of his tasks at http://taylorda01.weebly.com.

Andy Thompson

Andy is currently Lead Officer for maths and numeracy with the Northern Alliance Regional Improvement Collaborative. Prior to that he was a maths teacher, Principal Teacher and Deputy Head Teacher in Highland. Andy co-authored Leckie & Leckies's N5 and Higher mathematics textbooks. He has also worked extensively with, and for, the Scottish Qualifications

Authority and, until recently, was part of the examination team for Advanced Higher mathematics.

After moving to Shetland in 2018, Andy took on positions as an acting Head Teacher and Deputy Head Teacher, before taking the Northern Alliance role on a full-time basis. He has a keen interest in what research can tell us about mathematics teaching in higher achieving countries but retains a passion for all things related to good pedagogy. Andy can be found on Twitter as @thompo71

Anne Watson

Anne Watson is a retired Professor of Mathematics Education at the University of Oxford and her main focus now (of many) is the design of pedagogy throughout school. Output is at http://pmtheta.com. She contributes prolifically to the ATM journal Mathematics Teaching, often arguing that professional wisdom is a valid source of evidence for effective teaching.

David Wees

David is a former mathematics teacher turned educational consultant. He has 29 years of experience in education in a variety of roles and has taught in such far-flung places as NYC, London, Bangkok and Vancouver. David currently works remotely from his island paradise of Denman Island, British Columbia, writing curricula and running workshops for teachers. He blogs at https://davidwees.com.

Susan Whitehouse

Susan spent the first fifteen years of her career teaching A level Maths and Further Maths at London sixth form colleges, where she developed a particular interest in increasing access to Further Maths for disadvantaged students. Since 2010 she has been working as an educational consultant in a variety of roles, which currently include Pedagogy Lead and lesson observer on the MEI Teaching Advanced Maths (TAM) course. She is a co-author of the Hodder Education A level Maths textbooks. In 2011 she started sharing free resources on the TES website; they have since been downloaded 1.6 million times. These resources are also available via her website: https://susanrwhitehouse.wixsite.com/maths

Introduction

The respected educational researcher Michael Fullan coined the following phrase:

Focus on fundamentals: Curriculum, Instruction, Assessment and Professional Culture

(Fullan, 1997)

To improve the quality of learning in our classrooms, we need to constantly strive for improvement across these key areas. I like to think of these fundamentals in a simplified way:

- **Curriculum:** what we are to teach, and what the pupils are to learn.
- **Instruction:** how we are to teach.
- **Assessment:** how we are to establish the extent of learning and the effectiveness of our teaching.
- **Professional culture:** how we are to work together to become better at all of the above.

I've come back to this quote time and again. Every time, I give pause to the work I am doing. When I became a head of department, I regularly found myself very busy. I would reflect on how much of whatever I was busy doing had any impact on these fundamentals. The fundamentals helped to keep my eye on the goal.

On reflection, I began to realise that one of the things I spent significant amounts of time thinking about was tasks. I would scour the internet and textbooks to find tasks for my pupils to engage with. I would spend time creating new tasks. I would have conversations with colleagues about how tasks had played out in their classrooms. I would populate my scheme of work with tasks, to bring dry curriculum documents to life. Tasks were the focus of a significant amount of my time. It is this that leads me to say that tasks are the fifth fundamental. They are related to, yet independent of, all the other fundamentals Fullan listed. Doyle states that 'mathematics classroom instruction is generally organised around and delivered through pupils' activities on mathematical tasks' (Doyle, 1988). Given the central role tasks play, surely we can extend Fullan's list of fundamentals to include them?

Continuing my simplified definitions from above, we might consider:

- **Tasks:** devices through which pupils interact with the mathematics we are trying to teach.

This book begins with chapters exploring some theory of tasks before considering the role of tasks in the curriculum and the relationship between tasks and pedagogy. The second section of the book considers three broad types of task:

- tasks for developing procedural fluency and technical skill
- tasks for developing conceptual understanding
- tasks for use in the development of problem solving.

The final section of the book focuses on the creative process of task design. Before all of this, though, it is important to consider what we mean by mathematics and what it is to learn mathematics.

The first chapter spends time examining this, as our beliefs about the nature of mathematics influence how we teach. It is rare to find an author who does not have a bias towards a particular position. I am no different. My position is captured by Banwell and Pólya respectively.

In general, mathematics cannot be received; it has to be enacted.
(Banwell, Saunders and Tahta, 1972)

Learning begins with action and perception, proceeds from thence to words and concepts, and should end in desirable mental habits.
(Pólya, 1962)

I have attempted to be balanced, acknowledging the nuance that lies at the heart of every part of education. I am not an ardent defender of direct instructional approaches, married with drill exercises. Neither am I promoting entirely progressive approaches. Instead, I have sought a middle ground. I lay out an approach to thinking, rooted in pragmatic classroom reality, which I have arrived at after 15 years of teaching. I hope that this thinking will continue to evolve over time. I encourage you, while reading, to be critical and to interrogate the arguments I make.

This book does not attempt to convey mathematics teaching in a simplified or mechanical way. Instead, it is an attempt to bring to a wider audience some ways of thinking about mathematics teaching and the tasks we use. This is very much a book for teachers, written by a teacher. There is a plethora of knowledge about mathematics education, trapped in journals, and I have drawn upon some of this academic writing. I have interviewed some of the most illustrious names in mathematics education research, who have freely and generously given me their time. Similarly, I have called upon excellent classroom teachers to share their expertise and ideas. Much of the material in this book is fresh and won't be found elsewhere as it is drawn from these conversations. Where I quote somebody and provide no reference, it is because it was said directly to me in conversation.

I have written this book in the belief that every child can learn and every child is entitled to experience the joy of our subject. Education is not deterministic like agriculture or medicine. We can never say, 'this will work for every child'. However, I truly hope that what you find in this book will help to take your thinking and, more importantly, your practice, forward in a way that helps more of your pupils to learn better.

> *For every complex problem, there is an answer that is clear, simple and wrong.*
>
> H. L. Mencken

1 Learning mathematics

What is mathematics?

There is no universally agreed definition of mathematics. Aristotle described the subject as 'the science of quantity'. This and other definitions, which focus on magnitude and counting, fail to account for much of the content of the subject. Many areas of mathematics bear no obvious relation to measurement or the physical world. There are formalist definitions such as 'mathematics is the manipulation of the meaningless symbols of a first-order language according to explicit, syntactical rules' (Snapper, 1979). However, formalist definitions seem to make the symbols and notation the object of study. These definitions ignore both the physical and mental meaning of mathematics.

Henri Poincaré moved beyond simplistic ideas of number and symbols, stating that 'mathematics is the art of giving the same name to different things' (Verhulst, 2012). This quote hints at one of the essential ideas in our subject: the act of generalisation. Taking the specific, spotting patterns and relationships, and extracting an abstract generalisation that is independent of the specific. Karl Fredrick Gauss took the perspective that mathematics was about ideas, famously arguing that 'what we need are notions, not notations' (Gauss, 2009). A universal definition of the subject is unlikely to be agreed upon. The tension of the subject being viewed as both an art and a science is perhaps responsible for this.

Dave Hewitt describes mathematical knowledge as being either 'arbitrary' or 'necessary', hinting towards potential pedagogical approaches to establishing such knowledge. Some things require pupils to be told and other things can be found out by engagement with mathematics.

- **Arbitrary:** For example, one needs to remember the association between the word 'square' and a shape exhibiting a certain set of properties. You need to be told this – it is a convention.
- **Necessary:** For example, 'the angles in a triangle sum to 180°'. This can be established through many practical activities.

In his famous book, *A Mathematician's Lament*, Paul Lockhart takes a stand against a utilitarian perspective:

> *It would be bad enough if the culture were merely ignorant of mathematics, but what is far worse is that people actually think they do know what math is about – and are apparently under the gross misconception that mathematics is somehow useful to society! This is already a huge difference between mathematics and the other arts. Mathematics is viewed by the culture as some sort of tool for science and technology. Everyone knows that poetry and music are for pure enjoyment and for uplifting and ennobling the human spirit (hence their virtual elimination from the public-school curriculum) but no, math is important.*
>
> (Lockhart, 2009)

While I agree with Lockhart that mathematics is an art, it would be remiss to dismiss the practical applications of the subject in everyday life and in many other academic disciplines. Pupil experience of school mathematics should, where appropriate, acknowledge potential applications and engage pupils in meaningful contextual work.

Mark McCourt elegantly describes what it means to possess a mathematical disposition:

> *Mathematicians are curious in all aspects of their lives. Mathematicians, when faced with a problem, enjoy the state of not yet knowing the resolution (indeed, knowing there may not even be a resolution). Because they are curious, mathematicians, when faced with a problem, ask themselves questions of it. They can specialise, pattern spot, conjecture, generalise, try to disprove, argue with themselves, monitor their own thinking, reflect and notice how these new encounters have changed them as a human being. That is to say, mathematics is an epistemological model: a way of considering the very nature of knowledge.*
>
> (McCourt, 2019)

What is to be learned?

Contrasting perspectives on what mathematics is lead inevitably to contrasting views on what school mathematics should be. There is a necessity for pupils to learn facts and procedures: they need to develop fluency with key procedures and become intimately familiar with 'fact families'. However, Schoenfeld (Schoenfeld, 1992) makes the important point that:

> a curriculum based on mastering a corpus of mathematical facts and procedures is severely impoverished – in much the same way that an English curriculum would be considered impoverished if it focused largely, if not exclusively, on issues of grammar.

Similarly, Tom Francome argues:

> I don't subscribe to the idea that only experts can be mathematicians. I think anyone can be a mathematician by doing the sort of thing that mathematicians do: asking questions, making and testing conjectures, explaining ideas, being organised and systematic, etc. My teaching is about creating opportunities for pupils to do those things, but within the constraints of the curriculum. So, whatever I'm doing today there is the minimum of what everyone should get – 'the curriculum content' – but there is extra stuff around about it.

Tom's view captures my own thinking. It is important to acknowledge the curriculum material and to teach it, so that pupils can develop technical proficiency and gain a deep understanding of it. However, attention must also be given to pupils' mathematical identity:

> pupils need opportunities to develop a sense of themselves as mathematicians, as posers of problems, or inquirers.

Colin Foster shared a pragmatic perspective when I asked him what constitutes a positive mathematics curriculum:

> It's a value-laden question of what constitutes a good experience. For me, at the heart of maths is problem solving. It is being able to take an unfamiliar situation and make sense of it mathematically. However, I no longer think that problem solving has to be the main thing that happens in the classroom. Probably while I was teaching, I did have that view that real maths was solving problems and anything else I felt a little bit embarrassed about doing. I think that problem solving is the top of the pyramid but to make that really effective, we do need to do other things like develop fluency to get pupils into a position where they can make sense of mathematical problems. So now I'm

much less apologetic about focusing on things that aren't problem solving. But I still think that my main, ultimate goal is for pupils to be able to be powerful mathematically and be able to solve problems they'd not seen before – not just repeating stuff they've seen but being able to be creative and innovative. That doesn't just happen by giving pupils lots of problems; instead, I think there's work we need to do to get them to the point where they can do that.

The Singaporean curriculum places problem solving at its centre, with all other strands of mathematical thinking and behaviour supporting this.

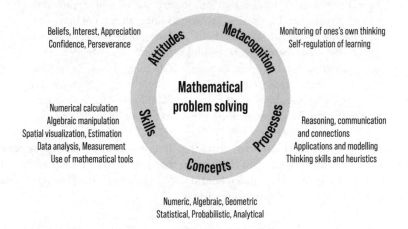

(Singapore Ministry of Education, 2012)

I write this book with the belief that all pupils can be mathematicians, can solve problems and can develop positive mathematical self-perceptions. I appreciate the real challenges of working in inner city schools in the UK, the accountability of the examination system and the negative attitudes many young people hold. However, I argue that we need to teach mathematics deeply, richly and in the fullest of senses. A focus on procedures and facts only is severely limiting and, in my view, part of the 'attainment problem' in our subject.

I use three broad categories of task throughout this book as the basis for thinking about mathematics learning:

- procedural tasks
- conceptual tasks
- problem-solving tasks.

It is only though engagement with tasks that pupils can begin to learn. All three of these task types are essential for a rich, meaningful, enjoyable and effective mathematics learning experience across the duration of schooling.

While much of the debate in education focuses on pedagogy, I hold the view that tasks are a key determinant of pupil learning. Informally, it's not 'how' we teach that matters, it's what we ask pupils 'to do' with what they are learning.

2 The role of tasks

The tasks teachers present pupils with and the way in which pupils discern mathematical meaning by working on tasks largely determine pupils' classroom experiences and their learning of mathematics.

(Hiebert, 1997)

This book has, as its main focus, mathematical tasks. One important question that needs to be addressed then is: Why do we have tasks?

I posed this to John Mason, who captured the idea nicely, saying:

from the most ancient historical records that we have, namely going back to Babylonian tablets and Egyptian papyrus, people have given pupils mathematical tasks. The reason is that it is only in approaching a task and working on a problem that you are doing mathematics. Mathematics is about solving problems. There are a lot of different uses of the word 'problem', from routine tasks, as often found in textbooks, through to completely unsolved things, which is what I tend to work on. I agree with Paul Halmos and various other mathematicians that mathematics is about problem solving. More specifically, I like to begin a session, even if it's a session on mathematics education, with some common shared mathematics, because I think it's only possible to talk about teaching and learning if you've had some shared mathematical experience that you can refer to.

Engagement with tasks results in activity from which discussion and reflection can follow. Anne Watson suggested that designing tasks might be about designing environments and situations which pupils can enter and possibly learn some mathematics from.

I want to use the word 'task' for anything that you give to pupils to do, be it complex or simple. For example, 'finding the missing number' problems such as '? + 3 = 7' are tasks. Likewise, something like 'find out the traffic flow on the Forth Bridge at different times of day and use that to predict if we need a new bridge' is also a task. You are setting up a situation in which somebody, through engaging with the task, has got to do some mathematics.

Tasks play a central role in mathematics classrooms. Lappan and Briars argue that 'there is no decision that teachers make that has a greater impact on pupils' opportunities to learn and on their perceptions about what mathematics is than the selection or creation of the tasks.' (Lappan and Briars, 1995)

Doyle, in his review of research on tasks (Doyle, 1988), suggested that tasks might be thought of as the point where curriculum, social order, classroom management, instruction and learning meet. This seems a significant burden to put on a task. Building on Doyle's writing, we might say that tasks are selected to help pupils engage with the curriculum content and that they are used as part of a teacher's instruction. The teacher might complete some tasks to teach – we call these examples. The pupils will then work on some tasks to interact with the mathematics. The tasks as examples or for pupils to work on are an important catalyst for learning to happen. The teacher might also choose specific tasks with social order or classroom management in mind. A rich collaborative investigation with practical equipment creates a very different feel in a classroom compared with silent work on a drill exercise. I can recall several challenging groups I have taught where the task selection was also informed by classroom management considerations.

According to Doyle, tasks can be thought of as having the following components. In every case I have expanded his definition to include more ideas.

Product	In many cases, the product of a task is the answer to the questions within the task. It might be an oral response, a worked solution shared by a pupil with other members of the class, a poster, or a completed card sort. Anything which is the result of pupil work (written or mental) is the product: the product is the end point of the task.
Process	The process involves the operations used to produce the product. For example, this might involve applying some 'rule', selecting appropriate answers from a list, formulating a solution to a novel problem, classifying objects by their properties, or representing an idea in an alternative way. The process is the activity the pupils undertake.

Resources	These are the tools available to pupils in the process phase, for example, notes and examples, textbooks, concrete manipulatives, or conversations with other pupils or the teacher. Anything which can help pupils to process the task is a resource.
Accountability	In some tasks, the stakes are high; summative examinations are the obvious example. In contrast, formative assessment tasks – while still important – are generally less weighted. Routine classwork, where the teacher might not check pupil solutions, may be perceived as 'low stakes'. For other tasks, involving group work, pupils might be accountable to each other through the implicit social contract among peers. Homework tasks might have high levels of accountability for a different reason – for example, there may be negative consequences for the pupil if the work is not completed.

In Doyle's research review, he notes that most of the classes involved in studies were set up for efficient production: in terms of the components listed above, he observed a focus on the product. The classrooms were set up around routine ways of working, such as warm-ups or sets of exercises. Typically, work was defined explicitly and pupils were given a lot of guidance. Tasks in these high-production classrooms were usually familiar and pupils were rarely required to assemble information or processes in ways that had not been demonstrated. The content was divided into small chunks and instruction focused on algorithmic 'steps' to be taken. Having pupils engage in routine work is a valid pedagogical choice. However, as I will argue throughout this book, pupils need engagement in a range of mathematical activities to develop a complete understanding and to develop their mathematical actions and patterns of thinking.

Of course, the product of pupil work is important. We can establish whether pupils have mastered some procedure, if they can produce correct answers. However, if pupils do not succeed then we need to examine the process. Further, in the development of conceptual understanding and problem solving, a focus on the product is insufficient. Tasks are the catalyst for the process. The physical dimension of the process is what the pupil does, but the key concern for us as teachers should be the mental dimension – what the pupil is thinking about. A core principle of this book is that the nature of pupil (cognitive) activity is what influences the acquisition of understanding, meaning and overall learning.

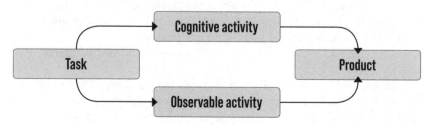

When choosing a task, we should first consider the question, 'what will pupils think about?'

Tasks and activity

Mathematics can be thought of as being made up of various topics. These topics are, among other things, collections of definitions, ideas, procedures, relationships, theorems, concepts, representations, language and behaviours. Tasks act as a bridge between the mathematics and the pupils. They serve as a basis for pupils to interact with mathematics in purposeful ways and, hopefully, to develop some level of understanding. This interaction takes the form of 'activity'. This activity is distinct from the task itself; rather, it is the mathematical processes in which pupils engage while doing the task. This distinction is important because pupils may work on a task without the desired level of mathematical activity. When actions become devoid of meaning, there is unlikely to be learning. Engagement is a poor proxy for learning.

Mason and Johnston-Wilder capture this concisely:

> The purpose of a task is to initiate mathematically fruitful activity that leads to a transformation in what learners are sensitised to notice and competent to carry out.
>
> (Mason and Johnston-Wilder, 2006)

In creating, selecting or adapting tasks, teachers need to consider how the likely actions of pupils will connect with the intended learning. In working on tasks, pupils may encounter specific mathematical concepts, practise techniques and have opportunities to behave mathematically. However, even having successfully completed a task and engaged in significant mathematical activity, there is no guarantee that pupils will have learned.

Christiansen and Walther explain that the tasks given to pupils, and their associated activity, are the basis for mathematical interaction between the teacher and pupils. They emphasise the social nature of learning:

> Learning cannot take place through activity performed by an individual in isolation, but must unfold in relation to activity mediated by other persons – the teacher, the parents, the peer group etc.
>
> (Christiansen and Walther, 1986)

Tasks play a key role in enabling meaningful interactions. When I spoke to Anne Watson, she said there were other purposes for designing tasks which we might consider. For example, some tasks might be about developing 'the social working climate of the classroom – tasks which promote discussion or develop groupwork'. If the interactions support the tasks we want pupils to work on, we can use other tasks to develop those interactions. It might be that we use some tasks which are 'maths-lite' to establish ways of working, before ramping up the cognitive demand.

Teachers cannot do the learning for pupils, but an important teacher action is to initiate reflection on the activity and to draw together the intended learning. This is good practice whatever sort of task pupils have been engaged in – be it a routine textbook exercise or a rich investigation: otherwise, despite meticulous planning, it is possible for pupils to engage in a task without recognising the point of the activity.

> *They can copy and complete a table of values without ever becoming aware of the relationships in the table; they can draw a diagram as an exercise in copying, without ever paying attention to how the diagram is built up, what can change and what relationships are invariant; they can do a suite of exercises, get most or all of them correct, and yet not learn anything from the effort.*
>
> (Mason and Johnston-Wilder, 2006)

Standing back to reflect on the task solution and the thinking used in completion of the task is essential. In some cases, the task may be constructed such that this reflection is a built-in design feature, but generally this reflection is explicitly prompted by the teacher. This might be a whole-class discussion, or an opportunity for pupils to talk in pairs. Over time, successful learners of mathematics can develop this metacognitive strategy and use it without prompting. Tahta expressed the notion of inner and outer tasks: the outer task is what the pupil is explicitly asked to do, whereas the inner task is the awareness and understanding the teacher hopes the pupil will encounter and develop through doing the task. The teacher needs to ensure the inner task is visible to all pupils (Tahta, 1981).

Askew offers words of caution:

> *If children are going to develop mathematical confidence, curiosity and a have-a-go attitude, there needs to be a certain 'gap' between the task that a teacher sets and the children's subsequent mathematical activity. Teaching which strives to narrow the gap between task and activity, for example through careful instructions that children have to follow, may lead to short-term success but not long-term learning.*
>
> (Askew, 2015)

With this in mind, we need to be careful when talking about what it means for a lesson to 'go well'. If a pupil fails to complete a task, we should not automatically assume this is a negative outcome. The pupil might have been engaged in a high level of productive cognitive activity and made significant steps in their learning, even if the product is not evident. The focus, again, has to be on the mathematical activity in which the pupil engaged. The role of the teacher is to use a range of strategies, possibly involving other tasks, to establish what the pupil now understands of the ideas. It is not the task itself which is important. Instead, understanding of the mathematics is the key focus. Johnston-Wilder and Mason emphasise the value of making the distinction between task and activity – that it:

> helps to free teachers from expectations that learners will all do the same thing in the same way, and to open up sensitivity to the richness of what emerges. This will also facilitate awareness of the kinds of questions to ask which might promote particular mathematical awarenesses and thinking.
>
> (Johnston-Wilder and Mason, 2004)

One of the problems we face is that it is much easier to think about tasks in terms of what pupils will do, rather than what they will think. It is easier to manipulate actions and behaviour than thought processes. Anne Watson explained the problem with this as follows:

> What is it that we create in a learner's mind about what it means to do mathematics? **Do** is the verb. What we do is teach them lots of things to do. We solve, we calculate, we simplify, we expand. Everything is an imperative verb, and yet we know that this is not mathematics. We are very busy giving them the view that mathematics is about deciding what to do, working out what do and remembering what to do. Think of the contrast in the questions:
>
> - What did you do in maths today?
> - What did you learn in maths today?
> - What was the big idea in maths today?
>
> When there is an emphasis on the word do we have pupils being able to say that we were factorising quadratics, but not actually being able to say very much about what quadratics are or how they relate to anything else they have previously learned. So, to me, the conjecturing,

proving, discerning etc are part of the mathematics and I think that those need to be embedded in the way the classroom operates. Even if I've got the missing number problem, ? + 3 = 7, this isn't about what you do, it is about what this means. The key question is about how we read this. We read it as 'I don't know what this number is, but I do know if I add 3 to it I get 7.' Then you can decide what to do. In secondary, learners encounter x + 3 = 7 and we are suddenly very busy balancing etc but have lost a sense of what it is we are doing. Tasks don't live alone, there has to be an associated pedagogy. I am deeply worried that a lot of the discussion at the moment is not about the pedagogy, it is about what do we do. Then somehow, we hope that learners make mathematical sense of it. But what we are actually training them in is what they have to do. When pupils see a test question, they ask 'what do I do?' not 'what does this mean?'. It is all about the culture. The culture of doing and remembering is not mathematical culture to my mind.

When I do maths for myself, I have noticed why I get stuck. It is usually that I haven't sufficiently thought 'what does it mean?' and I've gone into doing things, such as expressing in algebra and doing manipulation before I've really thought about the meaning properly.

General focus	Examples of specific actions
basic actions	calculating, doing procedures, stating facts
transformative	organising, rearranging, systematising, visualising, representing
concept-building	comparing, classifying, generalising, structuring, extending, restricting, defining, relating to familiar and intuitive ideas
problem-solving, proving, applying	conjecturing, assuming, symbolising, modelling, predicting, explaining, verifying, justifying, refuting, testing special cases
interdisciplinary connections	incorporating other epistemologies, identifying variables and structures, recognising similarities, comparing familiar/unfamiliar

(Watson and Ohtani, 2015)

The table above illustrates some specific actions related to intended task purposes. The actions below the top line are more likely to involve higher order thinking. When creating, selecting or adapting tasks, teachers should have in mind not only the task purpose but also the actions that will be involved. It is straightforward to have pupils perform basic actions such as calculating, doing procedures or stating facts. This is what makes up the majority of textbook questions in the UK. It is harder to create tasks which will invoke a range of concept-building actions. It is important that teachers recognise tasks which address these needs in addition to content requirements. A skilled teacher can elevate a routine task so that actions beyond the basic are required of pupils.

For concept building and development of problem solving, pupils need opportunities to think beyond basic actions. During and after engaging in these actions, dialogue is essential. Pupils require opportunities to express ideas and share their thinking with each other and with their teacher. The teacher plays an important role in prompting, questioning and offering potential actions for consideration. If we consider the actions associated with 'problem-solving, proving, applying' (in the table above), these terms need to become part of the descriptive language used in the classroom. The teacher can promote this while developing ways of working with a class.

Layers of experience

To learn mathematics means to develop an awareness of the object of study. This begins with the pupil interacting with the mathematics in some purposeful way. Through a succession of appropriate tasks, the properties of the topic can be appreciated and internalised. Completion of tasks alone is rarely adequate; reflection on the end product and the process undertaken to arrive there are also important. If one takes the view of a topic as being more than just a list of procedures to be practised or a series of definitions to be learned, there is an inevitable widening of the range of mathematical task types required for learning. John Mason has often said: 'Teaching takes place in time; learning takes place over time.'

That is, teaching is an observable act: it is something tangible that can be witnessed. Learning, however, is not observable and cannot be witnessed. Learning is the result of a range of experiences over time. This has consequences when planning to use tasks. In the short term, pupils need to interact with new ideas in a variety of ways to develop conceptual understanding. In the long term, the maturation of these ideas will support problem solving, if they are routinely revisited and built upon.

When selecting, adapting and creating tasks, we may have one or several possible purposes in mind. I offer a non-exhaustive list of potential task purposes:

- develop fluency with algorithms
- learn definitions and theorems
- recognise when to apply an algorithm
- practice for exams

- interpret ideas
- contrast alternative approaches
- use problem-solving processes
- develop understanding of concepts
- develop an awareness of how ideas connect to previous learning
- develop awareness of multiple representations.

If the purposes of tasks are rooted solely in the first four items above, pupils will not gain a rounded experience of mathematics. I argue that this narrow focus will limit what pupils can achieve. As Mason and Johnston-Wilder (2006) say: 'A succession of experiences, is not the same as an experience of succession.'

Consider the topic of quadratics. At the time of learning, this is often the most mathematically sophisticated topic pupils have encountered. There are numerous ideas to be understood, different representations to be interpreted and various procedural skills required. This topic is the springboard from simple linear functions to later study of calculus.

To demonstrate the enormity of what pupils must contend with, I have listed some of the ideas and skills they must learn:

- the relationship between algebraic representation, tabular representation and graphical representation
- that each coordinate on the graphical representation is an instance which satisfies the equation
- the various transformations of graphs
- the general form $y = ax^2 + bx + c$
- roots and how to find them
- the y-intercept and how to find it
- the algorithm for completing the square
- turning points and how to find them from any given representation
- axes of symmetry and their relationship with roots and completed square form
- axes of symmetry and their relationship with turning points
- the form $y = k(x - a)(x - b)$ and finding missing values
- the discriminant and related problems
- the quadratic formula
- iterative methods
- applications in context
- how all of the methods relate to each other.

Typically in textbooks, there is a succession of procedurally-focused tasks for pupils to engage with. A frequent experience in my career is that pupils are often able to perform the procedural tasks from the textbook well, but later, when presented with a question or problem in isolation, they are not sure which method to select. I argue for an alternative focus, beyond the learning of 'steps' and methods: I aspire for understanding of quadratics to complement pupils' algebraic competency. Another issue is that pupils often lack awareness that these ideas are highly connected and, as a result, are unaware of how to transform one representation to another (or even that they are related at all). This must be given explicit attention.

Procedural tasks are not enough. There need to be tasks which focus on conceptual understanding, tasks which pose non-routine questions, tasks where pupils have to make connections etc. In a recent Scottish national examination, pupils were given a quadratic and asked to sketch it, showing key points such as roots, the y-intercept and turning points. The vast majority of pupils did not perform well. Does this mean they had not been taught the content? No! The majority of teachers spend a significant number of weeks 'building up the pieces' of quadratics. The question is, what sort of tasks were those pupils engaged in during this time? The problem, in my view, is that many pupils still perceive quadratics as a plethora of discrete procedures to be learned. If, instead, pupils could see the topic as an interconnected web of ideas, they would gain a deeper conceptual understanding. Couple this understanding with some fundamental algebra skills and then you might have pupils who are able to engage more meaningfully with routine and non-routine questions alike.

One approach to making connections and to avoid ideas being seen as discrete is, when working through a succession of tasks, to have explicit classroom dialogue about the relationships between the tasks. We could draw a map of the relationships, perhaps in a network diagram, and build this up as we progress through the topic. As teachers, we know what pupils are 'meant' to learn from each task, and we understand where these tasks and the ideas therein are positioned in the big picture. We need to make these connections explicit, as the majority of pupils do not make enough of them. However, while drawing a network diagram might be helpful, it is not possible for pupils to fully appreciate these connections simply from being told about them. Pupils need experiences through which they can develop their own understanding and make connections for themselves. As the basis for this, we might use a task such as the following:

Factorised: $y = (x - 1)(x - 3)$	In expanded form: $y = x^2 - 4x + 3$	Completed square: $y = (x - 2)^2 - 1$
Table of values		**y-intercept:** (0, 3)
Roots: $x = 1$ and $x = 3$	Discriminant: $b^2 - 4ac = 4$	Turning point: minimum at (2, −1)

Table of values (from first grid):

x	y
−2	15
−1	8
0	3
1	0
2	−1
3	0
4	3
5	8
6	15

Factorised:	In expanded form: $y = x^2 - 6x + 9$	Completed square:
Table of values		**y-intercept:**
Roots:	Discriminant:	Turning point:

Table of values (second grid, empty):

x	y

Here, pupils are presented with a complete example, demonstrating different algebraic, geometric and tabular representations of a quadratic equation, along with some other key facts about the quadratic such as turning point etc. The idea is for pupils to recognise the body of knowledge around quadratics as more than a set of procedures to be recalled. Initially, it is useful to give pupils some time to read the completed grid individually. Then I ask pupils to work in pairs to cut out the cards and organise them in some way – the layout is entirely up to the pupils and how they see the relationships. I encourage pupils to draw arrows between the cards, to show which ones most directly connect to the others. For instance, there would not be a line between discriminant and y-intercept, but there would be lines joining the y-intercept with the expanded and factorised forms, the table of values and the graph, as it can be clearly seen from each of those. If the teacher leads this task, there is likely to be less cognitive demand placed upon pupils, less scope for conversation and, as such, less learning: it is essential to allow pupils to explore the information without prompting.

Next, I give pupils versions of the grid for different quadratics, with only one or two pieces of information in each grid. They have to complete each grid, including different representations, based upon this starting point. This is not like the exam questions they will be asked to do; rather, the task is about building connections, understanding equivalence of representations and developing an understanding that there are many ways to navigate this topic. For instance, there is no specific form in which a quadratic must be written to establish the turning point. However, there is a representation which makes this more convenient. I usually ask pupils to work together on one or two of these grids, to gain confidence with this less structured task and to gain insight from each other. Then I have pupils complete the remaining grids individually.

This task activates prior knowledge and serves as a prompt for dialogue. Pupils are unlikely to find a task like this easy but it nevertheless engages them in sophisticated mathematical activity. Because pupils complete several grids, reflection is built into the task. I have found it useful to provide some grids immediately after quadratics have been introduced for the first time, then space out the others over a few weeks, so pupils internalise the ideas for the long term.

Earlier, I outlined how the activity or process is what is valuable, not the end product. If pupils have been able to correctly answer fifty questions by carrying out some procedure, all we can infer is that, at this moment in time, they are able to replicate this procedure. It is often the case that, only one week later, the same pupil is unable to replicate this initial performance. All we can ever do is make inferences about learning using whatever assessment actions or devices we are aware of. Conversely, there are situations where pupils may not perform perfectly, yet make significant gains in learning. The quadratics task is one such example. There is an important place for tasks requiring deep thinking and utilisation of higher order mathematical behaviours. The gains from such tasks might be hard to quantify but still help pupils to develop their conceptual understanding and their range of mathematical actions. In summary, success in 'drill' exercises is no more evidence of learning, than failure to complete a richer task is evidence of no learning.

Tasks shape impressions of mathematics

Exams and textbooks are sources of tasks.

> *Pupils develop their sense of what it means to 'do mathematics' from the classroom activities in which they engage.*
>
> (Henningsen and Stein, 1997)

It may be the case that a teacher who views mathematics as a collection of procedures to be learned favours the use of 'drill' exercises, while a teacher who believes in the power of discovery learning presents initial teaching through inquiry prompts. The experiences of pupils in each of these classrooms is quite different. Haggerty and Pepin suggest that task selection by teachers influences and sometimes determines the degree of pupils' opportunities to learn (Haggarty and Pepin, 2002). I have argued that pupils need layers of different experiences to learn the various procedures, become comfortable with concepts and develop mathematical behaviours. This pedagogical stance is also important in shaping pupil attitudes to mathematics. A range of tasks and mathematical activity allow pupils to develop a better appreciation of what mathematics is. By having rich tasks which require a range of sophisticated actions beyond merely calculating, pupils begin to learn what it means to 'do' mathematics.

Textbooks, as collections of tasks, have a role in shaping pupils' impressions of mathematics. Senk and Thompson state that textbook tasks can be viewed as shapers of the curriculum rather than merely presenting a given curriculum. Textbooks are only ever an interpretation of the curriculum by an author. They are a collection of tasks which, if completed, should result in some learning. Textbooks are shaped by the beliefs of the author and the motivations of the publisher. If textbooks are to be a key resource in classrooms, it is vitally important that teachers do not fall into the trap of thinking the textbook is the curriculum. Coverage of the syllabus is rarely perfect, even in the best texts. A greater problem is that the range of exercises in textbooks, particularly in the UK, tends to be predominantly procedural. This is not a balanced mathematical diet for pupils. Nevertheless, many teachers hold on to textbooks as the primary, and in some cases only, resource (Senk and Thompson, 2003).

That some pupils experience a limited range of tasks is perhaps due to the fact that we live in a highly accountable exam-driven culture. Burkhardt and Swan explain that 'the tasks presented by high stakes examinations and textbooks largely determine the types of task that are used within classrooms' (Burkhardt and Swan, 2013). It is often the case that being able to do questions which resemble past examination questions is viewed as the 'goal state'. This can lead to an emphasis on procedures at the expense of concepts and development of other mathematical habits of mind. If the exam system does not value this other learning (which is essential in learning mathematics, as opposed to learning how to pass exams) then it is little wonder that it is often neglected. Teaching pupils to pass exams is a real problem. The popular booklet *Nix the Tricks* (Cardone, 2015) lists a whole range of 'tricks' which pupils are sometimes taught without any understanding – purely with a focus on passing exams. While these tricks may help pupils to pass the current level, they are seldom a sound basis for further study and often create problems for future learning. The inclusion of questions in exams which test conceptual understanding or require problem solving can encourage teachers to ensure pupils are mathematically proficient. While, as individuals, we may not have the power to change assessments at a national level, we can certainly influence the design of internal assessments in our own schools. I offer my mantra: 'if you teach the mathematics deeply and richly, the exams take care of themselves'.

Conclusion

We have established that tasks are the catalyst for mathematical activity and the means by which learning can occur. We have explored the necessity for layers of experience built up over time and for a focus on higher-order mathematical actions.

A prevalent theme in this chapter, and throughout this book is that telling pupils things is often necessary, but rarely sufficient for pupils to learn. Even when pupils are shown or told about a structure, picture or relationship, they must internalise it for themselves. Just because a pupil has been told something, it does not follow that they appreciate what has been said or can reconstruct it for themselves. This is where tasks, and the resultant activity, are so important. They, in conjunction with dialogue, help to bridge the gap between topics and learning.

Finally, I discussed the role of tasks in determining pupils' perceptions of the subject. I close this chapter with the following quote from Back et al.: 'task design is therefore meta-mathematics in the sense that it influences what is learnt, and how pupils understand the nature of mathematics' (Back et al., 2012).

3 Curriculum

Tony Gardiner

At the outset of writing this book, one person I was determined to talk to was Tony Gardiner. Tony is a truly unique voice in mathematics education. As well as being a former chair of the Mathematics Association, he founded the United Kingdom Mathematics Trust, an organisation which sets mathematical challenge competitions for school pupils. Tony has also written countless books of lovely mathematical tasks. So, when I contacted Tony, this great task writer, I was surprised, somewhat, by his response.

I believe there are two sides to this issue. First of all, we've got to look at the mathematics itself, because there's truth in the mathematics. The mathematics is the mathematics. The other side of this is that we actually need to look at the pedagogy and didactics, the actual mechanism of how we teach and the models that we know we can build up over time.

We need to address the question of how, supposing this task or activity has value, has it delivered any long-term benefit? My observation over many years is that the majority of tasks to which I have been subjected deliver no long-term benefits. A smaller number of tasks, I have emerged thinking "that was an hour and a half well spent". In that sense, the task has a certain positive something. However, I still don't see how these tasks deliver long term benefits. Further, the people presenting tasks don't explain how the tasks will deliver long term benefits. I compare it to the difference between going for a nice meal and dealing with obesity. Tackling obesity, promoting a decent diet and developing a healthy body, is different from going for a nice meal. A nice meal might be an enjoyable way to pass an hour and a half, but it isn't making people healthier. There's a complete difference between a nice meal and healthy eating. I don't watch any television cooking programmes because it seems to me there's something funny about them. I mean they are broadcast while, at the same time, obesity, type 2 diabetes, and everything else is running rampant. So clearly, whatever they are addressing, it doesn't seem to be helping us think more sensibly about good eating.

A good teacher is not a star, they are not performers. Some might be, but 90% of teachers won't be. They'll just be thoughtful, ordinary teachers, trying to do their best. I'm privileged to interact with a primary programme called Maths No Problem. I suggest that maths teachers would enjoy the books if they worked through them from 1A to 6B. You would see somebody had thoughtfully built something for almost all kids. It's not exciting, though I get excited looking at it because I'm interested not in nice meals, but in healthy eating. I see, in these books, somebody carefully avoiding doing what happens in a lot of English classrooms. They're avoiding focusing on a specific thing because now would be a bad time. And they focus slowly – boringly slowly – on all sorts of other little things. But I get excited because I know this is where things can improve for ordinary people. However, it isn't exciting on the surface, it wouldn't excite the inspectorate. It's not a collection of tasks, it's a map. It's a map with a colour scheme and a structure. Instead of giving snapshots of interesting cases to visit, which aren't linked together, the teacher is given a map which somebody has carefully designed. Think of a map that Columbus or Vasco da Gama or Captain Cook or whomever had to work with. They were crummy. And that's why lots of explorers disappeared and we never heard of them again. Having a map that somebody has thought out carefully, which you can trust, allows you to explore a city or a landscape in a completely new way and to get to know it.

Amazing things are possible when you learn to read an Ordnance Survey Map and use it to go out into places you didn't know. This is what the teacher's doing all the time. When teachers are in the first 10 years of their career and they really are raw, they don't fully understand how their subject hangs together or why we should teach a certain idea before some other. To an extent, at that early career stage, people are obliged to follow the scheme of work, without really knowing the way things should be arranged. Some schemes of work aren't good enough, which is what my book Teaching Mathematics at Secondary Level *is about. The National Curriculum in England has much of this arrangement of ideas wrong. It groups ideas wrongly and ignores connections. The National Curriculum isn't a map. It's open to interpretation. At the early career stage, a teacher can't know if an interpretation is sensible. This is why a map is necessary. It's telling you the way that ideas are built up over time. Of course, there are some choices one can make as to whether one does this before that, and those can vary. With a map, what you're getting is not dogma or a straitjacket, it is a carefully thought out route. I think the UK maths education community is guilty for having essentially concealed the map.*

So that's where I start from on why I have trouble with tasks. The tasks may be beautiful, just like a meal may be beautiful, but that's not the problem. The problem is how you link whatever you do to the long term. Task design looks sensible because you know that even if you were to draw a map, you would have to set some exercises. You'd need to have the anchor task upfront. It feels like it's connected to the long-term challenge. But my observation is that it never is, it's separate. Malcolm Swan was absolutely excellent in embedding the tasks that he imagined/ conceived/thought up or had presented to him into a kind of, I want to say a classroom setting or context. That would make wonderful sense if one were doing this chapter after chapter or square after square on a map in building up a progression – but that doesn't happen. As such, I don't see any alternatives to the textbook. Tasks encourage people to go and print out another bloody sheet from the web. I don't know any settings in which that works at scale. I can imagine it working in the odd classroom with the odd teacher but...I'm stuck."

I said in the introduction to this book that there would be nuance, that my stance would be somewhere in the complex middle ground. I had never intended to write a chapter on curriculum, since this is a book about tasks. However, after hearing Tony's words, I decided that a chapter exploring the mathematics curriculum would be an important addition. While I agree with much of what Tony says, I believe tasks have a significant role to play. They can be used to create the 'healthy diet' of activity required in mathematics learning and to provide a roadmap for teachers in conjunction with curriculum documentation.

In this chapter we will explore:

- the factors influencing the implementation of the curriculum in classrooms
- the role of textbooks

- a discussion of how tasks are used to exemplify two very different curricula
- ways to improve the system by changing examination tasks.

The factors influencing the implementation of the curriculum in classrooms

The word 'curriculum' has multiple meanings, but it is primarily used to refer to overarching frameworks that specify what should be taught. In some countries the curriculum means the resources teachers use when planning learning. In some cases, the textbook is essentially the curriculum. Remillard and Heck propose a useful model for understanding the complex interactions between curriculum, teachers, instructional materials and learning.

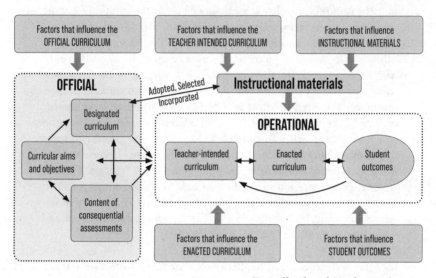

(Remillard and Heck, 2014)

As this diagram shows, a curriculum model is usually based on some broad **aims and objectives**. These might be high level, and somewhat applicable to all subjects, not just mathematics .

In Scotland, for example, the curriculum aims are such that all pupils become:

- successful learners
- confident individuals
- responsible citizens
- effective contributors.

For mathematics, there are more precise aims, written from a pupil perspective.

My learning in mathematics enables me to:
- *develop a secure understanding of the concepts, principles and processes of mathematics and apply these in different contexts, including the world of work*
- *engage with more abstract mathematical concepts and develop important new kinds of thinking*
- *understand the application of mathematics, its impact on our society past and present, and its potential for the future*
- *develop essential numeracy skills which will allow me to participate fully in society*
- *establish firm foundations for further specialist learning*
- *understand that successful independent living requires financial awareness, effective money management, using schedules and other related skills*
- *interpret numerical information appropriately and use it to draw conclusions, assess risk, and make reasoned evaluations and informed decisions*
- *apply skills and understanding creatively and logically to solve problems, within a variety of contexts*
- *appreciate how the imaginative and effective use of technologies can enhance the development of skills and concepts.*

(Scottish Government, 2016 [1])

These overarching aims and objectives may underpin the political narrative of education systems but are of little practical use to subject teachers. Many teachers, in my experience, desire a curriculum which suggests what they are to teach and provides some guidance as to how they might do this.

The visual model above includes the **designated curriculum**. This is a list of the content to be taught and may include some specificity on the design of teaching. While the designated curriculum varies little between countries, what varies a lot is how it is presented, the amount of detail, and the pedagogical and assessment guidance. It can be anything from a sparse list of aims and experiences to a detailed specification including exemplar tasks. Some countries rely primarily on curricular aims and objectives and assessments to communicate the official curriculum, while the specifics of instruction are left to the individual school or teacher. In other countries, the designated curriculum is simply an adopted mathematics textbook from a commercial publisher. In highly-centralised countries such as South Korea, the education ministry oversees the design of instructional materials and officially sanctions the textbooks which may be used in schools. In many school districts in the US, the designated curriculum consists of a host of assembled packages of materials, instructional resources, and structuring guidelines designed to shape the content, pacing, and often the processes and tools of mathematics instruction (Remillard and Heck, 2014).

A major shaper of curriculum is **assessment**. Cuban talks about the idea of the tested curriculum. Final examinations cannot assess every curricular objective and the ones which are assessed can be perceived, by some, to be those which are truly valuable (Cuban, 1993). In the US, for example, a number of states include problem-solving and communication skills in their curricular objectives, but do not assess these skills in state tests. Whether intended or not, the resulting message is that such competencies are less necessary than those tested. Ruthven captured this idea nicely, saying, 'what you test is what you get' (Ruthven, 1994).

As teachers draw on the designated curriculum along with other resources to plan for teaching, they create the **teacher-intended curriculum**. This is made up of the interpretations of curriculum documents and decisions based on teachers' own values, beliefs and goals for learning. The teacher-intended curriculum is also influenced by teachers' interpretations of assessment requirements. The **enacted curriculum** is 'the interactions between teachers and pupils around the tasks of each lesson' and in subsequent lessons. The enacted curriculum cannot be scripted because the enactment itself requires teachers to respond in the moment to the events in the lesson (Remillard and Taton, 2013). No matter the intended curriculum of the teacher, it is the pedagogical choices and interactions with pupils that result in the enacted curriculum. **Pupil learning** is primarily shaped by the enacted curriculum, with **instructional materials** commonly playing a prominent role as a source of tasks, worked examples, representations and explanations, as well as expectations for what pupils' work should look like.

In the UK, teachers often create schemes of work which interpret the curriculum and textbooks. This sort of document has more texture and detail and is designed for the local context, with particular cohorts of pupils in mind. This is the document that can come to life most readily, as it has been put together by teachers for teachers. Schemes of work regularly include many tasks and/or task sequences. When I spoke to Tom Francome, he recalled how in his department he had a 'canon of tasks', which he felt all pupils should experience during their schooling, such is their value.

It is clear that tasks, whether in designated curriculum documentation, in state-sanctioned textbooks, in formal examinations or in schemes of work, have a key part to play in the implementation of the curriculum in schools.

The role of textbooks

Mathematics is a subject that has long been associated with textbooks. The way in which textbooks can be used is varied. In some countries, such as South Korea and Japan, there are officially-sanctioned texts which clearly communicate what is to be taught and what models, representations and tasks should be used. There have been efforts to create textbooks or collections of tasks which are 'teacher-proof' but Komoski found significant mismatches between the contents of teachers' guides and classroom practice (Komoski, 1979). Teachers do not perform a script written by someone else!

Komoski is critical of commercial materials stating that 'if instructional materials continue to be developed in order to sell rather than on their ability to facilitate teaching and learning, education will suffer' (Komoski, 1985). Even with a good textbook in hand, teachers need training and support to use the textbook well. Teachers' notes are not necessarily enough. There is a complex relationship between pedagogy, curriculum, tasks and pupil learning. From experience, I know how uninviting a lengthy set of teacher's notes in accompaniment to a task or task sequence can be for a busy teacher.

In attempts to bring innovative, progressive curriculum materials into schools, Stephens found that teachers transformed the intended curriculum, imposing a rigid and narrow portrait of mathematics. Most teachers' instructional patterns focused on group management rather than mathematics. The materials alone did not have the desired outcome. Teachers have varying beliefs, levels of experience, pedagogical flexibility and content knowledge, which underpins their daily practice, making it unlikely that any new resource, alone, can transform pupil learning (Stephens and Romberg, 1982).

Where state-approved textbooks are the basis of curriculum, then certain shared professional knowledge can become common place. For instance, in Japan it is most common to teach the area of rectangles, then parallelograms before triangles. This is different to the typical UK ordering but has come about as a result of the shared practice and experience which informs these centralised materials.

Tom Francome suggested that, despite the best efforts of authors, the level of thought behind textbooks in the UK is often less than in countries such as Japan. Tom suggests that in a UK textbook you cannot just work from page 1 to page 300 and see everything pan out. This is likely because any textbook is simply an interpretation of the curriculum. In Japan, textbooks are entwined with the curriculum to such an extent that they **are** the curriculum: the textbooks are developed iteratively in line with the five-year cycle of curriculum refinement. Often what happens in the UK is that a new curriculum is launched, then people run around trying to get books published. In contrast, in Japan, publishers work to achieve approval of their textbooks before the curriculum change is implemented. This means that when the curriculum changes occur, comprehensive textbooks are immediately available. Japan also differs from the UK in that there is stability in the curriculum. There has been an ongoing, gradual refinement of the curriculum, informed by lesson study, for many years. The wholesale changes we see in the nations of the UK simply do not happen in Japan (Takahashi, 2016).

For teachers using textbooks, Tom suggest that we should be critical consumers. As a teacher you have to ask, 'what is the purpose?' To decide if a task is good or bad, you need to assess how it aligns with the purpose of the lesson. Many UK textbooks focus on procedural fluency rather than conceptual understanding of problem solving. However, even for technical fluency, the exercises might not meet the purpose. Sometimes there is too much or too little variety, for instance. It is not uncommon to see teachers pasting together exercises from various textbooks, to create something which 'does the job' for their pupils.

One potential advantage of a textbook compared with a worksheet is that, typically, a team has developed the textbook together and there is a narrative through a range of tasks. Textbooks can also give you an idea of what people think a certain topic is all about; they can shape how we might see mathematics. There is a place for high-quality textbooks, even if only to communicate some well-tested tasks and learning activities to teachers. This is not to suggest that textbooks alone are enough, but to acknowledge that they can be a good basis from which to build. They should:

- Encompass the proper progression of learning, based on the best research.
- Have a variety of quality tasks to help develop rounded mathematicians.
- Make use of effective representations (algebra tiles, for instance) and forward-facing methodologies such as the balance model for solving equations, instead of 'change side, change sign' etc.

The quality of textbooks is especially important for novice teachers. A good textbook allows them to stand on the shoulders of those who have gone before, using some of that accumulated professional knowledge.

Tom Francome raised two more interesting points about textbooks. First, a bit of advice. He suggests an interesting question to ask pupils when using a textbook is, 'why do you think the textbook writer chose these questions, in this order?' I suggest it is pertinent for us, as teachers, to consider this too. The next point was an observation. Hardly any textbooks are set up for spaced practice and interleaving. Given the recent prominence of cognitive science, it is surprising that these ideas are not more utilised in textbook design.

Hodgen and Wiliam, in their seminal paper *Mathematics inside the black box*, suggest that all textbooks can be used as a starting point for formative teaching.

> *For example, pupils could be asked to identify four questions, two which they consider easy and two which they consider difficult. They could then construct model answers – working individually on the 'easy' questions and with a partner on the 'difficult' ones. Pupils might then be asked:*
>
> - *What is similar ... what is different about the easy and hard questions?*
> - *Have you changed your views on which are easy and which are hard questions?*
> - *How could you make that question easier/harder?*
> - *What advice would you give on how to solve a hard problem?*

It is suggested that at the end of a lesson sequence, pupils could be asked to produce an alternative to the textbook with explanations and problems, providing advice and guidance to others. Doing this individually and then progressing to pairs or groups would provide an opportunity for pupils first to find out what they know, then to compare this with the ideas of others (Hodgen and Wiliam, 2006).

Tasks used to exemplify learning: South Korea and Scotland

A country with impressive mathematics attainment is South Korea, which has maintained a high placing on PISA rankings during a period when Scotland has been on a steady decline. There are clear cultural differences between South Korea and Scotland. However, there is much to contemplate when one examines the ways in which curricula are communicated in each country. I chose these two countries as there is a clear difference in approach.

Jeoung Suk Pang of the Korea National University of Education described important aspects of curriculum reform:

- objectives (why to teach/learn)
- content (what to teach/learn)
- progression (when to teach/learn)
- instruction (how to teach/learn).

The Korean curriculum is based on the idea of learning trajectories; although there is no explicit reference to this American construct in Korea, the principles clearly appear (Ferreras, Kessel and Kim, 2015).

Martin Simon (1995) describes learning trajectories as having three components:

1. A set of mathematical goals.
2. A clearly marked developmental path.
3. A coherent set of instructional tasks or activities.

Korean teachers are required to do demonstration lessons where they show understanding of both horizontal and vertical trajectories. The beginning of the teachers' manual gives vertical trajectories for all six grades and prior knowledge at the beginning of each unit, and teachers do the 'homework' of reading the descriptions in this manual. They have the belief that they can only teach well if they know what children learned previously, what they have to learn in this lesson and what they have to learn in future lessons.

Kyong Mi Choi discusses how textbook tasks in South Korea are developed by teams of mathematicians, mathematics educators and mathematics teachers to ensure mathematical correctness, and to consider how learners understand mathematics and possible misconceptions. These tasks have five core elements – intuitive exploration, explanation, examples, practice, and extension – and there is a richness to the pedagogy. To promote intuitive exploration of ideas, tasks borrow concepts from everyday life, ask pupils to fill in a missing piece of reasoning, or use mathematical knowledge from earlier grades (Ferreras, Kessel and Kim, 2015).

Tasks can be used to illustrate the key mathematical ideas to be conveyed. However, no single task can convey the entirety of an idea. A successive layering of experiences is necessary for that. There is a danger that if the curriculum is defined entirely in terms of procedural tasks, the key understandings for teaching will be unclear to both teacher and pupils. For instance, the topic of fractions can be considered in terms of procedures (adding fractions, finding fractions of an amount, creating equivalent fractions, etc.) and this topic is often presented in textbooks and in curriculum documents in these terms. However, considering fractions as these distinct procedures can obscure the deeper conceptual progression.

The diagram below shows the five subconstructs of fractions and the relationships between them. When running professional development workshops across Scotland, a question I regularly ask teachers is: 'what do we mean by a fraction?'. Particularly among teachers at primary level, the majority reply is 'part-whole'. I don't think this is because teachers have a lack of understanding of the other meanings of fractions. Instead, I believe that because teachers work with curriculum documents and textbooks which take a predominantly procedural perspective, these deep relationships are not at the forefront of their thinking when planning learning and teaching. The absence of a clear learning trajectory means it becomes much more difficult to develop coherence between mathematics lessons and across years of schooling.

The diagram is not a learning trajectory or a curriculum map in itself; it does not show all of the relationships. However, it spells out the required meaning of fraction to enable pupils to fully appreciate specific procedures. For instance, pupils need a sense of fractions both as part of a whole and as an operator to make sense of multiplication.

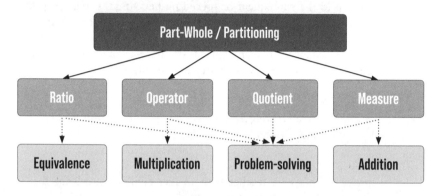

(Silver, Behr, Post and Lesh, 1983)

It seems clear that this should be part of the pedagogical content knowledge for teachers of mathematics at school level. However, in my experience, most teachers tend to talk in terms of actions associated with fractions rather than these wider meanings. This need not cause a problem, if there are clear learning trajectories. If these subconstructs have been considered by the curriculum writers and textbook authors then fractions can be taught at the appropriate developmental stage through correct sequencing of instruction and tasks, even if the teacher does not entirely appreciate the reasons for this order.

Tasks can play a powerful role in exemplifying the curriculum. Let's consider the different curricula in Scotland and South Korea regarding the multiplication of fractions.

In Scotland, the documents *Experiences and outcomes* and *Curriculum for excellence benchmarks* (Scottish Government, 2016 [1], [2]) define the mathematics to be taught. I have chosen the three benchmark statements that most closely relate to multiplication of fractions and the development of that knowledge.

- **First Level:** Calculates simple fractions of a quantity and uses this knowledge to solve problems in everyday contexts, for example, find ⅗ of 60.
- **Second Level:** Uses knowledge of fractions, decimal fractions and percentages to carry out calculations with or without a calculator.
- **Third Level:** Applies addition, subtraction and multiplication skills to solve problems involving fractions and mixed numbers.

There is also one exemplar task. It is not clear to the teacher how these statements relate to the subsequent or preceding benchmarks, related to this idea. There is little in the exemplar task to illuminate the sort of mathematical activity that pupils might embark on.

Scotland also produced a document called the *National Numeracy and Mathematics Progression Framework*. In this document, we find the statement:

> *Relationship between fractions, multiplication and division: There is a direct link between finding a fraction of an object or a quantity and multiplication and division.*
>
> (Scottish Government, 2018)

For a novice teacher or a teacher with weaker content knowledge this is quite inadequate. This is exacerbated by the variable quality of the available commercially-produced textbooks. This is not to say there are no good tasks in Scottish textbooks – there are, and there are some good sequences of tasks too. However, on a system level, there is a lack of cohesion such that the sequence of instruction, mathematical experiences and the tasks encountered is frequently not fit for purpose. The stronger UK texts – such as *Inspire Maths* or *Maths No Problem* – tend not to align well with the Scottish curriculum. One may question if this is a problem with the marketing of the books, or a reflection of weaknesses in the Scottish curriculum.

Comparing this with South Korea, fraction multiplication is brought together explicitly at the fifth grade. In the excerpt below, there are specific mathematical goals and some exemplar instructional tasks for teachers. The connections and depth of thinking required are much clearer. Understanding of multiplication of fractions is to be considered in three ways:

1. Repeated addition.
2. As an operator.
3. As a product of factors.

Having all three meanings brought together and contrasted helps teachers to more clearly understand the nuance of the conceptual development underpinning this learning.

The Korean teachers' manuals accompanying the textbooks explain why a particular task is in a particular place and identify situations that could lead pupils to misunderstandings, suggesting the actions teachers can take in these situations. The textbooks are designed with care and expertise. Different representations are used in accordance with the three different meanings of fraction multiplication.

1. Repeated addition: area model.
2. Multiplication as operator: measurement and set model.
3. Taking a part of a part of a whole: area model.

To encourage use of various computational strategies, textbooks provide various methods for calculation, ask pupils to decide which methods are more efficient, provide ways of making calculations easier (e.g. cancelling before multiplying) and emphasise the use of the distributive property. Typical Scottish textbooks, in stark contrast, provide only one method for reduction of complexity (or none at all), whereas Korean mathematics textbooks provide at least three reduction methods.

Developmental Path (Mathematical Goals)	Instructional Tasks
1. To understand (whole number x proper fraction) and (whole number x mixed number) calculate in multiple ways.	There are five pizzas of which $\frac{3}{8}$ of each pizza remain. How much pizza is there in total?
2. To understand (proper fraction x whole number) with manipulative; formulate algorithm and use it proficiently. To understand that if a multiplier is smaller than 1, then the product is smaller than the multiplicand.	12 m of wire was bought to make a wire sculptured animal with clay. If ¾ of the wire is used, how many m of the wire is used?
3. To understand (proper fraction x mixed number) with manipulative; calculate with two methods and compare two methods.	$12\frac{3}{4}$ m of wire was bought to make a wire sculptured animal with clay. If $\frac{3}{2}$ of the wire is used, how many m of the wire is used?

(Ferreras, Kessel and Kim, 2015)

The instructional tasks help to define the intentions of curriculum writers. The tasks in textbooks further help to bridge the gap between the designated curriculum and what is actually enacted in classrooms.

Korean teachers are used to this lesson structure:

- introduce the idea of the lesson
- develop ideas
- close the lesson.

The textbook structure uses this format because teachers use it (Ferreras, Kessel and Kim, 2015). The learning activities make sense to teachers, because they relate to the patterns teachers already use. Different textbooks may take different approaches, but each lesson has a clear format: approach ideas, have pupils practise, then wrap up.

Hugh Burkhardt argued that to specify a curriculum relatively unambiguously, you need three *independent* elements:

- the tools in the toolkit of mathematical **concepts and skills**
- the performance targets, as exemplified by **task types**
- the pattern of classroom **learning activities**.

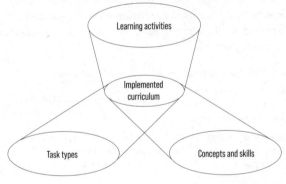

(Burkhardt, 1990)

This approach helps to communicate the curriculum more clearly. It also helps to avoid undesirable fragmentation of ideas. The Korean model of clearly-defined concepts and skills in the curriculum, exemplar task types, and textbooks and learning materials which correlate with typical teaching patterns, helps to ensure the enacted curriculum is coherent. As such, while there is a danger of the curriculum becoming a set of procedures, communicating it clearly in this way helps teachers to plan for joined up thinking: tasks bring the curriculum ideas to life and the sequencing of tasks in the curriculum documentation helps to exemplify the progression of ideas in an accessible form. In contrast, the Scottish model seems destined to result in a fragmented, incoherent experience for both teachers and pupils.

Improving the system by changing examination tasks

Most examinations include some element of problem solving but these questions are frequently beyond the grasp of many pupils. I conjecture that this is, partially, a result of teaching that focuses on a variety of procedures designed to show learners how to do standard exam questions, rather than conveying the underlying principles. To learn these underlying principles, pupils may have to engage in tasks that do not look like the final assessment questions.

As discussed above, 'what you test is what you get'. Final assessments convey what is valued and subsequently drive classroom activity. Swan and Burkhardt (2012) suggest that assessments should reflect the curriculum in a balanced way. 'Assessment should be based on a balanced set of tasks that, together, provide pupils with opportunities to show *all* types of performance that the curriculum goals set out or imply.' The sorts of assessment we use in the UK school systems do not capture all of the curriculum goals. Focus is on the statistical properties of the test and the 'fairness', not on what is assessed. Policy makers choose simple tests because they are cheaper and, if pressed, argue that the results correlate with more valid but elaborate assessments.

Final assessments tend to test each concept and skill separately with a short question that has no other cognitive load (for example complexity, long chain of reasoning) that would increase difficulty. Curriculum content is often defined in this way. The problem with this approach to final assessment is that, while success in these types of short task may be a stepping stone, it is by no means an end in itself. Burkhardt argues that a focus which is too much on atomised skills is, in fact, detrimental to pupil learning and no guarantee of success in situations where more substantial chains of reasoning are required.

> To be useful in solving substantial problems, from the real world or within mathematics, a technique needs multiple connections in the pupil's mind – to other math concepts and to diverse problem contexts within and outside mathematics. These connections are built over time.
>
> (Burkhardt, 2009).

If curriculum aims and objectives – such as developing strategic problem solvers – do not correlate with assessment, there is the possibility that the enacted curriculum will look quite different to what might have been imagined by the policy makers. I asked Hugh Burkhardt how system wide improvements might be made in the nations of the UK.

A central problem is that we know how to enable typical teachers to teach much better mathematics, much more effectively, to all pupils. However, nobody knows how to move a system to do that! It appears to be harder in the Anglo systems, where there is a tradition of letting the market provide the materials etc. A fundamental problem is addressing the question, 'how big of a step forward do we take?'. If we try to take a big step, then very few will follow. If we take a small step, then why even bother?

This is a pertinent point. There have been many attempts to import curricula and materials from southeast Asia but it is not as simple as lifting the materials from one country and placing them in another. Those countries have teachers who have developed their knowledge through those curricula and textbooks. The utilisation of the texts, in the UK, would inevitably be inferior. This is not because UK teachers are worse but because they haven't been trained to use these materials, just as Tony Gardiner described with the *Maths No Problem* books earlier.

Hugh Burkhardt describes a model that has worked in the UK previously.

We have developed modules, which take a number of days of teaching, to address particular things which are missing. We had a very successful realisation of it in the 1980s, called testing strategic skills. I was on the maths and research committee of the JMB [exam board]. I convinced the maths committee that the exam assessed only two or three of the eight "knowledges and abilities" which were outlined in the syllabus. We embarked upon a gradual process of change where each year, one new type of task would be added to the exam. That was around 5% of the curriculum. At the Shell Centre, we created teaching materials for around three weeks, which was the appropriate amount of time, and removed three weeks' worth of existing material from the syllabus. We provided the boxes: "Problems with patterns and numbers" and "The language of functions and graphs". Each box contained the following:

- *five examples of the types of task*
- *the three weeks of teaching material (carefully developed through three rounds of trialling)*
- *some professional development materials.*

The examples were non-routine, and, in the notes, we explained that the tasks in the exam would differ from the examples to about the same extent as the examples differed from each other. The key feature of this model is a digestible rate of change – profound change but on a small scale. Politicians treat education in a way that they would never treat medicine: "we are going to fix it". They always find money to support a new curriculum.'

Here is an example task and the curricular aims and objectives:

Skeleton Tower from 'Problems with Patterns and Numbers'
Knowledge and abilities to be tested
- The following list is intended to provide a general indication of the knowledge and abilities which the examination
  will be designed to test.
- Knowledge of mathematical notation, terminology, conventions and units. The language and notation of sets together with the ideas of a mapping and a function are basic to the syllabus.
- The ability to understand information presented in verbal, graphical or tabular form, and to translate such information into mathematical form.
- The ability to recognise the mathematical methods which are suitable for the solution of the problem under consideration.
- The ability to apply mathematical methods and techniques.
- The ability to manipulate mathematical expressions.
- The ability to make logical deductions.
- The ability to select and apply appropriate techniques to problems in unfamiliar or novel situations.
- The ability to interpret mathematical results.

Look at this diagram and answer the questions.
1. How many cubes are needed to build this tower?
2. How many cubes are needed to build a tower like this, but 12 cubes high?
3. Explain how you worked out your answer to part 2.
4. How would you calculate the number of cubes needed for a tower n cubes high?

(Shell Centre, 1984)

One tactical design feature is worth noting. Each of these units demanded significant changes from the normal teaching style of most teachers. Non-routine problem solving is destroyed if the teacher breaks up the problem into steps or guides the pupil through the mathematics – yet these are common teacher actions when pupils are having difficulty. These lessons are built around classroom discussion in which pupils explain and discuss each other's reasoning, not expecting answers from the teacher. Hugh and his colleagues were aware that many teachers would not read extensive notes, so decided the essential style changes should be summarised as a few key points on one page – the inside-back-cover of the teachers' guide.

These materials had significant impact. The modules were bought by most of the schools that used this examination. The pupil responses to the tasks in the actual examination showed a reasonable range of performance. The pupils acquired important new skills and the board's examination reflected more of its stated goals. There is a lesson in strategic design here. In contrast to attempts to raise standards in familiar areas of performance (adding fractions, using percentages, etc.), the introduction of important *new* areas, previously missing in examinations, almost guarantees substantial success if done well.

Predictably – and sadly – this work was not carried on in the long term due to restructuring of exam boards. While politicians focus on the benefits of reorganisation in education, they rarely focus on the costs. However, it is clear from this example that well-aligned changes in the system's high-stakes assessment, when achievable, can be a powerful lever for increasing impact.

4 Pedagogy

Teachers who want quick answers, won't find those answers. Teachers need to work on becoming the teacher that they want to become... The pupils' job is to learn the mathematics and the teachers' job is to learn the pupils.

Laurinda Brown

For teachers, everything we think about has to be rooted in the reality of the classroom. All too often, ideas about how to teach that come from 'top down' are unsuccessful in their implementation. There is no holy grail of teaching, there is simply what people are able to do, based on their past experiences. Pedagogy is deeply individual: it is a result of our experiences, our understanding of mathematics and our beliefs around how to teach it. It might be influenced by the external examinations which hold the system to account. At its core, pedagogy is rooted in the relationships we make with the pupils in our classes. We may employ different pedagogies with different groups. Even with the same group, our approach might change depending on the circumstances.

At the outset, it is important for me to say that I believe the argument centred on the false dichotomy of traditional versus progressive teaching is unproductive. It is deeply polarising and does not help any of us to improve. There are positives to be found in the practice and thinking of all teachers – I've yet to meet a teacher who hasn't thought about something in a way that has influenced me. We should discuss learning and teaching to listen and gain insight rather than to assert our own views.

Pedagogy can be thought of as the actions and decisions of the teacher. Schoenfeld (2014) states that 'people's moment-by-moment decision making in teaching, in medicine, in fact, in all knowledge-rich domains can be modelled as a function of their:

- **resources:** especially their knowledge but also the tools at their disposal
- **orientations:** a generalisation of beliefs, including values and preferences and
- **goals:** which are often chosen on the basis of orientations and available resources.'

This relates to the selection and use of tasks, which in turn is rooted in the pedagogical choices of the teacher. The sorts of task teachers choose to deploy, and the mileage a teacher may get from a task, are a function of his or her own beliefs about classroom practice and the pedagogical actions in their repertoire.

In this chapter, I intend to offer a few established models of thinking about mathematics pedagogy which support the perspectives that underpin the remainder of this book. We begin this chapter by considering some perspectives on learning from across the last century.

Associationism

Thorndike (1905) proposed a learning theory based on mental 'bonds' or associations between sets of stimuli and the responses to them. For instance, 'five plus five' as a stimulus, with 'ten' as the response. According to this theory, bonds become stronger as a result of frequent use, and weaker as a result of infrequent use. This way of thinking was manifested in the classroom with lots of 'drill' exercises. Associationism was a fairly straightforward model, which resulted in straightforward pedagogy.

Gestaltism

The perspective of the Gestaltists was much more sophisticated. They believed that complex mental structures needed to be recognised during planning of teaching. Wertheimer was a critic of rote learning and the associated drill exercises used in schools. While those drill exercises resulted in pupils who could master certain procedures, the knowledge acquired in this way was likely to be superficial and unlikely to be freely applicable to unfamiliar situations.

Wertheimer used this calculation to argue his point:

$$\frac{857 + 857 + 857 + 857 + 857}{5}$$

He pointed out that many pupils would laboriously add the terms in the numerator before dividing by five, rather than using the structure: the pupils could be fluent with the procedures, but quite lacking in appreciation of number sense. He remarked of one pupil that 'the child could add, subtract, divide and multiply with the best of them. The only problem was that the child never knew which method to use.' (Wertheimer, 1959)

Behaviourism

The behaviourists such as B. F. Skinner took a similar but more extreme stance to the associationists. Skinner argued that learning could be defined solely in terms of observable behaviours and was best thought of as the result of an individual's interactions with the environment (Skinner, 1958). Skinner and colleagues such as Terrace showed that 'errorless learning' was possible through shaping of behaviour by small successive approximations (Terrace, 1963).

The focus of a behaviourist approach to teaching is on careful sequencing and small steps. Robert Gagné described 'programmed instruction', which has the underpinning idea that the right sequence of experiences, repeated frequently enough, should generate the right learning (Gagné, 1965).

The influence of the behaviourist perspective is prominent in the practice of many teachers. 'The mathematics we teach is assumed to be a fixed body of knowledge, and it is taught under the assumption that learners absorb what has been covered' (Romberg and Carpenter, 1986). There is an assumption that pupils are blank slates: they are shown a procedure and, since the message doesn't always get across, they are shown again. If they are struggling, they might be shown different ways to do the procedure. However, all this is based on the assumption that the pupil 'hasn't learned it yet'.

Behaviourists tend to focus more on the *product* of the thinking, rather than the *process* (we discussed the product/process model in the previous chapter).

Constructivism

Constructivism, on the other hand, is focused on process rather than product. Perhaps surprisingly for some of those who are newly enthusiastic about cognitive science and its application to education, there is a significant overlap between the thinking in this field and that of the constructivists. The constructivist perspective is that we each build our own framework for making sense of the world, and we then see the world by interpreting it with regard to that framework. These frameworks are known as schemata. A schema describes a pattern of thought or behaviour that organises categories of information and the relationships among them (DiMaggio, 1997). It can also be described as a mental structure of preconceived ideas or a system of organising and perceiving new information.

A useful analogy for a schema is a complex web of interconnected ideas. Each node represents a discrete mathematical idea. The number of links and strength of links (indicated in bold) between ideas represent the extent of understanding.

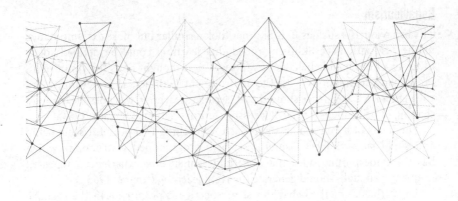

In teaching, constructivists hold beliefs such as that of Susan Carey: 'human beings are theory builders; from the beginning we construct explanatory structures that help us find the deeper reality underlying surface chaos' (Carey, 1985). Possibly the most prominent constructivist was Jean Piaget. In his theory of development, children construct a series of schemata, based on the interactions they experience, to help them understand the world. Schoenfeld describes lesson planning, from this perspective, as being concerned with how pupils will **interpret** what you show them rather than how much of it they will **absorb**. He suggests that, 'with this interpretation model, one has the opportunity to "get inside pupils' heads" and locate the cause of their difficulties' (Schoenfeld, 1987).

Constructivism in itself is not a theory of how to teach, it is a theory of learning. Various approaches to teaching – such as inquiry learning, problem-based learning and investigations – can be traced to constructivist thinking. However, it is possible to have a quite different pedagogical approach and still be a constructivist. My position is influenced most by the constructivist perspective but also acknowledges Vygotsky's notion of the Zone of Proximal Development (ZPD) (Vygotsky, 1978) – that is, 'the distance between the actual developmental level as determined by independent problem-solving and the level of potential development as determined through problem-solving under adult guidance, or in collaboration with more capable peers.' Essentially, this refers to the difference between what a pupil can do without help and what he or she can achieve with guidance and encouragement. Social interaction with others and appropriate task sequences can help pupils to cross through the ZPD.

These views have underpinned my own thinking in effective task design and the associated pedagogy. I argue that pupils cannot gain conceptual understanding simply by being told something. That may work for procedures and facts, but real conceptual understanding is not possible unless pupils have opportunities to interact with the mathematics, to develop awareness of phenomena beyond a superficial level, and to become sensitised to the principles governing these phenomena. Ideally, this should happen in a classroom where there is ample opportunity for discussion. There are times when a focus on the product – correct completion of a procedure – is necessary for mathematics learning. However, this is far from sufficient.

This idea, that connections are important to understanding, is a fundamental principle of what follows in subsequent chapters. Making connections is what understanding is about.

> The mathematics is understood if its mental representation is part of a network of representations. The degree of understanding is determined by the number and strength of its connections. A mathematical idea, procedure or fact is understood if it is linked to existing networks with stronger or more numerous connections.
>
> (Hiebert and Carpenter, 1992)

Teaching for Robust Understanding (TRU)

Schoenfeld has outlined a framework, based upon significant evidence from research, about powerful mathematics classrooms. The degree to which pupils emerge from the classroom as proficient mathematical thinkers and problem solvers is related to the five dimensions of Powerful Mathematics Classrooms (Schoenfeld, 2013).

The mathematics

In a powerful mathematics classroom, the integrity of the mathematics and the richness of the subject are central to everything. Teachers use mathematics correctly and avoid 'tricks'. They help pupils to focus on the key ideas and build on pupils' ideas, using sound reasoning and justification for the mathematical content, to support this dialogue. The classroom activity is set up to enable pupils to become knowledgeable, flexible and resourceful mathematicians. There is a focus on different perspectives, connection-making and mathematical thinking alongside techniques and procedures.

Cognitive demand

There is an appropriate level of cognitive demand, with a variety of opportunities for pupils to grapple with and make sense of mathematical ideas and their use. Pupils are challenged appropriately, with tasks ranging from moderate to demanding. Productive struggle is pitched at the right level at appropriate times in the instructional sequence. There is a range of tasks from procedural practice to non-routine, multi-step problems, which are previously unseen.

Equitable access to mathematics

Classroom activity is set up for the engagement of all pupils in the room. Classrooms in which a small number of pupils get most of the 'air time' are not equitable, no matter how rich the content. All pupils need to be involved in meaningful ways. Not only is it not equitable but the understanding of one or two is often used as a proxy for whole class understanding.

Agency, ownership and identity

Pupils are provided with opportunities to 'walk the walk' as mathematicians and to begin to see themselves as such. Mathematics learning is active, not passive. In a productive learning environment, pupils have the opportunity to see themselves as doers of mathematics – to develop a sense of agency – and to act accordingly. The roots of 'authority' reside in the word 'author'. The idea is that pupils create, or author, mathematical ideas and their justifications, thus becoming authorities. These ideas and justifications need to be aired. At the same time, pupils are not free to invent without constraint: they make conjectures, but are then accountable – to the subject itself, to the teacher, and to other pupils. The dialogic structures supported by the teacher can foster or inhibit agency, authority, and accountability.

Formative assessment

A key marker of effective teaching is the extent to which classroom practices elicit pupil thinking and where this thinking is subsequently acted upon. When assessment becomes an integral and ongoing part of the learning process – as opposed to an interruption of classroom activities – pupils' thinking takes a more central role in determining the direction and shape of learning. A fuller discussion of formative assessment follows.

It takes a number of years for teachers to develop each of these dimensions in their classrooms, if they ever manage to do so. As part of the TRU materials, various observation guides are provided. One that I find particularly powerful is shown below; this focuses on seeing a lesson from a pupil's perspective. I think we should all have this stuck to the wall in our classrooms, so these key ideas remain sharply in focus when we are planning lessons.

Observe the lesson through a student's eyes

The Mathematics	▪ What's the big idea in this lesson? ▪ How does it connect to what I already know?
Cognitive Demand	▪ How long am I given to think, and to make sense of things? ▪ What happens when I get stuck? ▪ Am I invited to explain things, or just give answers?
Equitable Access to Mathematics	▪ Do I get to participate in meaningful mathematical learning? ▪ Can I hide or be ignored?
Agency, Ownership and Identity	▪ Do I get to explain, or present my ideas? Are they built on? ▪ Am I recognized as being capable and able to contribute in meaningful ways?
Formative Assessment	▪ Do classroom discussions include my thinking? ▪ Does instruction respond to my thinking and help me think more deeply?

(Schoenfeld, 2016)

Formative assessment in detail

I'm sure most of us are familiar with conversations similar to the following.

'How did your class get on with vectors today?'
'It seemed to go well, they were fine with it.'

It 'seemed' to go well? What could this possibly mean? Does it mean the teacher used a range of formative assessment strategies including mini whiteboards, exit tickets and conversations with individual pupils to inform their judgement? Or does it mean the class were set a task and produced lots of work in silence? Maybe there was a call to 'put your hand up if you get stuck', which no child did. How did the pupils know they were doing OK? Were they allowed to discuss their answers? Was a mark scheme available?

'Seemed to go well' is simply not good enough.

As teachers, we need to be constantly gathering information about our pupils' learning and then, if required, acting on it. We should never be sitting at our desks distractedly working on the computer while pupils are in the room. There is always some information to be found out or some support for learning that can be given. While pupils are engaged in a task, we should be *teaching between the desks*. That is, we should be questioning and probing pupils, not just checking answers. We should provide scaffolding and support for pupils who are struggling, or offer ways to stretch those who are not finding the task challenging. Every pupil should be engaged in meaningful learning.

Formative assessment is a core component of effective teaching. It is about communication. By employing formative assessment strategies, teachers can get information on pupil performance, ideas and understanding 'in the moment';

this can then be used to inform what the teacher says or does next. Formative assessment also gives teachers feedback on the quality of their instruction, so they can refine explanations, sequences of examples or the choice of tasks given. For pupils, formative assessment should provide information on **both** their thinking and their written work. This information may come in the form of feedback from the teacher or from other pupils. Importantly, all of this feedback – between pupils, from the teacher to pupils and vice versa – has little impact unless it is acted upon. Teachers have the autonomy to decide what to do with the information they receive, but pupils need to have the space for this created for them. It is essential to provide time and opportunities for pupils to reflect and act upon feedback during lessons.

Tasks underpin formative assessment. The work pupils do, which is the subject of the formative assessment, is a result of engagement with a task. When we ask pupils to reconsider or to engage in some form of correction, that is a task. When pupils work together to discuss the work they have produced, that is also a task.

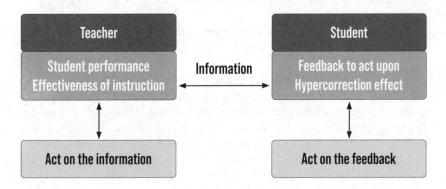

One of the most important papers of the past 20 years is *Mathematics inside the black box: assessment for learning in the mathematics classroom* (Hodgen and Wiliam, 2006). In this paper, Hodgen and Wiliam lay out five principles of learning:

Principle 1: Start from where the learner is
This usually involves starting with a question to establish what ideas pupils already have. We need to recognise that pupils have to reconstruct their ideas and that trying to overlay those ideas, without accounting for them, tends to lead to an understanding of mathematics as disconnected and inconsistent.

An interesting idea I first heard of from this book's editor, Mark McCourt, is to start a lesson with the hardest question the pupils will be asked that day. I extend this by including another question that is representative of the types of question pupils will encounter that day. This provides immediate information about pupil understanding. In some cases, particularly at early secondary level, pupils will be able to successfully complete the representative question. This means the lesson can begin by focusing on the harder standard of question. Even when pupils can't answer the questions posed, they will have ideas 'in and around' the representative question – assuming the curriculum is properly sequenced. This provides a useful starting point for discussion upon which to build the lesson.

I do not put prerequisite questions at the start of lessons; instead I use them in preceding lessons. Any small issues that arise can be dealt with in the moment. However, if there are significant issues, I am likely to require a full lesson to prepare pupils for the new learning. Once I have identified any issues, I can plan how to address them in the next lesson: I think it is better to know this in advance so I can create a well-designed lesson and task sequence to remedy these issues. I don't want to discover major issues with prerequisites on the day when new learning is planned!

Principle 2: Pupils must be active in the process

'Learning has to be done *by* them; it cannot be done *for* them.' If we use questions as suggested in the first principle for learning, the next consideration is how we act upon these questions. Teachers have to encourage and listen carefully to the range of explanations and ideas put forward by a variety of pupils. We are not listening for the right answer, or for what we want to hear. We are listening to learn what pupils understand. We don't aim to 'fix the pupil' but instead provide opportunities to address inconsistencies and errors, and to reformulate understanding of ideas. We cannot do the thinking for pupils but we are responsible for providing them with tasks and time in which to make sense of what we want them to learn.

Principle 3: Pupils need to talk about their ideas

When people discuss so-called CPA (concrete, pictorial, abstract) approaches, sometimes what is forgotten is the importance of language. 'Talking the talk is an important part of learning.' Being able to articulate mathematical ideas in words is a powerful representation in itself. As such, pupils need opportunities for whole-class, pair and group discussion. Of course, managing pupil discussion so it remains on-task can be a challenge. A common strategy is Think-Pair-Share. I sometimes build on this using an approach called snowballing, where individual work leads to paired work and then to group discussion.

For routine exercises

I will ask pupils to engage in the task individually, completing a short sequence of questions. After some time, I will ask pupils to pair up and compare their answers. I say, 'if you both have the same answer then we can assume, for now, that you are correct. If you have different answers, you need to talk about them and look at each other's work to resolve who is correct. If you can't agree, put a question mark.'

Next, I ask the pairs to pair up, so pupils are in groups of four. As before, I ask them to compare their answers: they can assume the work is correct if all four of them have the same answer, and they can discuss issues and examine their working if one or two of them have something different. If, at this point, there is a stand-off where pupils can't reach a resolution, they can ask me to join the discussion. I might confirm who is correct, then ask probing questions such as: 'Does it work if we change this?', 'Why can't this (other) solution be correct?', 'What would the graph look like?' or 'Can you build it with algebra tiles?' I might not say who is correct but instead ask pupils to think about a related sub-task and then come to some conclusion.

Finally, I read out the answers to the short exercise. I then ask if there is a group where everyone agreed on the answer but got it wrong. If so, this can be used as the basis for a whole-class discussion. This isn't necessarily more time-consuming than me going over the exercise at the board, but has the double benefit of giving pupils the opportunity to discuss their thinking and allowing them to be active in the process.

For rich, collaborative or problem-solving tasks

To begin with, I encourage pupils to read the task and formulate a couple of questions they have about it. I often ask pupils to write down 'something you are worried about'. Genuine problem-solving does invoke a sense of anxiety – we want to use this anxiety productively, if possible. With a problem-solving task, I will give individual pupils some time to start the process; if a task has been designed to be worked on collaboratively, I'll ask pupils to think about their first steps. Irrespective of task type, I give pupils time and space to play with their own ideas.

After a period of time, I ask pupils to pair up. They can ask each other the questions they wrote about the task and share any ideas they have. I then ask them to begin working on the task together. Again, at some later point, I ask them to join another pair to form a group of four. At this point, they can pool ideas or labour for the collaborative task or problem-solving question. They can ask questions, share their thinking and check their working.

It is important to clearly explain the purpose of this larger group work to pupils. Larger groups serve to open up pupil thinking to interrogation, but in an environment where it is safe to be wrong. This is an opportunity to listen to other pupils' ideas. It is important that pupils listen purposefully, rather than focusing on sharing their own thinking. Deliberately trying to understand the perspective of others will allow pupils to gain greater insight – particularly if other pupils have chosen a different approach. This group discussion is not about asserting a position; rather, if the task has been completed correctly, it provides opportunities to learn about alternative approaches. If pupils are stuck, it will allow them to share ideas about how they might proceed.

While pupils work in their pairs and groups of four, I move around the room, asking probing questions and responding to pupils who have questions for me; I am careful not to give answers or ease the problem significantly. Finally, all of this work might lead to a whole-class discussion or a final check of the answers, similar to that described for routine exercises above.

Principle 4: Pupils must understand the learning intention

> *Lists of criteria [are] rarely sufficient. Pupils need to engage in mathematical argument and reasoning in order that they and their peers can learn the ways in which the quality of mathematical work is judged. Peer and self-assessment are essential to this process, for they promote both active involvement and practice in making judgments about the quality of work.*

> (Hodgen and Wiliam, 2006)

Too often, learning intentions and success criteria become tokenised things that teachers have to write on the board at the start of a lesson, to satisfy some top-down policy from school leaders or the inspectorate. Starting a lesson with a question which is representative of what pupils will be asked that day gives pupils some sense of what might be involved. I would also suggest that the learning intention might emerge during the course of a lesson or sequence of lessons. Consider introducing calculus; the learning intention might be to know what it means to differentiate a function and be able to do so. This is a highly complex idea at the level of school mathematics, with a multitude of related ideas and principles. Actually calculating the derivative can also be technically demanding. To capture all of this will require many lessons with a layered succession of experiences and tasks. The extent of the learning will only become clear to pupils with reflection near the end of the block of lessons. There is an old saying in teaching, 'tell them what you are going to tell them, tell them it, tell them what you told them'. For direct teaching episodes, this might capture the essence of learning intentions.

I have concerns about writing lists of success criteria, in particular, since they require pupils to translate from a language representation to a mathematics representation. As stated above, we do want pupils to be able to do this; however, interpreting words about mathematics and extrapolating meaning is demanding for many pupils and so depending on this is problematic. Instead, co-construction of success criteria with pupils can be a useful strategy. Good examples of work, modelled clearly with key positive features highlighted, might be a better substitute. Sharing the work of individual pupils under a visualiser is also a good strategy: it is useful to collate pupil responses by taking photos of their work and saving these images to the cloud over a number of years, so that examples of strong and weak responses can be displayed anonymously to future pupils. Pupils can compare work with each other to critique. In doing so, they are not only improving each other's work, but also learning what good work is.

A major issue for consideration is that 'understanding' is hard to pin down. We can only ever make inferences if pupils have understood the intended learning through the completion of tasks. Further, there are occasions in maths classrooms – such as for discovery or investigation-based lessons – where a learning intention would give away the surprise. In those circumstances, they would be quite inappropriate.

Principle 5: Feedback should tell pupils how to improve

> When feedback focuses on the pupil as a good or bad achiever, emphasising overall judgment by marks, grades or rank order lists, it focuses attention on the self. When feedback focuses not on the person but on the strengths and weaknesses of the particular piece of work and what needs to be done to improve, performance is enhanced, especially when feedback focuses not only on what is to be done but also on how to go about it.
>
> (Hodgen and Wiliam, 2006)

This can be embodied through some of the strategies discussed above and other approaches, which will be discussed later in this chapter.

Mathematics knowledge for Teaching and professional noticing

Effective pedagogy is underpinned by Mathematical Knowledge for Teaching (MKT). This is a broad umbrella term capturing, among other things, a teacher's:

- knowledge of the mathematics
- ability to present mathematical ideas
- knowledge of appropriate representations and how to link them
- anticipation of pupil misconceptions

- knowledge of how to design instruction
- appropriate task selection
- appreciation of different instructional methods.

(van den Kieboom, 2013)

One way of considering effective teaching is to look at a matrix of MKT versus teacher responsiveness to pupil thinking, as captured in this diagram from Thomas *et al.* (2017).

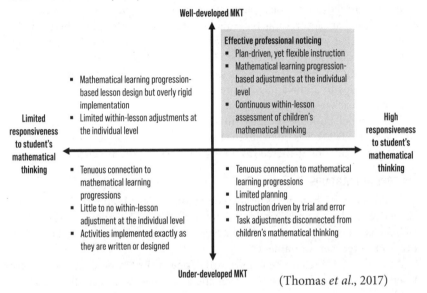

(Thomas *et al.*, 2017)

Professional noticing is a skill teachers use to identify and act upon salient mathematical actions of children. John Mason describes noticing as a collection of techniques for 'pre-paring' to notice in the moment and 'post-paring' by reflecting on the recent past to select what you want to notice or be sensitised to (Mason, 2001). That is, we cannot assume we will be responsive to pupils' mathematical thinking. This is something professional development can influence and it has been shown that experienced teachers with little focused professional development demonstrated professional noticing skills closer to those of pre-service teachers than their counterparts who participated in focused professional development. This suggests that teaching experience alone does not necessarily result in the development of such skills (Thomas *et al.*, 2017).

A framework in which to consider noticing is defined by Jacobs, Lamb and Philipp (2010) as the teacher's capacity to:

1. **Attend** to the pupil's mathematical conceptions and practices as they occur.
2. **Interpret** these conceptions and practices.
3. **Decide** on a productive instructional course of action based on this interpretation.

Use of noticing in a mathematical interaction between a teacher and a pupil should result in highly individualised and responsive instructional tactics. Of course, this depends on the teacher having well-developed MKT, so they can interpret correctly and choose next actions appropriately.

A phrase that captures much of this first framework is 'teaching between the desks': a teacher who moves among the pupils as they work, checking, probing, extending, questioning, observing, listening, reflecting, and interpreting what is going on. This teacher can choose to act or choose deliberately not to act, perhaps to allow a pupil more productive struggle, making for a truly responsive teacher–pupil interaction.

Professional noticing is clearly linked with effective formative assessment practices, while MKT is linked to the instructional decisions teachers make as a result of information gathered from formative assessment practices.

Teacher orientations

I would suggest that every teacher of mathematics should read the paper, 'Effective teachers of numeracy' (Askew *et al.*, 1997). This paper, written by a stellar cast of mathematics educators, lays out some of the beliefs and practices of effective teachers of numeracy.

As in the TRU recommendations earlier, one of the key practices of effective teachers is described as having 'systematic assessment and recording methods to monitor pupils' progress … to inform planning and teaching.' Teachers need to understand the progress pupils are making and where their understanding currently lies.

Pedagogical approaches might be important, and a teacher's subject knowledge is vital, but that is not enough. What teachers require is a profound understanding of fundamental mathematics and a repertoire of approaches for making this understanding accessible to pupils. These approaches will include a range of diagrammatic and verbal representations. For instance, teachers understand fraction operations but, to be highly effective teachers, they also need to understand the sub-constructs (conceptual meanings) of fraction and the approaches that might best support the development of each sub-construct. Further, they need to follow the developmental trajectories of how fraction develops. Teachers have to be able to externalise a perspective on fractions, which they have internalised to the extent that they, as mathematicians, rarely consider it explicitly. This is the mathematical knowledge for teaching.

Askew *et al.*'s (1997) paper lays out three orientations towards teaching mathematics:

- connectionist
- transmission
- discovery.

Models of teaching attempt to reduce a great deal of complexity into ideas we can grapple with and debate. Some of that complexity is inevitably lost in the process. No one teacher will fit exactly into one of these orientations; most of us will combine characteristics which could appear in any of the boxes. However, reporting on the observations from the study, an important conclusion is stated: 'teachers with a strongly connectionist orientation were more likely to have classes that made greater gains over the two terms than those classes of teachers with strongly discovery or transmission orientations.'

Connectionist orientation

Connectionist teaching focuses, as the name suggests, on making connections between mathematical ideas and across topics. Connectionist teachers use a variety of models and metaphors: physical manipulatives, diagrams, and written and verbal explanations. These teachers give the discussion of concept and images a central place in their classroom, which supports teacher explanation but can also be used formatively to assess pupils' understanding. It is difficult to visualise the understanding of another person; using different representations allows teacher and pupils to build a shared 'concept image' on which to base discussions. Connectionist teachers tend to believe that pupils come to lessons already in possession of knowledge but that the teacher has a responsibility to intervene and work with pupils to develop that knowledge further. These teachers build on the knowledge that pupils bring with them.

Connectionist teachers believe there is a balance to be struck between effective use of procedures and selection of efficient methods. For example, the subtraction 2016 – 1999 can be done using a procedure, but this is inefficient. Instead, the connectionist teacher would provide opportunities for pupils to engage with the number structure so they recognise opportunities to use less error-prone, mental techniques. Connectionist teachers believe that some of the complexity of mathematics has to be presented to pupils – for example, fractions, decimals and percentages are often taught together rather than as discrete topics. Pedagogically, these teachers do not easily fit either of the dichotomous 'direct teaching' or 'inquiry teaching' labels. Instead they use problem-solving tasks, investigation and inquiry where appropriate and teach explicitly at other times. These classrooms will have genuine whole-class dialogue. There will also be opportunities for group discussions and conversations between pairs of pupils.

Teachers with this orientation tend to believe that all pupils are able to become numerate and, as such, all pupils should engage in tasks which challenge and stretch them, not just those who are more able.

Transmission orientation

A transmission oriented teacher tends to believe in the importance of fluency in a collection of written procedures. For basic number, these teachers think pupils should have a procedure 'that works' for each of the operations, regardless of the level of efficiency of that method. What children know and bring with them to the class is of much less importance, unless it is related directly to a new procedure. Pupil-created methods are not used as a basis on which to build more efficient and effective methods.

Transmission oriented teachers tend to believe pupils vary in their ability to become numerate. If the teacher has explained a method clearly then any failure to learn must be a result of the pupils' inability, rather than a result of the teaching. Any errors made by pupils are seen as a failure to 'grasp' what was being taught. These errors are remedied by further reinforcement of the 'correct' method.

The focus on procedures inevitably leads to a segmentation of the curriculum. Mathematics is presented as discrete topics, where connections and relationships are not made explicit.

Problem solving tends to be nothing more than word problems, which are essentially a context for further practice of the methods. Any problem-solving teaching is around strategies for 'decoding' word problems, to identify which operation to use. This is quite far from the approach of a connectionist teacher, who would encourage pupils to create diagrams and make conjectures and would provide opportunities for collaboration around genuine problem-solving tasks.

Discovery orientation

Discovery oriented teachers have a perspective that tends to treat all methods of calculation as equally acceptable, regardless of whether the method is efficient. Pupils' creation of their own methods is central to this approach. These teachers place an emphasis on using concrete materials before proceeding to written methods. Calculation methods are selected primarily on the basis of representing the operation with physical manipulatives, rather than on what is mathematically more coherent for long term learning. Due to this, the curriculum can become fragmented, with connections not made across and between topics. Askew *et al.* (1997) note the emphasis on practical methods first of all:

> *The primary belief here is that becoming numerate is an individual activity derived from actions on objects. Learning takes precedence over teaching and the pace of learning is determined entirely by the pupils. Pupils' own strategies are the most important: understanding is based on working things out for themselves.*

Further, discovery oriented teachers believe pupils need to be 'ready' before they can learn new mathematical ideas. Pupil misunderstandings are often attributed to pupils not being 'ready' to learn the ideas. This illustrates an implicit assumption that pupils vary in their ability to become numerate.

Teachers with this orientation value problem solving. Problem solving is rooted in practical equipment and, as such, is typically introduced through practical problems.

Implications

The overwhelming conclusion from this study was that pupils in the classes with connectionist teachers made the most significant gains in their learning. Some of the key ideas are summarised below:

Connectionist	Transmission	Discovery
Teaching and learning are seen as complementary	Teaching is seen as separate and as having priority over learning	Learning is seen as separate and as having priority over teaching
Teaching is based on dialogue between teacher and pupils to explore understandings	Teaching is based on verbal explanations so pupils understand the teachers' methods	Teaching is based on practical activities so pupils discover methods for themselves
Believe pupils learn through being challenged and struggling to overcome difficulties	Believe pupils learn through being introduced to one procedure at a time and remembering it	Believe pupils need to be 'ready' before they can learn certain ideas
Believe most pupils are able to become numerate	Believe pupils vary in their ability to become numerate	Believe pupils vary in the rate at which their numeracy develops

(Adapted from Askew *et al.*, 1997)

Transmission approaches are still the most common in schools. This approach also seems to dominate much of Edu-Twitter and has been captured in popular books. The debate, however, has become oversimplified. At times the arguments can be superficial, missing the important ideas that can be drawn from the vast canon of literature around mathematics teaching while acknowledging the contributions that can be made by, for instance, cognitive science. It is not a case of 'either-or'.

Ollerton *et al.* (2020) describe this superficial debate and the reality of classroom practice thus:

> *'direct instruction' is interpreted as telling learners everything they need to know (and we see many examples of this when we visit classrooms) while 'inquiry' is interpreted as leaving them to construct all methods and knowledge for themselves (which we seldom see, although we do often see inquiry).*

This correlates with my own experience during my time travelling across Scotland to deliver CPD and consultancy to schools. While I encountered small numbers of teachers who could be described as having strong discovery or transmission orientations, most teachers seemed to draw on a range of beliefs and practices. Most common overall, in the lessons I observed, were teachers whose practice lay somewhere between connectionist and transmission orientations, with the majority of those leaning more towards transmission.

Later in this chapter, I will outline further the importance of pedagogic knowledge for teaching of mathematics. Ollerton *et al.* echo this, stating:

> *The limited time for educational input on many routes into teaching mean that generic teaching skills are often the major focus for new teachers rather than pedagogic knowledge for mathematics, that is the specific knowledge about how children learn mathematics and how our concepts build up in sequences of lessons (see ACME, 2015). In most of Europe new teachers study the conceptual structure of, say, multiplication or axiomatic reasoning as part of their training, as well as experiencing mathematical inquiry as a feature of being mathematical. They therefore understand the role of inquiry in learning.*

A later piece of work by Malcolm Swan advocates a collaborative approach (Swan, 2006). This most closely resembles the connectionist perspective.

The diagram below shows beliefs as being on a continuum between transmission and collaborative orientations. I think this is helpful, as it appreciates the nuance. We are all somewhere along that continuum and should, as professionals, be capable of moving along it based on professional reading and reflection on our own experiences. This thinking underpinned the development of Swan's (2005) publication, *Improving learning in mathematics*, which we will discuss in more detail in the chapter on conceptual tasks. Swan states that many pupils view mathematics as a series of unrelated procedures and techniques that have to be committed to memory. Instead, we want them to engage in discussing and explaining ideas, challenging and teaching one another, creating and solving each other's questions and working collaboratively to share methods and results.

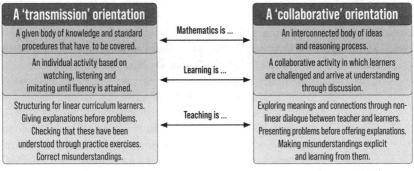

A 'transmission' orientation		A 'collaborative' orientation
A given body of knowledge and standard procedures that have to be covered.	Mathematics is ...	An interconnected body of ideas and reasoning process.
An individual activity based on watching, listening and imitating until fluency is attained.	Learning is ...	A collaborative activity in which learners are challenged and arrive at understanding through discussion.
Structuring for linear curriculum learners. Giving explanations before problems. Checking that these have been understood through practice exercises. Correct misunderstandings.	Teaching is ...	Exploring meanings and connections through non-linear dialogue between teacher and learners. Presenting problems before offering explanations. Making misunderstandings explicit and learning from them.

(Swan, 2005)

In this publication, Swan argues that 'traditional, "transmission" methods in which explanations, examples and exercises dominate do not promote robust, transferrable learning that endures over time or that may be used in non-routine situations.' The key here is the word 'dominate'. There is a place for explanations, examples and exercises – but they are inadequate on their own. The model of teaching proposed here 'emphasises the interconnected nature of the subject and it confronts common conceptual difficulties through discussion.' An interesting feature of the recommendations is that pupils are, sometimes, given opportunities to tackle problems *before* the teacher offers guidance and support. The tasks chosen must be relevant and within grasp of the pupils' current understanding, of course.

Swan's (2005) paper highlights eight practices of effective mathematics teaching, as summarised below. The overlap with some of the other writing we have discussed is evident.

Teaching is more effective when it:

1. Builds on the knowledge students already have. *This means developing formative assessment techniques and adapting our teaching to accommodate individual learning needs* (Black and Wiliam, 1998).
2. Exposes and discusses common misconceptions. *Learning activities should expose current thinking, create 'tensions' by confronting students with inconsistencies, and allow opportunities for resolution through discussion* (Askew and Wiliam, 1995).

3. Uses higher-order questions. *Questioning is more effective when it promotes explanation, application and synthesis rather than mere recall* (Askew and Wiliam, 1995).
4. Uses cooperative small group work. *Activities are more effective when they encourage critical, constructive discussion, rather than argumentation or uncritical acceptance* (Mercer, 2000). Shared goals and group accountability are important (Askew and Wiliam, 1995).
5. Encourages reasoning rather than 'answer getting'. *Often, students are more concerned with what they have 'done' than with what they have learned. It is better to aim for depth than for superficial 'coverage'.*
6. Uses rich, collaborative tasks. *The tasks we use should be accessible, extendable, encourage decision making, promote discussion, encourage creativity, encourage 'what if' and 'what if not?' questions* (Ahmed, 1987).
7. Creates connections between topics. *Students often find it difficult to generalise and transfer their learning to other topics and contexts. Related concepts (such as division, fraction and ratio) remain unconnected. Effective teachers build bridges between ideas* (Askew et al., 1997).
8. Uses technology in appropriate ways. *Computers and interactive whiteboards allow us to present concepts in visual dynamic and exciting ways that motivate students.*

The question that needs to be addressed now is: is there anywhere in the world where this sort of teaching happens regularly? The answer to that question is: yes, in Japan.

The Japanese approach to mathematics teaching

Let us take some time now to consider Japanese teachers' perspectives.

In a study by Zhou *et al.* (2006), Japanese teachers commented on what they considered to be the components of a well-taught maths lesson:

- pupils' understanding of the material
- not too much talking by the teacher
- a slow enough pace to allow pupils at all levels to understand
- proper use of materials where appropriate
- proper use of the blackboard to illustrate a variety of solution strategies (neatly written).

In contrast, the same study asked some American teachers what they considered to be the components of a well-taught maths lesson:

- behavioural indications of pupil engagement – pupils 'on task'
- clear language and explanations by the teacher
- not too little talk by the teacher
- a fast-enough pace to ensure bright pupils won't become bored
- use of materials and the blackboard, especially by the teacher and knowledgeable pupils.

From the limited number of teachers interviewed here, we can infer that the Japanese teachers tend more towards the connectionist/collaborative perspectives outlined above, while the American teachers tend towards a more transmission approach. While it is naïve to make generalisations about teachers in an entire country, there is evidence that within-country differences in teaching approach and beliefs are much smaller than the differences that exist between countries (Askew *et al.*, 2010).

It is worth noting how the Japanese teachers use physical manipulatives. Unlike discovery-oriented teachers, described above, the Japanese teachers used these materials in parallel with more abstract representations. This is in contrast to starting from the physical, with the expectation of this providing a foundation for the abstract, before gradually withdrawing the physical manipulatives. The Japanese teachers' approach is similar to the most effective teachers from the *Effective teachers of numeracy paper* (Askew *et al.*, 1997), who worked with a connected range of representations in parallel.

Lesson phasing

It is common in Japan, in primary and early secondary, for lessons to adhere to the following structure:

1. Presentation of a problem.
2. Individual problem-solving by pupils.
3. Whole-class discussion about the methods for solving the problem.
4. Summing up by the teacher (exercises/extensions).

(Shimizu, 1999)

The focus is on comparing and contrasting various solution strategies for an opening problem, while building connections with previous learning and maintaining a forward-facing perspective to what comes in later years. Each of the lesson components listed is so well established that there is vocabulary to describe the associated teacher actions.

- Presentation of a problem is known as **Hatsumon**. Lessons usually begin with a practical or word problem, which might be displayed on the board or selected from the textbook. The teacher presents the problem and gives pupils time to read, then confirms that pupils have understood the problem. If not, the teacher may ask the pupils to reread it or, in some cases, might ask some pupils to share their initial thoughts about how to solve the problem.
- The next phase involves pupils engaging with the problem. During this phase, pupils develop their ideas individually to begin with. The teacher is involved in the process of **Kikan-shido**, which means 'instruction at pupils' desks' or, as I like to think about it, 'teaching between the desks'. When appropriate, the teacher will support any pupils who are struggling, perhaps with a suggested direction or some questions for reflection. (They will not simply tell the pupil which procedure to apply.) During this phase of purposeful scanning, the teacher moves around the room, making mental notes of pupils' work and identifying pupils who have good ideas. In the subsequent discussion, the teacher will select some pupils who have completed the task as anticipated, some pupils who have used alternative approaches, and perhaps some pupils who have reached an incorrect solution; all these processes can be useful teaching points. Pupils are sometimes given time to collaborate with a peer to share and discuss strategies, before the whole-class discussion.
- The lesson then moves into the phase which involves whole-class discussion. 'The term **Neriage** describes the dynamic and collaborative nature of the whole-class discussion during the lesson. In Japanese, the term Neriage means kneading up or polishing up' (Shimizu, 1999). This is essentially a metaphor for polishing the individual pupils' ideas and drawing them together towards some key mathematical idea, through whole-class discussion. This is considered to be an essential element of the process. Pupils identified during Kikan-shido will be called upon, in a considered order, to present their solution methods on the blackboard to the rest of the class. This will be done so there is a degree of encouragement for pupils who have used a naïve approach. Once pupils' ideas have been presented, they will be compared and contrasted through discussion. The teacher's role is not to tell pupils which is the best solution but to guide the discussion towards an integrated idea. Pupils will critique each other's ideas, identifying strong and weak points.
- The final phase involves summing up the findings and reflecting upon them. In Japanese, the word **Matome** – which literally means 'summing up' – is used to describe this phase. This part of the lesson encompasses the identification of important ideas and generalisations. The teacher

leads the process, reviewing the key ideas and emphasising important points; they will also make a considered judgement on pupils' work in terms of mathematical sophistication. At this stage, if appropriate, some practice questions will be issued for pupils to work on.

To draw a contrast between this and the typical Anglo-American approach, we can consider the following lessons on area of a triangle, observed by Zhou *et al.* (2006).

> *Both lessons introduced the formula for finding the area of triangles to upper primary school pupils but differed in the approach to establishing this. The Japanese lesson was structured around children manipulating images to find informal methods for calculating the areas of triangles and with the teacher subsequently drawing these together into the accepted formula at the end of the lesson. The American teacher introduced the formula early in the lesson: the pupils then applied this to several problems.*

The Japanese approach here sits much more comfortably within the frameworks of collaborative or connectionist orientations outlined previously. Of course, the problem task the teacher selects needs to be appropriate and within the grasp of pupils' current understanding, so they can begin, at least, to identify key features and ideas.

Levels of teacher expertise

The sort of teaching described is more challenging than that which uses mainly transmission approaches. This is recognised in Japan too. In their first teaching posts, teachers are considered to be apprentices: they work with an experienced colleague, who coaches and mentors them closely with a focus on subject-specific pedagogy. According to Sugiyama (2008), teachers are generally regarded as passing through three stages in their practice:

- **Level 1**: The teacher can tell pupils important basic ideas of mathematics such as facts, concepts and procedures.
- **Level 2**: The teacher can explain the meanings of and reasons behind the important basic ideas of mathematics for pupils to understand them.
- **Level 3**: The teacher can provide pupils with opportunities to understand these basic ideas and support their learning so pupils become independent learners.

We might consider a progression such as:

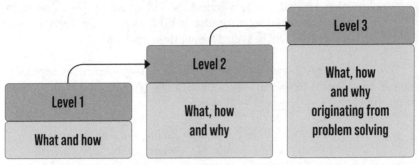

To implement a Level 3 lesson, teachers must be able to choose a good task, to identify the pre-requisite knowledge, and, most importantly, must be able to nurture pupils to apply their knowledge to a new situation.

Contrasting with other countries

Japan performs very well on international comparative studies such as TIMSS and PISA. However, other countries, with different approaches also do well. Is it possible to attribute the connectionist philosophy to the high levels of achievement in other countries?

> *You can have an egalitarian education and high standards (Finland), or you can have a selective one and still have high standards (Singapore). You can have a problem solving pedagogy (Japan) or you can have a teacher centred one (Korea) and either can lead to high standards.*
>
> (Askew *et al.*, 1997)

There are commonalities between these countries, particularly those in East Asia. Curricula tend to be well thought out and supportive of long-term learning.

In a video analysis study comparing countries in east Asia and the West, Neubrand (2006) noted from his observations that 'making connections' could be a central distinctive issue of teaching in high-achieving countries. Looking at tasks alone, however, does not reveal how teachers use these tasks in practice. Procedural tasks can give rise to cognitive acuity that becomes focused on conceptual understanding. Similarly, potentially rich tasks can be made procedural by the teachers' interventions. Neubrand stated that, in high-attaining countries, problems classified as 'making connections' tended to retain this focus in the course of teaching. However, in lessons based around problems initially classified as 'using procedures', 20–55% of these problems evolved, through teaching emphases, into 'making connections' or 'stating concepts' problems. The role of the teacher in drawing more from the task is vital; the teacher can take a resource and draw pupils into richer mathematical thinking.

What appears clear is that thinking that is rooted in making connections is a key consideration in successful mathematics teaching. The pedagogical approaches may vary, the task selections might sometimes seem uninspired, but the teacher actions and prompts have the potential to 'make or break' the richness of a lesson.

Pedagogy and tasks

Doyle (1988) describes the work that pupils are required to do as being about processes and product. Work is the context in which a significant amount of classroom time is spent.

Teachers often present lessons or structure tasks which focus on computational procedures and accuracy of calculations. In many tasks, pupils know in advance which strategy is required. For example, word problems involving multiplication will immediately follow an exercise on practising multiplication. This is problematic, as part of learning procedures is knowing when to apply them to unfamiliar situations. If pupils know, in advance, that all of the problems will require multiplication, this decision-making process has been removed.

From observational study, Doyle suggests that teachers often emphasise a smooth-flowing work system with high levels of production. This is normally focused on familiar work or on tasks where pupils are heavily guided. As I have already outlined, procedural fluency *is* important, but a mathematics education focusing solely on procedural fluency is incomplete. Of course, a focus on production of answers is easier to manage as a teacher and pupils might accomplish a large amount of work in a classroom where they are faced with only familiar, scaffolded or procedural practice. But is production our aim? Production alone cannot be taken to mean understanding. Pupils can practise procedures or follow algorithms but fail to understand the underlying principles and relationships which underpin these exercises. Another problem, where smooth flowing of the work system is seen as a priority, is that the focus is predominantly on producing answers. It is entirely possible for pupils to produce correct answers while still holding on to misconceptions, which go unnoticed by the teacher because pupils have been given little opportunity to articulate their thinking. A mathematics classroom in which pupil thinking is not aired and non-routine problems are rarely encountered might look successful on the surface – because pupils are producing correct answers – but often does not result in long-term learning or meaningful comprehension.

Teachers often interpret the curriculum and smooth it out by removing the inherently problematic content; 'they won't be able to do that'. By using a large amount of prompting to keep production rates high, teachers limit pupils' opportunities to develop autonomous learning capabilities. The dependency on the teacher is accentuated. Yet, what we really want is for pupils to become independent problem solvers, who are confident enough to face new mathematics on their own. Where teaching is set up so pupils are overly dependent on the teacher, pupils will say things like, 'Mr Smith got me through the exam. I'll only do maths next year if he is taking the class.' This is not a badge of honour for a teacher. Instead, we should aim to be so effective that the pupils don't realise the extent of the role we have played in their success. A goal is for pupils to confidently proceed to further study, with knowledge, procedural fluency and conceptual understanding but also with a sense of themselves as mathematicians.

Smooth-flowing lessons focused on routine or familiar work are suitable for managing the complexities of classroom environments. They provide a clear structure and boundaries, are accessible to almost every pupil, and have tangible outcomes – the work pupils produce. However, teachers need to describe the connections between lessons to build broad understanding of content and to place individual tasks within a wider context of understanding. This is not easily done using transmission.

Teachers have an important role in ensuring pupils engage meaningfully in mathematical thinking at all times. This is challenging to do when pupils are engaged in either rich collaborative or problem-solving tasks. Both of these types of task are typically more complex than routine problems and require more time in deep thought. If we want pupils to develop the capacity to think, reason and problem solve, those pupils need exposure to high-level, cognitively complex tasks.

The potential of a task can be made or broken by teacher actions, both in the immediate context and also as a result of the classroom culture that has been established over time. 'Although attention to the nature of mathematical instructional tasks is important, attention to the classroom process surrounding mathematical tasks is equally needed' (Henningsen and Stein, 1997).

When pupils engage with problem solving or rich tasks, there is a degree of ambiguity as to what is expected compared with routine exercises. Pupils will get stuck – and quite rightly so; after all, a problem is not really a problem if we know the solution path at the outset. Whenever a pupil encounters a problem, they should think to themselves, 'I do not know the solution to this problem *yet*.' There is a natural desire from pupils for a reduction in task complexity; how the teacher reacts to this is key. The teacher might decide to give pupils some information that eases the task significantly – for instance, stating which procedure to use. This reduces the demand and robs pupils of the opportunity to engage in high-level mathematical thought. Pupils are now applying a procedure, as in a routine lesson. Anderson describes a specific type of scaffolding for when a pupil cannot work through a task on their own: essentially, a teacher or peer provides assistance that enables the pupil to complete the task alone but does not reduce the overall complexity or cognitive demand of the task (Anderson, 1989).

There is a number of reasons for pupils not engaging in high-level mathematical thought. Primarily, the task needs to be within grasp of pupils' current understanding: there must be adequate prior knowledge to provide a secure basis for meaningful engagement with the task. There are also issues surrounding a pupil's motivation – is the problem one they want to solve? Placing accountability on pupils to participate in the task also plays a role. If the teacher views a task as an 'add on', pupils are likely to pick up on this. For some tasks, particularly practical work, pupils may enthusiastically manipulate the materials and, on a surface level, appear to be engaging meaningfully, when in fact they are not thinking mathematically at all. It is the role of the teacher here to make explicit connections between the activity and the mathematics.

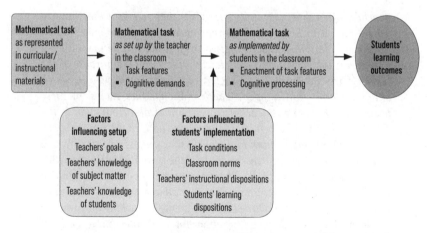

(Henningsen and Stein, 1997)

The diagram above illustrates the transformation of the task designer's intentions through to actual pupil learning. The role of the teacher is clear. First, the teacher will have specific goals in mind, in terms of what he or she hopes the learning outcomes will be. They might not appreciate the extent of what is involved in a task if they have not either attempted the task or consulted the teaching notes. This isn't necessarily an issue with routine exercises, but with rich tasks the teacher risks failing to utilise the full potential of the task – as I have learned from experience! When I first used the excellent resources from the Standards Unit (Swan, 2005), I chose to simply use the printout materials, without reading the notes. The following year, when I did read the notes, I realised how much potential learning I had left off the table.

At this set-up phase of any task, the teacher might want to encourage specific ways of working. For instance, they might encourage pupils to use multiple representations to support their explanations and justifications, or to try multiple solution strategies to confirm their answer. These ways of working are examples of task features. There are many factors which influence pupils' implementation of a task. The level of cognitive demand placed on pupils is influenced by the types of support offered and by the extent to which a teacher is willing to let a pupil struggle with a difficult problem. The extent to which pupils are willing to engage in productive struggle is another major factor. The classroom culture, ways of working and shared understanding of what it means to do mathematics all come into focus here.

Hugh Burkhardt explains how his design work takes these issues into account:

> Teachers often don't let pupils struggle – they feel as if they have to 'sort it out'. Ann Brown had a lovely phrase: 'lethal variance'. When we design a lesson we don't expect it to go exactly as defined, but we don't want the variance to completely undermine the purpose of the lesson. Early intervention to 'sort it out' is a typical way in which lethal variation can happen. The 'common issues tables' in those lessons are there to give teachers a very practical introduction to the research. They serve as a guide to the errors pupils make. For instance, we know many pupils think of distance–time graphs as a picture and come to generalise, incorrectly, that 'if the graph goes up then this means the journey is uphill'. These common issues are listed, but so are the suggested interventions. These are all about making the pupils think harder, not about telling them the answer. Teaching non-routine mathematics is about blending observing and intervening, only in a way which moves pupil thinking forward. It's not about putting forward what the teacher is thinking.

In tasks where high levels of cognitive demand are intended, such as problem solving or rich collaborative tasks, it can be difficult to sustain a high level of thinking. In their study, Henningsen and Stein (1997) established three typical sorts of 'cognitive decline' and their possible causes:

Type of cognitive decline	Possible causes
Decline into cognitive activity which is focused on mechanical use of procedures with no connection to underlying meaning	▪ Can be a result of teachers 'taking over' difficult pieces of a task and performing them for pupils ▪ Focus becomes on completeness or accuracy of answers at expense of thinking processes ▪ Too little time allocated ▪ Classroom norms aren't established for rich working: pupils rarely engage in these sorts of task, normally doing routine problems
Decline into unsystematic exploration	▪ Inappropriate task selection relative to prior knowledge ▪ No clear expectations of mathematical activity outlined ▪ Too little scaffolding in task to support pupils – teachers need to know their pupils to establish how much is needed, without overly reducing cognitive demands ▪ Too much time allocated
Decline into activity with no mathematical focus	▪ Inappropriate task selection relative to prior knowledge ▪ Classroom management problems ▪ Too much time allocated ▪ No clear connections between activity and the mathematics

Henningsen and Stein assert that 'the mere presence of high-level mathematical tasks in the classroom will not automatically result in pupils' engagement in doing mathematics.' They reason that the ambient classroom environment, established by the teacher, has to support this engagement. The mathematical learning community in the classroom will have ways of working and values which are enacted, if not stated explicitly. A teacher might say 'take your time' but then praise a group for finishing first. What is clear is that establishing a classroom culture and ways of working which will result in pupils being able to engage in and then sustain high-level thinking is challenging. The pedagogical actions of the teacher influence the type of classroom culture which is established.

Tasks are important: they are the basis of the activity. Fortunately, there exist superbly-designed materials from the Standards Unit and the Mathematics Assessment Project. These tasks, due to their excellent design features, usually result in high-level pupil thinking. They also come with excellent teacher notes which can be highly impactful forms of professional learning. Teachers interested in developing their pedagogy are advised to start by trialling some of these lessons.

Classroom discussion

When making sense of ideas, pupils need opportunities to work both independently and collaboratively. At times they need to be able to think and work quietly, away from the demands of the whole class. At other times, they need to be in pairs or small groups so they can share ideas and learn with and from others. And at other times they need to be active participants in purposeful, whole-class discussion, where they have opportunities to clarify their understanding and be exposed to broader interpretations of the mathematical ideas that are the present focus.

Providing opportunities for pupils to express, discuss and argue about ideas is particularly important in mathematics teaching. However, effective ways of managing class discussion are complex and take time for teachers to develop. Hodgen and Wiliam (2006) describe the key elements involved in developing classroom discussion:

- challenging activities that promote thinking and discussion
- encouraging pupil talk through questioning and listening
- strategies to support all learners to engage in discussion
- peer discussion between pupils
- rich and open whole-class discussions.

The following teacher moves can also be productive, according to Michaels, O'Connor and Resnick (2008):

- revoicing (when the teacher restates something a pupil has said, attributing it to the pupil)
- asking pupils to restate someone else's reasoning
- asking pupils to apply their own reasoning to someone else's reasoning
- prompting pupils for further participation
- asking pupils to explicate their reasoning
- challenging pupils' reasoning by asking for counterexamples.

Reflections

We end this chapter with a series of reflections from various educators about their own pedagogy. There is much insight to be gained from these excellent thinkers. Each of these reflections is direct quotation.

Mike Ollerton

I want the pupils to work towards the understanding of the key mathematical concepts. The task is there for them to do some initial work on. I want to set up a task where the main ideas underneath the concept begin to reveal themselves. That means I'm not having to explain the concepts. What I don't want to do is to explain what I understand about the concept because I want the learners to make their own sense and understanding of it. I don't necessarily want them to understand and see things the way I see things.

For instance, if I put myself in the position of a pupil, my most powerful learning is when somebody gives me something to think about, or to work on or to discuss. Things fall into place for me through that interaction with the task and with other people. I'm thinking, 'Yes! That's what the essence of this is about' kind of thing. ... Later on, I can then see isomorphisms between the structurer's own concept and how it links with other concepts. So it's not just the concept in isolation; it's the concept and how it links with other concepts. I don't want somebody to tell me those links, I've got to create those links for myself. But that doesn't mean to say that my teacher can't give me some direction and ask questions along the lines of, 'What about this and what about that?'

On the contrary, I'll describe something I didn't think was good teaching. I was at a conference and during a session there was a really interesting idea the presenter had given us delegates to work on. After about five minutes, they stopped us all and told us what the answers were. They had this lesson plan where they wanted to do this, this, this and this. We were just passengers on their journey. Yet the starting task was so powerful, I could've worked on that for 15–20 minutes, then come back to see what other people were doing with it, so on and so forth. It was a new task to me: I'd never thought about the idea that way before, it was just so exciting for me. All of that excitement got torn away and then the rest of the session became a lecture. It became the teacher showing off. It became what I describe as 'teacher lust', where the teacher is either lusting for the learners to know what they know or the teacher's wanting to show off what they know. It was all kind of pre-scripted. That, to me, wasn't really about the learning experience. Instead of that, I would rather find ways of me, as the teacher, not being in control. I'd rather have a situation where I wasn't expecting people to believe what I tell them just because I'm the teacher.

Tom Francome

Pedagogically – it depends. There is never a 'I'll never do that'. I use the same tasks a lot. I think it's important that teachers can extend and adapt tasks in the moment. I like using the same tasks, year on year, in a scheme of work because then I have experience of where to take it – what sort of questions to ask etc. I know the sorts of things pupils might say, where they might get stuck. I know good things to do before the task, how to follow it up etc. Doing the same tasks across the department is a way of building in quality assurance. I think we should have some canonical tasks, which are tasks everyone has to do, written in bold on the scheme of work. 1089 would be one such example! (Write down a three-digit number whose digits are decreasing. Then reverse the digits to create a new number, and subtract this number from the original number. With the resulting number, add it to the reverse of itself. The number you will get is 1089!)

In preparing to use a new task I think it is important to do it, get a feel for it, pre-empt pupil questions, think about how to extend or ease, think about possible misconceptions and get a sense of what pupils are attending to. Of course, there are things which we take for granted, so that is hard. Part of the skill of a teacher is being able to distance yourself from doing the maths. Part of you does the maths and part of you watches yourself doing the maths. Then you get the insight for pupils etc.

Other times, I'm happy to just go into a lesson with a new task, but you need to have built up confidence and a way of working in the classroom to do this. You need to feel comfortable in not knowing what to do, in front of the pupils. Sometimes it is fun to say, 'Mr Smith sent me this task, he thought you'd have fun with it. Let's see what we can do with it.'

Susan Whitehouse

My view on teaching maths is that the teacher's role is to help the pupils to form their own understanding. It's not the teacher's role to convey their own mathematical understanding to their pupils, and it's certainly not to convey a collection of set methods. Having said that, I would rather a pupil ended up with the teacher's understanding than with no understanding at all!

Multiple representations – in particular looking at things in both an algebraic and a graphical way – are important to me. I also think mathematical discussion and collaboration are very important. Asking questions that challenge a pupil's understanding and force them to justify themselves, sometimes by creating cognitive conflicts, is certainly part of my teaching. This might be part of a task, but it might be in direct questioning. I will always have mini whiteboards out in my lessons, not necessarily for 'show me' Q&A (though I do a bit of that) but more because I find the pupils are more willing to have a go and take mathematical risks knowing that it can be erased.

A good task will be accessible to all the pupils but still challenging to the top end. It will allow me to circulate and to listen to the pupils discussing maths. This will let me pick up on misconceptions and see how the pupils view the concepts, which will inform my teaching.

It may sound trite, but as teachers we need to always plan our lessons keeping in mind our aims. I don't just mean our narrow 'learning objectives' type aims, but also our wider mathematical and pedagogical aims. For example, suppose I was teaching a lesson on completing the square. With every class I've ever taught that topic to I've probably had very similar objectives ... [in terms of the central] process of completing the square. But I will also have other aims to do with a focus on proof or problem-solving or mathematical language or collaborative working or resilience or curve sketching etc. These aims will vary from group to group and the task I choose has to be appropriate for supporting these aims. Something that is a great task when I'm teaching a topic to one class won't necessarily be a great task when I'm teaching the same topic to a different class, because it will depend on my wider aims.

John Mason

$$1 + 2 = 3$$
$$4 + 5 + 6 = 7 + 8$$
$$9 + 10 + 11 + 12 = 13 + 14 + 15$$

I know I didn't come up with this, but I have no idea where I found it!

I do it in silence. I write 1 + 2 and then I pause, write =, then pause and scratch my head before writing 3. Then I pause before writing 4 + 5 + 6 =, then pause again and scratch my head before writing 7 + 8. Almost always, in any reasonable size group, I'm going to hear a sound of surprise from somebody in the room. The reason for this is because everybody else is expecting 15 instead of my 7 + 8. That sets me up and now, depending on the maturity and sophistication of the audience, I might play. I might put my chalk or my pen where the 9 is going to be and pause for a minute and try to get them to anticipate what's coming next. So, this task I use to try and underline the notion that I want everyone to be anticipating what is coming, making conjectures and then modifying that conjecture on the basis of what happens.

Then I do the 9 + 10 + 11 + 12 = and pause, write 13 + 14 + 15 and then I have options. I can turn and say to them 'and is it?', or I often pause at this point and pretend I am checking it. Then the next line, I'm about to write 16 when I stop and say something like, 'I know that you know what I am likely to write next. Am I right?' and everybody says 'yes!' even though they haven't got the slightest idea, as I could do all sorts of unpleasant things at this point! So, we do the 16 and then we work on different ways of checking that these [calculations] are correct.

I've been shown something like 11 different ways of checking that they are correct without actually adding them all up. For example, 9 + 10 + 11 + 12 = 13 + 14 + 15 can be thought of as 9 + (9 + 1) + (9 + 2) + (9 + 3) = (12 + 1) + (12 + 2) + (12 + 3). Consider the 13 and the 10, we have (12 + 1) and (9 + 1). They differ by 3. The same for 14 and 11, 15 and 12. We have 3 of these 'differ by 3' which gives us the missing 9! That's just one of many ways of thinking about this.

Next I usually say that my wife is thinking of a number and I don't know what it is, so I'm going to call it a cloud and draw a little cloud. That tells me the line that we want to do next. We've done the first, second, third line and we now want to do the cloud-th line. So I ask, what will be the first number in the cloud-th line? Somebody is usually able to offer that it is cloud squared. I then check that everyone has caught on before asking them to write out the cloud-th line. Next, I ask them to check it. They may look confused, but I suggest that they use the same method they use to check the specific cases. They can use the same method to check the generality. Specialising and then generalising arise from this task.

This can take me 10 to 30 minutes depending on the group I am working with. Then, at the end of the session, once there has been a break, I show them these four pictures, one after the other.

Once they've talked to each other about what is the same and what is different about [the pictures], I ask them to count how many little cubes there are in the right-hand slice of the bottom-left diagram (16) and then in the next slices (17, 18, 19, 20). Next I ask them how many little cubes there are in the front slice of the bottom-right diagram (21), then in the other slices (22, 23, 24). What we've done here is to look at the line beginning 16, from the original task! There is often an audible reaction from people as they come to realise the connection with what we worked on earlier.

Now we have a basis to carry on. We can consider how the fifth line would look, in blocks etc. We could then suggest making up another one which is a bit different in its layout.

And you can go on and do all of that, with an audience of appropriate sophistication. But we don't have to – we can come at it many different ways!

5 Classification of Tasks

So far, I have argued for a rich and varied diet of mathematical tasks, to develop the whole mathematician. I consider procedural fluency, conceptual understanding and mathematical behaviours of equal priority. To help our exploration of different task types, I considered that it would be useful to classify the tasks in some way. There are many possible ways of doing this.

The demands of different tasks

In Chapter 2 we encountered the idea of tasks as being the vehicle for mathematical activity and asserted that the mathematical activity itself is no guarantee that learning will happen. We require pupils to think hard about the right things and then to internalise those ideas. The role of the teacher in all of this is to ensure that the ideas are aired and that pupils' thinking is given a platform, so it can be refined if required and to allow the teacher to compare and contrast the thinking of different pupils before bringing things together.

The tasks we set pupils determine the nature of their interaction with the mathematics. In our task selection, we need to have a clear focus on the sorts of thing the task will require pupils to think about. Crabbe says of tasks that 'they serve a communicative purpose between teacher and pupil, by conveying the teacher's intent for learning and the pupil's conception of that intent' (Crabbe, 2007). If we seek to develop some fluency with a procedure then drill exercises may suffice; however, if we seek both conceptual understanding and procedural fluency of some given idea then drill exercises are likely inadequate vehicles for this learning.

Stein and Smith (2011) describe levels of cognitive demand as summarised in this table:

Level of cognitive demand

Lower level	*Higher level*
Memorisation • Reproducing facts, rules, formulas or definitions with no connection to underlying meaning • Cannot be solved using procedures, because a procedure does not exist or because the time offered is too short to use a procedure • Not ambiguous	Procedures with connections • Attention on purpose of procedure and understanding of mathematical concepts • Suggest pathway to follow that is connected to conceptual idea • Represented in multiple ways • Requires cognitive effort
Procedures without connections • Algorithmic, use of procedure is specifically called for • Little ambiguity • No connection to meaning that underlies procedure • Focus on correct answer, rather than developing mathematical understanding • No explanation required	Doing mathematics • Requires complex and non-algorithmic thinking • Requires exploration and understanding of mathematical concepts, processes or relationships • Requires considerable cognitive effort • Requires students to analyse the task and examine constraints that may limit the solution or strategies

A helpful elaboration of this for evaluating task selection in lessons in Singaporean classrooms is shown:

Levels of cognitive demand	Characteristics of tasks
Level 0 – Very low Memorisation tasks	• Reproduction of facts, rules, formulae • No explanations required
Level 1 – Low Procedural tasks without connections	• Algorithmic in nature • Focused on producing correct answers • Typical textbook word problems • No explanations required
Level 2 – High Procedural tasks with connections	• Algorithmic in nature • Has a meaningful / 'real world' context • Explanations required
Level 3 – Very High Problem solving / doing mathematics	• Non-algorithmic in nature, requires understanding and application of mathematical concepts • Has a 'real world' context / a mathematical structure • Explanations required

(Kaur, Wong and Chew, 2018)

To learn well, we need to think hard and this thinking has to be productive. I broadly agree with the classification categories shown above but have one reservation. In some cases, the technical demands of a procedure require a high level of cognitive demand, even without thinking about connections. For instance, when pupils first learn calculus, the level of practice and attention to detail required in differentiating something like the function shown below results in many errors.

$$y = \frac{\sqrt[3]{x^2 - 1}}{3x}$$

There are several places where pupils can, and invariably do, trip up during initial learning. At this point, adding the burden of thinking about connections seems too much.

The aim should always be to teach in such a way that pupils are making connections. However, in practice, experience suggests that procedural fluency sometimes comes before understanding. I begin my teaching of differentiation, for instance, with a lot of conceptual work, but am never convinced that pupils have grasped the ideas. It is only when pupils are armed with some tools with which to tackle problems on their own, that the sense of things begins to materialise. Richard Skemp (1976) talks about instrumental and relational understanding. He describes relational understanding as 'knowing both what to do and why' whereas he considers instrumental understanding to be 'rules without reasons'. He acknowledges that 'one can often get the right answer more quickly and reliably by instrumental thinking than relational', but still considers instrumental learning as a proliferation of little rules to remember rather than fewer general principles with wider application.

Like any model, Skemp's is there to be tested. Subsequent thinking has suggested that procedural and conceptual understanding develop iteratively (Rittle-Johnson, Siegler and Alibali, 2001). This seems a sensible suggestion to me; when I reflect on my earlier career – where I had fewer models, metaphors and mathematics knowledge for teaching – pupils still developed conceptual understanding through the routine textbook exercises that dominated my task selection. However, my conjecture is that more pupils would have developed this level of understanding if I had used more tasks with that specific purpose in mind.

Consider the two example tasks shown below. They are almost identical but the way in which the teacher has asked pupils to complete the tasks dictates the nature of the activity. Task A is an example of a procedure without understanding: it is unlikely that work on tasks like this will result in significant gains in understanding. The mantra shown – 'Divide by the denominator and multiply by the numerator' – exemplifies Skemp's idea of rules without reasons. In Task B, the subtle addition of an alternative representation potentially changes the nature of the task. Pupils now have to think about the meaning of the operation performed, so concept and procedure are complementary to each other.

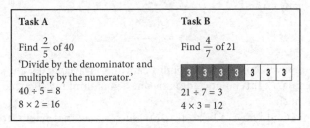

Task A	Task B
Find $\frac{2}{5}$ of 40	Find $\frac{4}{7}$ of 21
'Divide by the denominator and multiply by the numerator.'	
$40 \div 5 = 8$	$21 \div 7 = 3$
$8 \times 2 = 16$	$4 \times 3 = 12$

Another way of considering tasks is by their overarching purpose. Doyle, in his study, described a class which was observed over six weeks. According to Doyle (1988), tasks fall into one of four categories.

1. **Reinforcement tasks:** Guided practice on new skills.
2. **Review tasks:** Covering a skill learned earlier in the year.
3. **Application:** Problems requiring a mix of different skills.
4. **Assessment tasks:** Tests in which pupils demonstrate attainment and retention of skills.

This approach seems fruitless as a basis for discussing tasks or the resultant pupil activity. The actual task content and cognitive demand here seem interchangeable. We use tasks at different points in lessons but, in my view, this is a superficial way of thinking about task selection. The interesting discussion is around questions such as: What do the review tasks look like? How do the tasks selected by one teacher differ from another?

The most striking and useful model of task classification I have encountered is from Malcolm Swan (below). The three broadest classifications align clearly with what we have discussed in the preceding chapters. There is a recognition here that all three forms of mathematical understanding are important; pupils need to develop procedural fluency, acquire conceptual understanding (which serves as a basis for reasoning) and apply what they know to solve problems.

Framework for selecting tasks and activities

Goal	Student Product	Task and activity 'genres'
Factual recall Procedural fluency	• Performance	• Memorise and rehearse through 'études' that practice specific skills
Conceptual understanding	• Classification • Representation	• Sort, classify, define and deduce • Describe, interpret and translate • Exploring principles with deliberate interaction with attributes
Reasoning and communicating	• Analysis • Argument	• Explore structure, variation, connections • Test, justify and prove conjectures
Solving problems	• Model • Solution	• Formulate models and problems • Employ strategies
(Mathematical literacy)	• Critique	• Interpret & evaluate solutions, strategies, models

(Swan, 2006)

The separation between product and activity/process is also clearly made. For instance, we might have a goal of pupils developing conceptual understanding. As part of this conceptual understanding, we may want evidence that pupils understand different representations. The sorts of activity in which pupils are required to engage (describe, interpret and translate) are all shown.

Authentic versus inauthentic

Kaur states that some tasks may be considered 'authentic', which is problematic as it suggests that some tasks might be classified as 'inauthentic'. Authentic seems to suggest an 'assumed correspondence between the nature of the task and other mathematical activities that might be undertaken outside the classroom for purposes other than the learning of mathematics' (Kaur, Wong and Chew, 2018).

Swan's model grapples with authentic mathematical tasks by breaking down modelling in some detail.

Framework for selecting tasks and activities

Student product	Task and activity 'genres'	
Model	Formulate models and problems	• Identifying accessible questions that may be tackled within a situation • Making suitable assumptions to simplify a situation • Representing a situation mathematically • Identifying significant variables in situations • Generating relationships between variables

(Swan, 2006)

Applying mathematics to 'authentic' situations is a desirable activity for pupils to engage with. A challenge facing teachers is that many school mathematics problems are contrived versions of reality. The problems which best stand up to scrutiny tend to be those that do not present a utilitarian façade, but are instead problems for their own sake within mathematics, for example a geometrical puzzle.

It is important to appreciate that, as pupils are learning mathematics, the tasks they encounter to learn the subject need not be the same as those used in the actual practice of the subject; that is to say, the practice of a profession is not the same as learning to practise the profession (Gulikers, Bastiaens and Kirschner, 2004). Daisy Christodoulou suggests that practice of the profession 'depends on the detailed, knowledge-rich mental models stored in long-term memory. The aim of performance is to use those mental models. The aim of learning is to create them. The activities which create such models often don't look like the performance itself' (Christodoulou, 2016). As such, I argue we should have no hesitation is using 'inauthentic' mathematical tasks as the basis upon which pupils can develop an understanding of the subject and appropriately develop the skills required to tackle 'authentic' problems.

My approach

Considering the models above and being most heavily influenced by the work of Swan, I have created a classification table of my own. This separates the desired strand of mathematical learning from the sorts of task in which pupils might engage. These activity types are not intended to be exhaustive, but hopefully give a sense of what is possible within each strand of learning.

Task type	Potential activity
Procedural fluency	<ul><li>Developing fluency with calculations and algorithms</li><li>Identifying the most suitable calculation/algorithm to apply to a problem</li><li>Learning names, definitions and other arbitrary ideas</li><li>Recalling and recognising necessary facts, such as multiplication facts and standard integrals.</li></ul>
Conceptual understanding	<ul><li>Sorting and matching</li><li>Classifying</li><li>Multiple representations – interpretation and generation</li><li>Scaffolded proof</li><li>Guided discovery</li><li>Discussing mathematical statements</li><li>Combining ideas</li><li>Interpreting and creating stories</li></ul>
Problem solving	<ul><li>Mathematical investigations</li><li>Mathematical inquiry</li><li>Contextual modelling</li><li>Non-routine problem-solving tasks</li></ul>

In the coming chapters, the reader will find it useful to keep in mind that developments in one strand of mathematical thinking will potentially develop thinking in other strands. The framework serves as a way of organising our discussion.

It is impossible to meaningfully discuss the use of mathematical tasks without exploring real examples. In the following chapters, I include many examples of the sorts of task that might result in the activities shown above.

6 Procedural tasks

Well mastered routines free conscious attention to focus on aspects of
a task which are novel or problematic

(Cockcroft, 1982)

Mathematics teachers know the importance of pupils developing procedural
fluency. However, much of the literature on task design seems to focus on
conceptual understanding and problem-solving. There is, perhaps, a sense that
developing procedural fluency in pupils is easier than focusing on concepts
or problem-solving. This is a perspective I struggle to reconcile with my own
experience. I look at the examination papers in Scotland and can see that the
majority of questions are procedural. If pupils had procedural fluency, they
would be passing the exams comfortably and attainment would be higher
nationally. Developing procedural fluency clearly isn't a trivial goal. In this
chapter I will outline a variety of procedural tasks and consider the cognitive
activity in which pupils might be engaged.

Tasks will typically contribute to the development of more than one strand
of mathematical understanding, but those described in this chapter have
procedural fluency as the primary aim.

Procedural fluency includes, but is not limited to:

- developing fluency with calculations and algorithms
- identifying the most suitable calculation/algorithm to apply to a problem
- learning names, definitions and other arbitrary ideas
- recalling and recognising necessary facts, such as multiplication facts and
  standard integrals.

Activities which might help to develop this include:

- practice
- engagement with études
- attention to the 'fine details'

- matching
- selecting procedures
- recognition activities
- recall activities
- taking attention **off** what we are doing
- learner generation.

There are two main conditions for using these tasks:

- interleaving
- spacing versus massing.

Spacing versus massing

The NCTM summarises some of the key principles we will encounter in this chapter, stating that 'practice is essential for building fluency; however it should be brief, engaging, purposeful, and distributed' (NCTM, 2014). Practice has a place. Sometimes an unpretentious exercise where pupils have the opportunity to engage with technical details can be useful. However, it is my view that exercises of 20-plus repetitive questions are often not effective tasks. Frequently, as pupils work through long exercises, the focus becomes less on principles and more on 'cranking the handle' or replication without attention. Pupils get into a groove of doing repetitive manipulations and any deep mathematical thinking dissipates. Of course, there are situations where longer exercises can be useful – for instance, with calculus, where there are so many twists and turns in 'regular' questions that extensive practice can be beneficial. Generally however, we need to consider the idea of spaced practice.

Rohrer and Taylor (2006) tell us in their research that it is better to space practice problems over time rather than doing all the practice at the same time. An excerpt of an exercise is shown below (the original exercise had 40 questions). Imagine we have two groups of pupils, Group A and Group B. Group A completes the exercise in one go: they sit in class, working through all 40 questions and perhaps finish them off at home that night. Group B, instead, works on 10 of the problems in class. They then do three more sets of 10 questions spaced over a number of weeks.

Convert each mixed fraction to an improper fraction

$9\dfrac{1}{9} = \underline{\quad}$ $3\dfrac{8}{9} = \underline{\quad}$ $8\dfrac{7}{12} = \underline{\quad}$ $7\dfrac{7}{9} = \underline{\quad}$

$3\dfrac{11}{15} = \underline{\quad}$ $3\dfrac{2}{5} = \underline{\quad}$ $4\dfrac{2}{7} = \underline{\quad}$ $7\dfrac{1}{3} = \underline{\quad}$

$5\dfrac{1}{7} = \underline{\quad}$ $2\dfrac{7}{10} = \underline{\quad}$ $3\dfrac{4}{5} = \underline{\quad}$ $4\dfrac{5}{7} = \underline{\quad}$

$3\dfrac{3}{8} = \underline{\quad}$ $6\dfrac{1}{8} = \underline{\quad}$ $5\dfrac{5}{6} = \underline{\quad}$ $7\dfrac{4}{15} = \underline{\quad}$

The research shows that pupils who distribute their practice over time have significantly stronger retention. Even more striking is that if group B does only the first set of 10 questions, with no subsequent practice, the retention difference between the two groups is negligible. Dwell on that for a moment. Group A did lots of extra practice but this did not result in stronger retention, due to the fact that it was massed together. All of the extra questions might give pupils and teachers a sense of security, but this is false. The implication is that if we think it is necessary for pupils to do all 40 questions (which I don't) then it is much better to space them out over time.

In the initial lesson, I would ask the class to answer ten of the questions but then move on to tasks that require them to attend to the structure, principles, relationships and various representations of the ideas they are working on. I would also be sure to use a visual representation in the teaching of the ideas, so pupils are not simply applying a procedure 'blind'.

To be clear, I am not against traditional exercises – I use them with my own classes and they certainly have a place. But how we use such exercises matters. An idea for using a mixed exercise, which I have found useful, is as follows. Rather than have pupils work through this task from start to finish, I like to pick out four key questions. On the board, I display something like this:

Question 5	Solution: $x = 10$	Question 15	Solution: $x = -3$
If you get this wrong, do: Q2, 3, 4, 7, 9 **Answers:** 2. $x = 3$ 3. $x = 9$ 4. $x = 2$ 7. $x = 3$ 9. $x = 1$		If you get this wrong, do: Q11, 12, 13, 17, 19 **Answers:** 11. $x = -2$ 12. $x = -5$ 13. $x = -10$ 17. $x = -5$ 19. $x = 1$	
Question 24	Solution: $x = \dfrac{5}{2}$	Question 35	Solution: $x = \dfrac{-5}{2}$
If you get this wrong, do: Q22, 23, 25, 27, 29 **Answers:** 22. $x = \dfrac{3}{2}$ 23. $x = \dfrac{9}{5}$ 25. $x = \dfrac{1}{2}$ 27. $x = \dfrac{2}{3}$ 29. $x = \dfrac{1}{4}$		If you get this wrong, do: Q30, 31, 32, 37, 38 **Answers:** 30. $x = \dfrac{-3}{5}$ 31. $x = \dfrac{-9}{7}$ 32. $x = \dfrac{-1}{6}$ 37. $x = \dfrac{-4}{7}$ 38. $x = \dfrac{1}{3}$	

There are two reasons for this. First, I don't want pupils wading through lots of questions they can already do. This approach means they do one question which is representative of a 'class' of questions and only do more of that 'class' if they answer incorrectly. Secondly, I want pupils to be able to reflect on their own learning and feel a sense of ownership. I want them to feel there is flexibility in the task, to allow them to get quickly to the point where they do require practice. Developing this as a way of working with classes, I find that pupils tend to take it seriously, without cheating: they quickly realise that they would only be cheating themselves, so instead, they engage with a real sense of purpose in the exercise. If pupils demonstrate perfect solutions to the four representative questions, I either offer them some rich problem-solving task or ask them to work with other pupils who are struggling with a particular question type.

This chapter offers several ideas and approaches for incorporating practice into lessons, which look a little different from 'traditional' exercises. Some look like they may belong in a textbook but have design features that are uncommon in most UK texts.

Practice tasks

Equivalence and simplification of fractions

Many textbooks have exercises, often on consecutive pages, focused on writing equivalent fractions and then on simplification of fractions. Pupils can come to see these two ideas as distinct and unrelated. The task below is intended to show how they are one and the same. Through engaging with the procedural aspects of simplification and making equivalent fractions, pupils can make connections and begin to see that the two process are essentially the same.

$$\frac{3}{4} = \frac{\square}{8} = \frac{\square}{12} = \frac{\square}{16} = \frac{\square}{28} = \frac{\square}{320}$$

$$\frac{\square}{5} = \frac{\square}{10} = \frac{\square}{15} = \frac{\square}{30} = \frac{\square}{60} = \frac{480}{600}$$

$$\frac{\square}{3} = \frac{\square}{9} = \frac{8}{12} = \frac{\square}{18} = \frac{\square}{30} = \frac{\square}{150}$$

$$\frac{\square}{8} = \frac{\square}{16} = \frac{\square}{32} = \frac{25}{40} = \frac{\square}{64} = \frac{\square}{400}$$

The first two rows deal with equivalence and simplification in turn. Some of the fractions can be completed sequentially while, for others, pupils will need to refer back to the original fraction to scale. The purpose at this stage is to focus attention on the proportional relationships between fractions. It is in the third and fourth rows that the task comes together. In these rows, pupils have a choice of which fraction to find first. There are then several possible paths through the task.

There are opportunities here for rich dialogue around the mathematical structures. Particularly, the theme of 'doing and undoing' permeates throughout. Simplification is multiplication of denominator and numerator by some value k, where $0 < k < 1$, whereas creating equivalence involves multiplication of numerator and denominator by some value k, where $k < 0$ or $k > 1$. If we multiply numerator and denominator by k, we then need to multiply them by $\frac{1}{k}$ to undo this process; multiplication by $\frac{1}{k}$ requires multiplication by k to undo.

Collecting like terms

This task was designed as an alternative way for a low-attaining group of pupils to meaningfully interact with collection of like terms. I had done some work with algebra tiles but felt the pupils still weren't demonstrating the levels of understanding I would hope for. I knew the class needed 'purposeful practice' – practice where they were not only carrying out the process but also thinking deeply about the ideas at hand. Another consideration was that of pupil engagement. A sure-fire way to turn off this class would have been to give them a sheet with a large number of repetitive questions on it. (Perhaps this is true of every class? Maybe this lower-attaining group was less willing to comply with expectations to engage with such activities?) There were also considerations around learning, classroom management and pupil engagement when I wrote this task.

(1)	$5x$	(2)	$2x$
(3)	$-3x$	(4)	$-x$
(5)	$2y$	(6)	$-3y$
(7)	y	(8)	4
(9)	-7	(10)	

I issued the set of cards above and asked pupils to cut them up (a small loss in learning time perhaps, but it would have taken a lot of my prep time to organise all this in advance). Once the cards were cut out, I asked pupils to group them in piles, any way they liked. Some pupils grouped by like terms, some into piles of positive or negative terms, others had a pile with constants and another pile of cards with variables. This was an interesting moment: we had been working on like terms for a few lessons, but the pupils' responses demonstrated to me that likeness wasn't the most immediate idea that came to their heads when encountering some algebraic terms. I then asked the pupils to regroup the cards into piles of like terms, if they had not done this already.

Next, I asked the pupils to start on the task shown below.

Task One

1. What do cards 1 and 2 make?
2. What do cards 3 and 4 make?
3. What do cards 1, 2, 3 and 4 make?
4. What do cards 1 and 8 make?
5. What do cards 1, 2 and 8 make?
6. What do cards 1, 3 and 8 make?
7. What do cards 1, 4 and 9 make?
8. What do cards 2, 4, 7 and 9 make?
9. What do cards 1 and 7 make?
10. What do cards 1, 2, 6 and 7 make?
11. What do cards 3, 4, 5 and 6 make?
12. What do cards 5, 6, 7, 8 and 9 make?

I offered no re-teaching as we had spent time on collecting terms in previous lessons. I wanted pupils to transfer that learning to this new scenario. As I moved around the room, I noticed some pupils getting incorrect answers. As I observed them, I could see that they were not physically laying out the terms side by side for each question. I suggested they could lay the required tiles next to each other, then regroup those tiles for likeness, and this was the prompt some pupils required to start being successful. Many pupils intuitively did this, but it was interesting to me that some did not. Was this further evidence that the mental actions I would hope to see were not yet embedded in these pupils? It would have been harder to pick up on these small insights if the pupils had been working on a routine exercise on paper: I can tell pupils to lay out their work in a certain way, but I need to see how they naturally lay it out first.

The second part of the task, shown below, involves working backwards from a target to find the cards required; this proved slightly more challenging. I find that after working on a 'doing process', it is often useful to ask pupils to focus on the 'undoing process'.

Task Two

1. Which cards are needed to make x?
2. Which cards are needed to make $-2x$?
3. Which cards are needed to make 0?
4. Which cards are needed to make $7x + 3y + 4$?
5. Which cards are needed to make an expression with 3 negative terms?

The final part of the task involves using the blank card from the set to complete Lucy's expression. At this point, I could have asked more questions of the sort used in Task One. Instead, I opted to continue to increase the demand. The questions here are more challenging versions of those shown in Task Two.

Task Three

1. Lucy says it is possible to make $3x + 3y + 3$. How close to this can you get?
2. Fill in the blank card so you can make Lucy's expression.
3. Using the new card from Q2, is it possible to make the following expressions? If so, which cards do you need?
   a. $-x - 2y - 8$
   b. $-4x - 3y - 4$
   c. $-3x + 4y - 9$

All of these questions could have been posed without using the cut-out cards but, in the context of this class, the cards made a significant difference to the activity pupils undertook; this in turn affected the insights I was able to discern from that activity. A number of colleagues have tried this task and reported similar observations. A key point to take from this task is the significant role of classroom dynamics in effective task selection and design. The fundamental teaching point here, to maximise the benefit of the task, is to move around the room, teaching between the desks.

Multiplication

Sam Blatherwick shared his thinking about teaching lower-attaining pupils, setting out to provide many opportunities for spaced practice of ideas with these pupils.

> *We found with these students that very little maths was entirely secure from previous stages and that we wanted to go back over topics again and again. We believe this will make a difference with these pupils.*

Sam gives the following example:

> Which one do you think will be bigger?
>
> 84 × 93   **or**   83 × 94
>
> What's the difference?

This is an opportunity for pupils to practise a procedure. However, the task also has an additional layer: there is an opportunity for forming and testing a conjecture. This is not only about the procedure but also about making sense of calculations.

This would be followed by a similar task (such as the one below), so the insights from the first task could be used to inform thinking.

> Which one do you think will be bigger?
>
> 25 × 54   **or**   24 × 55
>
> What's the difference?

The procedure is practised but attention is paid to the relationships between the products. Some generalisations emerge in words, through whole-class discussion and conversation with some groups; Sam would then formalise these generalisations with algebra as appropriate.

Sam might then extend the task with a subsequent prompt such as:

> 123 × 456   **or**   156 × 423

Parts of circles

This is two tasks for the price of one!

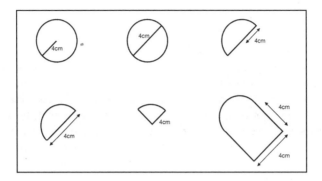

I usually ask pupils to find the perimeter of each shape and then the area of each shape. In my experience of teaching circle calculations, pupils often struggle to attend to the variables at play – for example:

- What is the value of the radius?
- What is the value of the diameter?
- When do we halve to get the final answer?

There is lots of halving and doubling in these types of circle question and pupils can become bogged down. This task, by keeping the numbers the same (although not always referencing the same variable) aims to focus pupil attention on the role of halving and doubling of radii/diameters and of areas and circumferences. Pupils have to develop an appreciation of situations where we double the radius but halve the answer, or halve the diameter and then halve the answer, and so on. One might argue that it would be useful here to work through lots of example-problem pairs, (a sequence where pupils are alternate between studying examples and doing similar problems) but I have not found this to be the case. It is useful for getting pupils started but there is just too much possible variation in types of circle problem. As such, engagement with a range of problems and deep thinking are required. I could build a list of 'atomised' example types and teach every single one explicitly, but there will always be a possible situation that I haven't taught. It is better for pupils to use a few examples to establish principles, rooted in understanding about how to tackle these problems, rather than trying to memorise steps.

The key feature of this task is that there is a degree of invariance. The number four appears in every question, and the aim of this is to reduce the 'noise' that arises when different numbers are used. I encourage pupils to reflect on each question at the outset: 'What does the 4 represent this time? What information do I need to get started with this problem?'. I allow pupils to discuss strategies with each other, although every pupil is accountable for producing their own solution. Because 4 appears throughout, pupils sometimes make conjectures about relationships between the shapes. Often these are perceptive – for example, recognising that the shapes in questions 1, 3 and 5 all belong to the same 'whole' circle. At other times, pupils make incorrect assumptions around the effect of squaring the radius; for example, if one circle has a radius which is double that of another circle, pupils incorrectly assume that the area of the second shape will be double that of the first. If pupils have demonstrated some real fluency with the problems, I might encourage them to investigate the idea of area scale factors while other pupils continue to practise. A nice follow-up task is to ask pupils to generate some more shapes for the exercise. The sorts of question they come up with are often far more imaginative than those on the original sheet.

Increasingly difficult questions

Dave Taylor came up with the idea of his task format, Increasingly Difficult Questions (IDQs), after learning about the textbooks commonly used in Shanghai. Dave saw that Shanghai textbook exercises had a lower starting point than English textbooks but a much more challenging end point with quicker increases in difficulty levels.

Dave recalls:

> I took the idea to school to share with the department and worked with some friends on a few tasks. I'd write the first question, a colleague the second, a different colleague the third and then back to me – the idea was to make it more difficult, but not too difficult. I then started doing this in the departmental workroom, writing the first two questions to an exercise and asking others to write the next one (and only the next one), with people contributing once someone else had. After a few rounds, I started creating them at home and sharing them online.

Dave generally uses these tasks as a substitute for a traditional textbook exercise. He normally works through some example-problem pairs to scaffold pupils' initial thinking. After this, he gives pupils the IDQs, which provide an opportunity for pupils to step back to more basic knowledge before quickly experiencing increments in difficulty. Dave also uses these exercises as a diagnostic tool, to ascertain pupils' current level of understanding and fluency.

Let's look at two examples of Dave's work, beginning with a task about perimeter. The idea of perimeter is something pupils have been working with since primary school – it is not new content at secondary level. As such, work on routine exercises – for example, finding the perimeters of rectangles – is likely to be rather pointless for the majority of pupils. This task begins with a familiar example and the challenge gently increases with each new question; the level of challenge by the end of the exercise is significant. There is no immediately obvious solution path, so pupils have to do a little thinking.

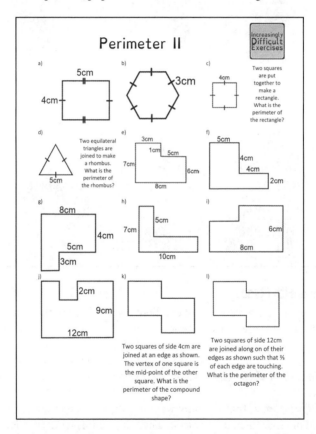

This second example focuses on fractions, taking a familiar exercise and ramping up the challenge significantly. Again, identifying fractions of an area is something pupils will have experienced at primary level. This task gives pupils an opportunity to develop their thinking and reasoning about areas and fractions considerably.

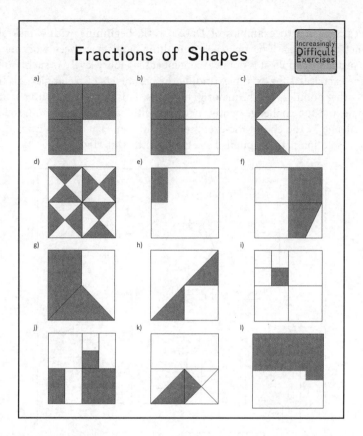

Engagement with études

Colin Foster has written a series of excellent tasks called 'mathematical études', and we discussed these tasks in depth. I could have placed them in either the problem solving or procedural chapters of the book – they are quite novel! These tasks aim to find creative, imaginative and thought-provoking ways to help learners of mathematics develop their fluency in important mathematical procedures.

It is often assumed that the only way to get good at standard procedures is to drill and practise them *ad nauseum* using dry, uninspiring exercises. Études, instead, embed extensive practice of important mathematical procedures within more stimulating, rich problem-solving contexts. Colin's research suggests that études are as good as exercises in terms of developing procedural fluency – and it seems likely that they have many other benefits in addition (Foster, 2018).

Here is an example of an études task:

ACTIVITY: EXPRESSION POLYGONS

The figure at right is an *expression polygon*. Each pair of algebraic expressions is joined by a line segment. Each line segment represents an equation equating the expressions that it connects. For example, the line segment at the top represents the equation $x + 5 = 2x + 2$.

1. Write the six equations represented by the six line segments in this expression square.

2. Solve your six equations.

3. Describe any patterns you notice among your six solutions.

4. Construct another expression polygon containing different expressions. Can you make the solutions to your expression polygon a "nice" set of numbers?

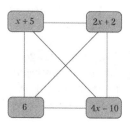

The remaining two extension questions might prompt further discussion:

5. How could you make an expression polygon in which all the solutions were 7?

6. How many solutions will an expression 10-gon have? What about an expression n-gon? Why?

THINGS TO CONSIDER

Number of Expressions

An expression triangle would be easier to begin with than an expression square. An expression pentagon would be challenging. An expression cube, in three dimensions, could be very challenging!

Type of Solutions

Here are some possible challenges:

• Make all the solutions integers.
• Make all the solutions distinct (i.e., different) integers.
• Make the solutions a "nice" set of numbers, such as consecutive even numbers, or square numbers, or prime numbers.

Is it always possible to design an expression polygon that will produce any given set of numbers? Why or why not?

Type of Expressions

It is best to start with linear expressions of the form $ax + b$, where a and b are constants. Including one or more quadratic expressions of the form $ax^2 + bx + c$, where a, b, and c are constants, could give some equations with two solutions, so two numbers might be needed on some line segments.

(Foster, 2015 [1])

A concern in some mathematics classrooms is that some pupils rarely get to experience true problem-solving. The teacher might say, 'when you reach this level (wherever it may be) then you'll be ready to tackle some interesting problems'. With certain pupils, we might be inclined to think they would be better working on basic procedural work, rather than problem-solving. The concern is that these pupils are always stuck doing routine tasks, which has implications in terms of their perception of the subject. How will they ever get excited by or passionate about mathematics?

Colin explains:

> *I think there has to be a little bit of balance and maybe there is a place for tackling problems at an earlier stage. I think what I've been trying to do with my work on études, has been to marry those two things so that pupils do get experience in problem-solving. However, those tasks are not totally open-ended; they are written such that the pupil experiences the task in a structured way so that they're developing their essential processes along the way.*

Colin describes the real tension in classrooms between developing procedural fluency and allowing pupils time to work on non-routine problems:

> *Pupils have to develop fluency in things. They have to be able to do things, almost automatically. If they're going to be able to do harder stuff, we have to help automate the basic things, so that they are able to think about more complex things. If they always have to work out the basics, it really limits what they are able to do in terms of problem-solving. I remember talking to colleagues and we broadly agreed about that. Despite this, there was a kind of reluctance. It was a case of 'I suppose we have to have some boring lessons some of the time, otherwise the pupils will never develop enough fluency in everything.' I felt that was a bit depressing.*

> *I also reflected upon when I'm presenting stuff to teachers. I'd say, 'let's try some rich tasks together'. I sometimes thought that that can almost make teachers feel guilty, because we have a lovely time together as maths teachers. It was as if I was saying, 'don't you know there's all these wonderful, rich tasks out there?' and the teachers think, 'of course I know that and I'd love to do them', but the reality is that they need to spend time on other stuff to develop fluency in their pupils.*

> *It seemed like, as task designers, it would be easy to sit around making up lovely, rich tasks knowing that most of the time teachers won't be*

able to use them because they've got other constraints. I talked to people at Nottingham about designing tasks for fluency. The reaction seemed to be, 'well, why would you be interested in fluency, we've got exercises for that'. The feeling was that fluency was kind of sorted. We know that exercises work, we know how to do that.

I began to think, as a task designer, do I want to keep designing more and more tasks, which get used during a Friday afternoon or whenever there's time at the end of the term, or do I want to design tasks that support the day-to-day business of teaching? So, my interest shifted towards the sort of tasks that teachers have to use on a daily basis. I wondered if I could invent tasks that would be a replacement for exercises. Not extra stuff that teachers had to find time to do. As such, the intention with the études was a more interesting way of developing fluency as an alternative to exercises. The teacher can explain, can teach however they want to, some new ideas, and when they get to the point where they would say, 'go and practise twenty of them', instead they issue an étude. An étude aims to generate that same concentrated, focused practice of a particular, specific skill, but hopefully in a more interesting, maybe problem-solving kind of context.

A confession; when I first looked at this task, specifically when I saw the diagram, and I hadn't yet read any of the text, my reaction was to think that Colin could have simply written out the six equations as a conventional exercise for pupils to solve. This, of course, was a terribly superficial way of thinking about the task. The follow-up prompts Colin has listed are the key ingredients in making this étude result in some rich activity.

This feature is true of all the étude tasks: they start off with something that's equivalent to an exercise. This is a deliberate design choice by Colin. He makes the argument: 'if pupils are capable of doing exercises, then they're capable of doing études'. The initial task is a form of assessment: can pupils solve equations? This part of the étude presents four linear expressions in four boxes, with each expression joined to every other expression by a line. The lines that join the expressions make them into equations – so, for example, the top two boxes are joined by a line to form the equation: $x + 5 = 2x + 2$. The lovely fact that arises from doing the task is that the solutions to these equations turn out to be 1, 2, 3, 4, 5 and 6. Colin explained that it was actually quite difficult to come up with expressions to have this solution set. When he uses the task with teachers, they might say, 'that's quite nice', but fail to appreciate how challenging it is to create a polygon with nice solutions like this.

The main task is for pupils to generate expressions to form their own equations. This is demanding and involves a lot of trial and error. The idea is that pupils are trying to create a polygon with nice solutions, but at the same time they are doing a lot of practice in solving equations. Colin wants pupils to undertake a specific sort of cognitive activity: thinking about the undoing processes and considering things like, 'to make the solution 4 instead of 3, what do I need to change?' Because there are four joined-up expressions, a change in one expression changes everything else. This means pupils have to keep going back, revisiting the whole polygon. When pupils do this, there's an awful lot of crossing and scribbling out and modifying. If a pupil already knows how to solve a set of equations, they might become demotivated to learn if they are just asked to do the same thing over and over. Hopefully, the étude will give them something a bit more interesting to think about: that pupil is not really focusing on how to solve equations anymore. Instead, they're thinking more broadly about this big problem.

Colin explains that the task can be adapted easily to meet the specific needs of pupils:

> There are some quite demanding problems that can arise from this. For example, what set of six numbers can you generate using four expressions like this? I've had teachers working on group theory trying to answer that question. The sky's the limit in terms of extensions. At the other end, when you've got pupils who are really struggling and only just managing to solve their first equations, then it can be made much simpler. You can start with three expressions in a triangle which is a lot easier than the four expressions. You can invite them to simply find whole number solutions. That's enough of a challenge to begin with. It's very easy to self-differentiate these tasks. As pupils become more fluent at solving the equations, they naturally begin to look for more demanding scenarios.

The teacher plays an important role, moving around the classroom, being interested in the work of individual pupils. For instance, if a pupil is finding the task too hard, the teacher can make it easier to begin with and then build the complexity back in. If pupils are finding the task too easy, we can suggest extensions or, better still, ask the pupils what they can do to extend the task.

With this task, there is a natural self-checking and peer-checking that goes on, which means there's less need for the teacher to keep checking the answers. Colin says a common question from teachers is, 'how do you cope with an étude where pupils are making up their own numbers?' Colin replies:

I think that often takes care of itself because if a pupil says, 'Oh I've got 2, 4, 6, 8, 10, 12 as my numbers', then you can bet the child next to them is going to check that and say, 'Oh no you haven't, that one doesn't work!' It creates a scenario where pupils care about the answers a bit. Ordinarily if you're doing a page of exercises and you get x = 6, it doesn't matter; you just go on to the next question and do another one and if one's wrong you probably wouldn't notice. Whereas with this, pupils tend to pick up your errors either because that answer has an effect on other answers or because they're challenged by someone else.

Attending to fine details

As the complexity of procedures increases, it is useful to use tasks that deliberately focus pupils' attention on the small but important technical details. The following tasks demonstrate a couple of ways in which we might do this.

Complex numbers

This table shows a sequence of questions where pupils have to convert complex numbers to polar form. The table layout serves as a scaffold for their thinking during this process. I have included the 'principal argument' column because, in my experience, many pupils forget to adjust their angle to be in the correct range of values. The table is a device designed to focus pupil attention on the principal argument: telling pupils to remember is one thing, setting up some activity where they encounter the often-forgotten point is quite another.

Carteisan form	Argand diagram	Modulus	Argument	Principal argument θ	Polar form
$-4-3i$		5	3.78	-2.5	$5(\cos(-2.5) + i\sin(-2.5))$
$2+2i$					
$-3+2i$					
$5-12i$					
$-24-7i$					

This second table is more demanding. At this level in particular, I think it is important to keep the level of cognitive demand high. The hardest element in this task is likely to be converting back to the $z = a + ib$ representation in the first four rows – this is shot through with trigonometry and Pythagoras. Pupils have to find triangles where the hypotenuse is the length of the modulus value but also need to satisfy the requirements for the argument. In creating the task, I had to reconfigure my triangles a few times to make them work.

Carteisan form	Argand diagram	Modulus	Argument	Principal argument θ	Polar form
		$\sqrt{2}$	$\dfrac{7\pi}{4}$		
		2		$\dfrac{-3\pi}{4}$	
		$\sqrt{2}$			
		$\sqrt{5}$			$\sqrt{2}(\cos\left(\dfrac{-3\pi}{4}\right) + i\sin\left(\dfrac{-3\pi}{4}\right))$
					$5(\cos(-2.5) + i\sin(-2.5))$

Chain rule

Differentiation using the chain rule, particularly with regard to trigonometric functions, is a significant developmental jump for pupils. The idea here is that pupils need to be able to establish the 'layering' that exists in each of these questions to apply the chain rule (if required).

The notation for powers of trig functions is not intuitive. While this looks neat, pupils need to be able to translate it (at least mentally) to the form to understand how to process it. The task below employs careful use of variation theory. In each column, the trigonometric terms remain invariant; further, the digit used is always 2 (in the first column) or 3 (in the second column).

$y = 2sinx$	$x = 3cosx$
$y = 2sin2x$	$x = cos3x$
$y = sin^2x$	$x = cos^3x$
$y = 2sin^2x$	$x = 3cos^3x$
$y = sin^2 2x$	$x = cos^3 3x$
$y = 2sin^2 2x$	$x = 3cos^3 3x$

Despite encountering a sequence of carefully chosen examples and working through example-problem pairs, many pupils struggle with textbook exercises on this topic. Often there is too much variety in the questions, so pupils struggle to get a sense of the principles. These textbook exercises make good mixed practice once pupils have begun to develop some degree of fluency and confidence but often place too much expectation on pupils at an early stage in their learning. I wonder if, because we are working at the 'top end' of school mathematics, authors think exercises with a steady gradient are less important?

The task above can be used in several ways. I like to display it on the board and ask pupils to do their work on mini whiteboards. I work down the page, zig-zagging between the columns. To start, I'll pose the top sine question; once pupils have held up their solutions, I'll go over it if required or point out errors to individual pupils. Next I'll pose the cosine question from the second row and repeat the process, before posing the sine question on the third row. Pupils receive immediate feedback as they work through the exercise.

At this point, I'll wipe the board clean and then ask pupils to go back and answer the questions we missed out as we zig-zagged. This means the scaffolding is gradually removed, and provides an opportunity for pupils to go back and apply what they learned from the first three practice attempts. This is not the same as the commonly used 'example-problem pairs' approach; by this stage, we would already have done that. Instead, this is about consolidating the instruction and learning acquired during 'example-problem pairs' or similar and moving towards variety. At this halfway point, I'll write the solutions only, without working, and ask pupils to peer-correct each other's work. We then repeat the whole sequence for the bottom half of the task. I have found that this gradual 'handing over' can help pupils to quickly make the leap to fluently working with mixed examples on these problems.

Matching

Susan Whitehouse writes a lot of excellent resources for A-Level. She regularly uses matching tasks, which, as she explains, result in pupils receiving useful feedback by undertaking the task itself. Here is an example of one of her tasks.

First column				Second column			
1	$\sqrt{x}$	11	$\frac{1}{x^2} \times \frac{1}{x^3}$	A	$x^{\frac{-3}{2}}$	K	$x^{\frac{-1}{2}}$
2	$\frac{1}{x}$	12	$\left(\sqrt[3]{x}\right)^2$	B	$\frac{1}{2}x^{-3}$	L	$x^{\frac{9}{2}}$
3	$\frac{1}{\sqrt{x}}$	13	$\sqrt{x^7}$	C	$\frac{1}{2}x^{-1}$	M	x^{-2}
4	$\sqrt[3]{x}$	14	$\sqrt{\left(\frac{1}{x^8}\right)}$	D	x^{-4}	N	$x^{\frac{3}{2}}$
5	$\frac{1}{x^2}$	15	$\frac{1}{\sqrt{x^{-8}}}$	E	x^{-1}	O	$2x^{-1}$
6	$\frac{1}{2x^3}$	16	$x \times \sqrt{x \times x^6}$	F	$\frac{1}{2}x$	P	$x^{\frac{1}{2}}$
7	$\frac{2}{x^3}$	17	$\sqrt{\left(\frac{4}{x^2}\right)}$	G	x^4	Q	x^{-5}
8	$x\sqrt{x}$	18	$\sqrt{\left(\frac{1}{4x^2}\right)}$	H	x^2	R	$x^{\frac{2}{3}}$
9	$\frac{\sqrt{x}}{x^2}$	19	$\sqrt{\left(\frac{x^2}{4}\right)}$	I	$2x$	S	$2x^{-3}$
10	$\frac{1}{x^{-2}}$	20	$\sqrt{4x^2}$	J	$x^{\frac{1}{3}}$	T	$x^{\frac{7}{2}}$

When I interviewed Susan for this book, she said: 'I like the way that matching activities give you a bit of a check on learning – if your answer isn't there then you know you have a problem – but without giving you the answer.' Susan explains that she deliberately included common errors and misconceptions – this is always a good strategy with this type of tasks. When creating a task like this, it is important to ensure pupils can't do the matching by looking at some other discriminating feature. For instance, the only coefficients Susan uses are 2 and 4, whereas if she had used different coefficients in the first column it would have made the task significantly easier (because pupils could simply direct their attention to the coefficients). They would still be engaged in activity, but below the level intended. Instead, the task has been written in such a way that it forces pupils to consider the powers and roots and make conversions between them.

Susan suggests this is a collaborative activity, in that pupils can discuss and argue with each other about the matchings, but says each pupil should produce a written record of their own work. This is a subtle but important point. The process of working through and discussing the matchings is in itself valuable but requiring all pupils to have a product at the end of the activity adds an element of accountability.

Susan reminds pupils of the tactic of substituting in numerical values to check the matchings, so pupils can resolve any disagreements without teacher intervention. Finally, she says:

> *I might get different pupils up to the front to justify different matchings or get them to write out their working for a particular one in full. I find that students are quite motivated to finish these activities, regarding it as a bit more of a game and more fun than a traditional textbook exercise.*

Even at this level, motivation and engagement are considerations in a classroom. This task is the basis of active learning, where pupils are meaningfully involved and the level of mathematical demand remains high.

Procedure selection

An important part of learning various procedures is knowing when to apply them. In this section, there are examples of tasks that focus on procedure selection.

Subtraction procedure selection

At first glance, this task appears to be a rather mundane set of questions. Typically, when presented with a set of questions like this, pupils are inclined to apply the standard subtraction algorithm to each one irrespective of whether that is the most efficient approach or not. Instead, I suggest that this task can be used in a different manner.

302	356	782	312	645	900
− 190	− 187	− 653	− 185	− 498	− 563
873	506	783	756	635	532
− 854	− 289	− 405	− 478	− 212	− 342

In many cases, rewriting the question given, using the principles of constant difference, will make it easier to calculate mentally. For instance, it is laborious to calculate 629 − 304 using the written method but rewriting as 625 − 300 makes the calculation much easier.

There are different strategies which might be applied to the questions. At the outset, before attempting any of the questions, I ask pupils to group them in terms of the strategy they might employ. This requires pupils to attend to surface structure features which are common to each strategy group. Once they have identified their groups, they can then attempt the questions. While working through the questions, pupils sometimes realise they have mis-grouped one of the calculations and it would work more efficiently using a different strategy. I often make the point that, 'if two exchanges are required, you are probably using an inefficient strategy'. I suggest that for three-digit subtraction we should never have to exchange twice.

This task captures the idea of taking a routine, repetitive task and raising the level of cognitive demand for pupils, to establish some more meaningful learning.

Sorting trigonometric equations

Let's consider a second example where a conventional exercise can be used with more attention, this time with trigonometric equations. Often, pupils learn the techniques for the different equation types discretely and, when presented with one question in isolation (for instance, in an exam) don't know which technique or procedure to apply. Of course, we want to teach the processes with a focus on understanding the notation, so pupils understand the principles rather than simply relying on memory. Nevertheless, procedure selection for this topic is often problematic.

(a) $3\tan^2 x - 1 = 0$	$0 \le x \le 360$	(b) $2\cos 2x + 3 = 2$	$0 \le x \le 360$
(c) $4\sin x - 3\sin 2x = 0$	$0 \le x \le 360$	(d) $2\cos 2x = 1 - \cos x$	$0 \le x \le 360$
(e) $4\cos^2 x - 1 = 2$	$0 \le x \le 2\pi$	(f) $5\tan(2x - 40) + 1 = 6$	$0 \le x \le 360$
(g) $2\sin 2x + \sqrt{3} = 0$	$0 \le x \le 2\pi$	(h) $3\sin 2x - 3\cos x = 0$	$0 \le x \le 360$
(i) $\cos 2x = 5 = 4\sin x$	$0 \le x \le 360$	(j) $4\tan 3x + 5 = 1$	$0 \le x \le \pi$
(k) $2\cos(2x + 80) = 1$	$0 \le x \le 180$	(l) $6\sin^2 x + 5 = 8$	$0 \le x \le 2\pi$
(m) $5\sin 2x - 6\sin x = 0$	$0 \le x \le 360$	(n) $3\cos 2x + \cos x = -1$	$0 \le x \le 360$
(o) $\tan^2 x - \dfrac{1}{3} = 0$	$0 \le x \le 2\pi$	(t) $5\sin 2x + 3 = 1$	$0 \le x \le 360$
(q) $5\sin 2x + 6\cos x = 0$	$0 \le x \le 360$	(t) $2\cos 2x - 4\cos x + 3 = 0$	$0 \le x \le 360$
(s) $3\cos 2x + 3\sin x = 3$	$0 \le x \le 2\pi$	(t) $4\sin(2x + 10) - 3 = 0$	$0 \le x \le 360$

A simple, yet powerful modification to this exercise can be achieved by asking pupils to group the questions by strategy; this is the same pedagogical choice as in the subtraction task above. Once pupils have made their groupings, I ask them to check with a peer and give them space to justify and argue about their choices. The key idea here is that pupils recognise the essential surface features that determine the type of equation to solve. Double angles do not always mean application of a double-angle formula, for example.

Percentages

Craig Barton (2018) coined the term 'Same Surface, Different Deep' (SSDD) for his take on procedure selection tasks. Craig describes the issue with many textbooks in which, after some routine Pythagoras questions, there is a mix of contextual problems in various contexts: ladders, diagonals of shapes etc. All of these problems have differing surface structure, but the same deep structure – they are all Pythagoras problems. Pupils don't have to select a strategy: they know to use Pythagoras at the outset. In contrast, SSDD problems present a variety of questions that appear to have the same surface structure – for instance, they may all look like Pythagoras questions at first glance – but require different underlying mathematics. It is just as important to recognise when **not** to use Pythagoras as to know when to use it.

I have written some of these sorts of task with my own classes, such as the example below.

1. I get a 12% pay rise. I now earn £2000 per month. **What was my previous rate of pay?**	2. I get paid £2000 per month. I get a 12% pay rise. **What is my new rate of pay?**
3. I buy £2000 in shares. They increase in value by 12% per month for four months. **What are my shares worth now?**	4. I buy £2000 in shares. I sell them 12 months later for £2400. **What is my percentage profit?**

This example highlights a classic topic where pupils sometimes struggle to select the correct strategy. Pupils may have excellent procedural fluency and a good conceptual grasp of the individual types of percentage problem represented here. However, without an awareness of the subtleties of the language, they are unlikely to correctly determine which strategy is required. This SSDD example gives pupils practice with different types of percentage question, but also forces them to read carefully to decide which method to use.

When this type of task is first used, many pupils don't succeed with it at all, so it is important to have a whole-class dialogue about the cues in the wording.

I have found a useful follow-up, a few days later, is to give the class the set of questions again, with different numbers and the questions arranged in a different order. I will often then ask pupils to create a set of questions of their own; at this stage, I like to challenge them to make the question types harder to distinguish. Pupils enjoy swapping their question sets and challenging each other.

Integration techniques

The question below, set by Jonathan Dunning, is a powerful example. There is less variance between the examples than in a 'normal' exercise, but this is perhaps more difficult. When using this task with pupils, I often hear them say, 'but surely that's just the same as that one?'

$\int \dfrac{x}{x - x^2} dx$	$\int \dfrac{x-1}{x^2-1} dx$	$\int \dfrac{1}{x - x^2} dx$
$\int \dfrac{x}{x+1} dx$	**Can you add one to the collection?**	$\int \dfrac{x}{x^2-1} dx$
$\int \dfrac{x^2}{x+1} dx$	$\int \dfrac{x+1}{x} dx$	$\int \dfrac{x+1}{x^2} dx$

Pupils working with this level of calculus have to be able to pay attention to the small differences (I think that's a calculus joke). These questions may look similar but they require different strategies: integration by substitution, by parts, by partial fractions or by using algebraic manipulation are all represented here. To an expert, a quick glance is likely to reveal a strategy for at least some of the questions; for pupils, however, the distinctions between them are often not immediately clear.

What Jonathan has produced here, in this seemingly simple task, is really well-thought-out, excellent advanced-level practice. I have found that pupils always enjoy this task and become really engaged with it. There is something about it looking as though it 'should be easy', as one pupil said to me. A nice feature is the lack of question numbers: there is no set path through the questions. If they choose to, pupils can start with the ones that are immediately obvious to them, before spending time thinking about the others.

Jonathan has included the nice prompt: 'Can you add one to the collection?' Once one has been created, a follow-up prompt could be, 'and another? and another? ...' I like to take questions generated by members of the class for all of us (including me) to work on. Often, pupils come up with excellent demanding questions; there is an expectation that the questions pupils generate will be doable at this level, so they can't arbitrarily write down anything. I recall one pupil who eagerly suggested $\frac{x+1}{x+1}$ for us all to do. He was astonished by how quickly the rest of the class completed it: unlike him, they noticed that it simplifies to 1, which is quite a trivial integration.

Recognition activity

Quadratic inequalities

Above, I described Craig Barton's idea of SSDD problems. However, I think there are many opportunities where Different Surface, Same Deep (DSSD) problems are powerful.

For example, the four questions shown below look nothing like each other, but each of them potentially leads to a quadratic inequality. Many pupils find the topic of quadratic inequalities challenging. They need to learn how to solve these inequalities and recognise them when they arise in other situations. As Craig rightly says in his book, giving pupils an exercise where they know the solution strategy in advance will not necessarily enable them to apply the idea to problems beyond the confines of that exercise. Once more though, I argue that pedagogical choices around the use of a task are a key determinant.

State the domain of $$f(x) = \dfrac{4}{\sqrt{x^2 + 6x - 16}}$$	Find the values of k for which the equation $$x^2 + 2(k+2)x + 20 - 2k = 0$$ has no solutions.
Find the intervals for which the function $$f(x) = x^3 + 9x^2 - 48x + 15$$ is strictly increasing.	Find the values of k for which the line $y = 2x + k$ intersects the circle $x^2 + y^2 - 8x - 10y + 36 = 0$.

I tend to offer the set shown above to pupils several weeks *after* having focused on quadratic inequalities. I give pupils no clue that quadratic inequalities will be important for this task; I like to let them stumble upon this (or not) for themselves. I ask pupils to work individually on this problem set for a period of time before I open it up to peer discussion. They tend to be able to get started with all the questions, but unless they recognise and know how to solve quadratic inequalities, they will not be able to complete them. Many students work through several steps with each of the problems, but are unable to successfully complete any of them. When these pupils begin to realise that the step they are finding problematic is the same for every question, there is a palpable sense of dawning realisation.

This task serves several purposes. First, it is intended to provide mixed practice from across the curriculum. The main purpose though, is to sharpen the pupils' radar for quadratic inequalities, as well as providing some practice in solving them. It is about being sensitised to spot quadratic inequalities when the topic arises 'unexpectedly'.

Structural arithmetic

Here is a task in which the distributive law is key to solving the problems, but this is not clear at the outset as no mention of it is given. I was inspired to write this task after creating question 7 by adapting a task by Max Wertheimer.

Try to calculate the answers to each of the following in the most efficient way. There is a smart, efficient way of doing each question.

1) $12 \times 11 + 12 \times 9$

2) $\dfrac{1}{4} \times \dfrac{2}{5} + \dfrac{4}{4} \times \dfrac{2}{5}$

3) 18% of 72 + 82% of 72

4) 15% of 60 + 70% of 30

5) $0.3 \times 100 + 0.07 \times 1000$

6) $0.62 \times 37.5 + 3.75 \times 3.8$

7) $\dfrac{389 + 389 + 389 + 389}{4}$

8) $\dfrac{143 + 143 + 143 + 143 + 143}{5}$

9) $\dfrac{757 + 757 + 757 + 757 + 757 + 757 + 757}{757 + 757 + 757}$

10) $\dfrac{212 + 212 + 106 + 106}{6}$

Generally, pupils have no difficulty in identifying the distributive law if it is in bracket form $a(b + c)$. However, starting with $ab + ac$ and then using this structure is a different prospect. The task is designed so that insights on each question can influence pupils' thinking in the subsequent ones. I might not present it as a worksheet; instead, I might display one or two questions on the board, give pupils some time to work on them and discuss in pairs, and then pull everything together in a whole-class discussion. I would then present the remaining questions.

I don't want to take ownership from the pupils by doing worked examples: such an approach can lead to pupils simply comparing problems and examples and thinking, 'it's one of those ones. I do this'. Instead, the purpose here is for pupils to actively engage in the hunt for structure themselves. As teachers, we need to have faith that some pupils will spot the structure, but it is the subsequent discussion and reflection that will draw the attention of *all* pupils to the inner purpose of the task. The wording of the question is quite deliberate: 'There is a smart, efficient way of doing each question.' Pupils can busily engage in activity, but if they apply crude strategies, which do not take the distributive law into account, then I anticipate that meaningful learning will not occur.

Recall activity

Multiplication grids

Developing fluency with multiplication tables and associated division facts is complex. It requires a succession of experiences and representations layered over time. There is no single activity or task that will lead to pupils fully learning their times tables.

For pupils to become successful learners of mathematics, it is important that they do not rely on figuring out common results every time they wish to use them. This would be a significant added burden on working memory, which we should seek to avoid. There is an important distinction between being able to 'figure it out' and 'knowing it'.

Another problem with not knowing common results – such as those in the multiplication tables – is that pupils are unlikely to recognise patterns that indicate their presence. This is particularly pertinent to division. Once pupils recognise that $8 \times 7 = 56$, the related division facts of $\frac{56}{7} = 8$ and $\frac{56}{8} = 7$ are in reach. Without this knowledge, pupils are forced to resort to 'working out'.

Choral chanting of times tables might be perceived as being archaic; however, one of the powerful things about chanting, if done in unison, is that if a pupil loses their place, the others in the class will know the answer and he/she will quickly be able to get back 'on track' with the chant. The idea of the chanting is to develop recognition of the numbers involved.

I wouldn't want to ask individual pupils to chant multiplication tables in front of the whole class. Those who can do it will do so and those who can't won't. I don't see any outcome from this other than humiliation for those who are struggling. Nevertheless, pupils do need individual tasks on recall and recognition of the facts, to accompany the deep conceptual work they will undertake in learning about multiplication.

The humble multiplication grid is a short task which pupils can use to practise recall of multiplication facts. I find these grids helpful with pupils in early secondary who haven't yet learned the facts by heart.

×	7	9	8	5	6
6					
5					
9					
7					
8					

I like such grids for a couple of reasons. If pupils get stuck, there are many patterns and additive structures they can use to 'work out' the value that has not yet been found. Perhaps controversially, I do tend to use a time limit with these grids, albeit quite a generous one. After completion, I want pupils to focus on the facts they didn't know. In subsequent lessons, pupils can attempt to improve on the number they manage to get correct in the time.

How we use the grids and structure their design depends on the pupils in front of us. I tend to include an 'easy' table such as 2 or 10 if working with a group who are just beginning to learn times tables. I find this helps to give them a sense of being able to get started.

Grids are also useful as they can be easily tweaked to incorporate associated division facts, as shown below.

×	7	9	8	5	6
		54			
			40		
	63				
				35	
					48

Some might argue that this is instrumental process without any concern for meaning – 'rules without reasons'. However, this is only one task in the sequence of tasks pupils will engage with when working on multiplication. We also know that gains in fact recall can lead to gains in conceptual understanding – the two are not mutually exclusive. The Nuffield report on high-attaining countries (Askew *et al.*, 2010) suggests that, in the UK, an unhelpful separation exists between the two, with procedural fluency and conceptual understanding in mathematics largely seen as mutually exclusive aims. In contrast, teaching in Pacific Rim countries is largely dominated by procedures and hence supportive of procedural fluency, but rooted in mathematical principles such that it is more mathematically coherent and meaningful.

Taking attention 'off' what we are doing

Factors

When I interviewed Tom Francome, he described the idea of taking attention off what we are doing. Tom offered a lovely task on factors. Before using the task, he suggests that pupils should know what a factor is; he asks pupils to give some factor pairs of numbers, just to be sure the idea is clear. Even in a procedure-focused lesson (finding factors of numbers), Tom tries to make space for pupils to develop their mathematical thinking and habits of mind. He is reluctant to give much more information, unless required. In his own words:

I don't say 'two didn't go in, so I don't need to try four.' I want that to come out. I don't want to teach every possible variation of every possible question. I want kids to use reasoning and thinking. Of course, there is some stuff you need to tell pupils and sometimes you need to tell some pupils more than others.

The task begins with pupils taking a piece of paper and, by folding, dividing it into 16 equal rectangles. On each of these rectangles, pupils write a number from 1 to 16. The paper is then cut up so pupils have 16 pieces of paper, numbered from 1 to 16. The pupils are then instructed to sort the numbers into piles, based on how many factors they have. The distinction between the direct call to action, 'find the factors of all the numbers' and the more open question, 'how many factors does each number have?' is clear. It is not a case of 'do this'; rather, pupils are invited to think and use their own strategies. Tom suggests that this is more powerful than simply telling pupils a process for listing factors of numbers. 'Often I see people teach kids a procedure, they can do it at the moment and then two weeks later nobody even knows what it was.' In this task, pupils will get plenty of practice, but will have to think a little harder because the level of cognitive demand hasn't been lowered too much.

1	2	3	4
5	6	7	8
9	10	11	12
13	14	15	16

Number of factors:
1. 1
2. 2, 3, 5, 7, 11, 13
3. 4, 9
4. 6, 8, 10, 14, 15
5. 16
6. 12

It helps to think about this task through the lens of product and process. The product is the numbers sorted into piles. The process is pupils finding the factors – but this is subordinated to the sorting. Tom suggests that:

the way you get fluency is by taking the attention off what you are doing. You've got to be able to do it without thinking about it. If you ask kids what they are doing, they might say, 'I'm sorting these cards by how many factors they have'. The thing I really want them to be able to do is to find factors. They are doing this, but the simple tweak of the cards means it's not their sole focus. This, for me, helps to develop fluency. I want them to be able to think about it if they need to.

This is an interesting theory on how we might develop fluency, which Tom is pursuing further in his PhD research.

The task is easily extendable. Tom describes the opportunities for generalisation, saying:

we've got some particular examples, but we can move towards the generality. As Gattegno said, "every maths lesson should be shot through with the generality".

Once pupils have created a solution, we can ask questions such as, 'Which numbers have one factor? Which have only two factors? etc...' We can begin to attach some meaning. We can see that numbers with exactly two factors are primes. A nice situation that arose when I tried this task with a group of teachers was that we established that numbers with three factors are square. However, it does not follow that all square numbers have three factors. This is a great example of making conjectures and having opportunities to discuss them. Through more investigation we might establish that having an odd number of factors is what determines if a number is square. Further exploration could involve questions such as considering the properties of numbers with four factors. Pupils often realise that they are a 'prime times a prime', but sometimes it's a prime cubed. Seamlessly, the focus is moving towards writing numbers as a product of primes.

The beauty of this task is that everyone can start, everyone is working on the same ideas. There is extension in this even for pupils who have done it before. I would argue that this is a far richer experience than finding lists of factors for numbers in an arbitrary manner from a textbook.

Tom made some important points about pupils discovering things.

It's trendy at the moment to diss discovering things [but this] is nonsense. If there is an opportunity for pupils to make a step to discover things, this is powerful. The problem arises if we depend upon [discovery learning] as the only place you will encounter this. Maths is all interconnected.

Tom emphasises that ideas can be discovered in different ways at different times and stages of learning. For example, we could have pupils measure the angles of triangles in circles in early secondary, as practice in angle measuring. Some pupils might discover some facts about circle theorems at this point, but the key focus is practising measuring. We can recognise pupils' ideas and chat about them, but we don't depend on their discovery here. If pupils have had that experience, this is positive as it helps us to lay the groundwork for later teaching. Tom says:

> *Similarly the laws of indices can be built up over time where, by the time of formal teaching, pupils have internalised much of [the theory]. I want pupils to feel like they are mathematicians, but I don't want them to be tied to and dependent on me.*

In some respects, allowing pupils to encounter material which is harder than currently needed, makes the easier material simpler. We can think, 'what will they need in two years?' and engage with that – it's just about laying some groundwork.

Surds

Gerry McNally described a lesson on surds, which had a similar structure to the factors task described by Tom.

Initially, Gerry showed his pupils this rule

$$\sqrt{ab} = \sqrt{a} \times \sqrt{b}$$

and worked on the basics of that idea. Then, to begin the task, he issued 100 sticky notes to the class, each showing the square root of a number from 1 to 100 (e.g. $\sqrt{50}$). Pupils were put into groups and each group was given a random selection of the sticky notes.

At this point in the lesson, Gerry made some deliberate choices around language: 'Bear in mind, they had an idea around the simplification of square roots but at this stage I wasn't using the term "surd".' Pupils were asked to classify their square roots as 'fully resolvable' (for example, the square root of 25 is 5), 'partly resolvable' (for example, the square root of 8 is $2\sqrt{2}$) or 'not resolvable'. Gerry drew the following chart on the board and asked the groups to place their sticky notes in the appropriate sections:

Fully resolvable	Partially resolvable	Not resolvable

That was the task. I'd given an introduction and then I stood back and watched. I just loved what I saw. I loved the amount of engagement. I loved the amount of moving around the room and discussing things. That took a whole lesson; more, to be honest. Between them they didn't get it all completed and didn't get it all right, but it gave so much opportunity for discussion. It highlighted, I hesitate to say, misconceptions; it highlighted cases which were wrong. This gave us an opportunity to have discussions as a class, but in the main the pupils were having those discussions themselves. For the main part of the lesson I did very little other than just observe what was taking place. I like to give tasks that give pupils the opportunity to speak about what they have done, to question things, make conjectures and justify ideas.

Sometimes we may be inclined to think that all procedural tasks should be about pupils achieving a correct solution – that we should be product focused. Being able to correctly perform common processes is important, but so too is building on pupils' own thinking and understanding. This task is about drawing out pupils' self-generated ideas and strategies and then, through discussion, moving towards more sophisticated formal approaches.

Learner generation

Watson and Mason (2005) suggest that:

mathematics is learned by becoming familiar with examples that manifest and illustrate mathematical ideas and by constructing generalisations from examples. The more of this we can do for ourselves, the more we can make the territories of mathematics our own.

The idea of learner generation is a useful pedagogical tool. A pupil's passive acceptance of given examples, or given definitions, does not necessarily result in deep understanding of a concept. Sowder (1980) describes a phase in learning such that, once pupils are adept at distinguishing examples and non-examples, they need to construct their own examples before stating and using formal definitions meaningfully.

There is a further discussion on learner generation as a task design principle in Chapter 9. For now, we will examine some tasks that involve pupils generating examples of their own.

Quadratics

Pupils typically do work on quadratics which are given to them, often scaffolded with questions such as 'Find the roots' or 'State the axis of symmetry'. I suggest that this level of scaffolding is not always necessary or desirable. Here is an example of a task providing little scaffolding:

In each cell, sketch a quadratic which meets the criteria and write a possible equation to go with your sketch.

	No real roots	Equal real roots	Two real roots
y-intercept > 0			
y-intercept = 0			
y-intercept < 0			

Here, pupils are presented with some constraints within which to operate. The task requires pupils to interact with the definitions of the terms 'roots' and 'y-intercept' in a meaningful way, and aims to help pupils view these terms as something with which they are comfortable , rather than simply as received definitions.

Drawing sketches gives pupils the chance to externalise their understanding of the terminology and underlying concepts. The additional challenge of having to create potential equations for these graphs makes the task more complex. I have refrained from asking for the values of the roots or the y-intercept, since this would demand further thinking from pupils; the task could be used for that purpose, but I typically use it fairly early in pupils' learning about quadratics. At this stage, I want to assess the extent to which they have grasped the ideas of 'roots' and the 'y-intercept'. Also emerging from this task, but not directly stated, will be the generation of some parabolas with either maximum or minimum turning points.

The first cell in the middle row – 'no roots, y-intercept = 0' – provokes a little moment of tension for pupils as there is no graph which fits these criteria!

A task with similar goals, taking into account learner generation, is shown below:

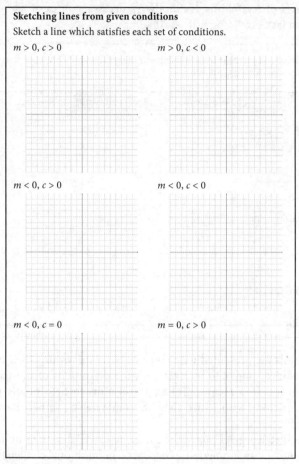

Logarithms

Logarithms can be reduced to some cold, austere definition such as:

$$log_b(x) = y \text{ exactly if } b^y = x \text{ and } x > 0 \text{ and } b > 0 \text{ and } b \neq 1$$

While this captures the definition formally, in my experience it is of little value to pupils who are learning about the idea. Pupils need some interaction with logarithms through examples. Let me suggest an alternative approach, using this task:

$$\log_4 16 = \log_2 \square = \log_\square 9 = \log_\square \square$$
$$\log_4 16 = \log_{10} \square = \log_\square 81 = \log_\square \square$$
$$\log_{16} 4 = \log_{100} \square = \log_\square 2 = \log_\square \square$$
$$\log_2 \tfrac{1}{2} = \log_3 \square = \log_\square \tfrac{1}{5} = \log_\square \square$$
$$\log_4 8 = \log_{16} \square = \log_\square 27 = \log_\square \square$$

The task involves a mix of interpreting log expressions and then generating other expressions with equivalent values. In each row, pupils first have to interpret the given expression. The second and third expressions in each row require pupils to consider the relationship between the base, the argument and the value of the logarithm, and use this to identify values that satisfy the constraint. In the final expression in each row, there is more freedom. The expression generated has to be equivalent to others on the line, so once pupils decide on a base, there is only one valid argument. The mathematics itself imposes a constraint upon the values for the argument.

This task is increasingly challenging on each subsequent line, with pupils later having to consider fractional and negative powers (although these powers never explicitly appear on the page – they are hidden in the thinking involved in the task). It is important to give pupils opportunities to verbalise their understanding of the invariant relationships. For instance, on the penultimate line, each expression is equal to −1, but a pupil may successfully complete the task without realising that, in general, $\log_a \tfrac{1}{2} = -1$.

The task can be developed further with simple prompts such as, 'write four log expressions with a value of x'. These sorts of activity take advantage of the generation effect to strengthen pupils' learning.

Algebraic fractions

No matter how much 'telling' or 'drilling' happens, pupils still make errors. I suggest that pupils require various experiences before they begin to appreciate an idea, learn to recognise it in other situations and then produce mathematical work which takes the idea into account. That is to say, the idea needs to be encountered, understood and then assimilated to their wider understanding of mathematics. The simplification of algebraic fractions is a topic where pupils often appear to have developed some degree of procedural fluency at the time of completing a routine drill worksheet. However, when an algebraic fraction appears as part of some other task it is common for pupils to make technical errors with the simplification.

While pupils may seem to have grasped the key idea – that a term must be a common factor to numerator and denominator for simplification to be permissible – this is not always the case. It may simply be that, on a given worksheet, they have been imitating the process demonstrated by the teacher. True fluency comes when pupils are able to recognise a phenomenon and then employ strategies they have worked on previously.

Consider the task shown below.

Here are some algebraic terms:

$4x$	2	x^3
y	$8x^2$	9

Selecting from the terms above, create expressions of the form below that **can** be simplified. Do the correct simplification.

$$\frac{\boxed{} + \boxed{}}{\boxed{}}$$

Selecting from the terms above, create expressions of the form below that **cannot** be simplified.

$$\frac{\boxed{} + \boxed{}}{\boxed{}}$$

Using **any** terms, create four expressions of the form below that **can** be simplified. Do the correct simplification.

$$\frac{\boxed{}}{\boxed{} + \boxed{}}$$

Using **any** terms, create expressions of the form below that **cannot** be simplified. Try to make them so that somebody might think they can be simplified.

$$\frac{\boxed{}}{\boxed{} + \boxed{}}$$

I use this task sometime after the initial teaching – usually after some homework exercise in which several pupils have tried to simplify algebraic fractions where simplification was not possible. By the time this task arises, pupils can probably simplify algebraic fractions. It is the recognition of when this is allowed that we need to work on, and more drill practice of this is unlikely to reap significant rewards. In the task above, there is some element of doing procedures, but the main focus is on examining the conditions where the simplification is possible. This encountering of examples and non-examples can help to develop appropriate awareness. The whole task uses learner generation. The first couple of questions are constrained by pupils selecting from the terms given, while the later tasks involve pupils generating their own terms.

The task can be extended so there are two terms in the denominator and in the numerator. It can then be extended further still to include quadratics and polynomials in the numerator and denominator if appropriate.

Circle theorems

Here is a task I have used many times with my pupils, in this form and with several variations.

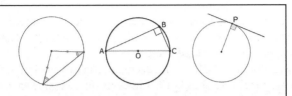

1. In words, describe each of the circle facts shown above as accurately as you can.
2. For each circle fact, create an easy question for your partner to solve.
3. Create three questions, each of which uses two of the circle facts, for your partner to solve.

Usually, I use this task to help pupils revise their knowledge of circle theorems sometime after having initially worked on them. Pupils are invited to generate their own explanations of the circle theorems shown. This is more demanding, but likely more useful, than regurgitating a teacher-given definition, since it requires them to think carefully about the mathematics and how to articulate its meaning; pupils must focus on the features present in each theorem to arrive at accurate articulations. To check they have appreciated this, they are then asked to create simple problems for a partner to solve. There is a built in checking process, which becomes apparent through their collaboration with a peer.

Next, pupils are asked to create questions that draw on two of the theorems. This is intended to get them into the mindset of the task designer. Pupils can consider ways to make the problems more challenging. They have to think carefully about the range of permissible changes and ensure the theorems still hold in the problems they generate. It is important that pupils work through their problems before swapping with a partner and working through each other's questions. Again, checking is built in through the discussion.

Interleaving effect

One of the most frequently misinterpreted ideas from research on memory is that of interleaving. I know that I have previously fallen into the trap of confusing interleaving and 'spacing', for example. This is easily done as the ideas are closely related. Let's take a moment here to ensure a common understanding of interleaving.

Interleaving

What it is not:

- Spacing practice over time – this is called spaced practice. Although interleaving and spacing are different interventions, the two are inextricably linked because interleaving inherently introduces spacing
- A curriculum design tool for chopping up lots of topics. That would also be an application of spaced practice.
- An excuse to shoehorn fractions, decimals, angles, negatives or whatever else into every single exercise. Again, this is an application of spaced practice.

What it is:

- A consideration at the time of initial study, where **related** ideas are taught in close proximity.
- A *desirable difficulty* (as described by Robert Bjork) – that is to say, a feature introduced at the time of learning that deliberately disrupts the learner and creates an apparent tension, cognitive conflict or obstacle. This acts to refocus or reset the learner's attention (Bjork, 1994).

Spacing involves revision throughout the course, whereas **interleaving** involves switching between ideas while you study.

Interleaving might work because it helps pupils to distinguish between concepts and learn when to apply which strategy (Rohrer, 2012). However, interleaving completely unrelated ideas results in no additional gains in learning (Hausman and Kornell, 2014). Much more research is needed to interpret how we can use interleaving in the mathematics classroom. However, Rohrer *et al.* have taken steps in completing some interesting work with this focus, testing the effects of interleaving in a mathematics-specific domain and beyond laboratory conditions (Rohrer, Dedrick and Stershic, 2015).

The task below is designed for pupils learning the basics of the chain rule for differentiation, integration of linear expressions to a power, and integration and differentiation of trig expressions. I tend to work through a few example–problem pairs involving differentiation and integration, then follow up with the set of questions below. Usually, I would have taught all of these related ideas separately; however, the premise of interleaving is to create 'interference' of some sort. Making the learning harder in the initial stages can lead to long-term gains in terms of both memory and the ability to retrieve those memories. However, it can be uncomfortable for teacher and pupil alike. For pupils, there is the struggle involved in switching between two different, but related ideas. For the teacher, the lesson may 'seem' to go less well than a lesson with a narrower focus. However, this sort of thinking is a result of confusing instantaneous performance with learning.

It is important to remember that they are not the same thing. How pupils react to these desirable difficulties can be a result of the culture built up in the classroom. If time is taken to explain the principles behind the desirable difficulties, in an age/stage appropriate way, this can help pupils make better sense of it too and embrace the challenge rather than feel demoralised or frustrated by it.

Differentiate	Integrate
$(3x + 2)^2$	
	$(2 - 5x)^3$
$\dfrac{2(1 - 4x)^3}{5}$	
	$\dfrac{3(2x - 4)^2}{7}$
$\sqrt{4x + 5}$	
	$\sqrt{3 + 2x}$
$\sqrt[3]{1 + 5x}$	
	$\dfrac{1}{\sqrt[3]{1 - 5x}}$
$(2x^2 + 1)^4$	
$\cos(2x - \pi)$	
	$\sin\left(3x + \dfrac{\pi}{2}\right)$
$2\sin\left(\dfrac{\pi}{3} - 4x\right)$	
	$3\cos(\pi - 2x)$
$\cos^2(x)$	

Rather than blocking these three or four skills over separate lessons and then bringing them together at the end, the idea here is to work on all of them together, from the start, and continue to do this across a sequence of lessons.

Robert Bjork often tells a story that sums up this approach beautifully. Describing his attempts to learn how to play tennis, he tells us about the normal coaching practice of weeks and weeks of learning how to serve (and nothing else), followed by weeks of backhand, weeks of lobbing, weeks of smashing and so on. The aspiring tennis player builds up confidence and deftness in each individual skill or technique, before finally bringing them together in a game. The experience for the learner is one of assured mastery of each separate pointer the coach gives them – they practice and practice until the serve is natural and unthinking, and so feel like they are making excellent progress. Bjork then describes an interleaved approach. This time, the poor sap of a beginner tennis ace arrives at their very first lesson and is asked to try all techniques immediately – they serve, play backhand, smash at the net, try to master footing, learn how to defend a serve and do everything else involved in a full game. They are left defeated and dumbfounded. Every subsequent lesson is the same – a mix of all techniques in every session.

As teachers, we are often tempted by the first, smooth path to mastery. But the interesting and remarkable outcome is that the second player more readily becomes the tennis ace, not the first. By interleaving the related techniques, the learner is forced to focus their attention on the differences between the moves rather than on the sameness within each move. Our mathematics task above achieves the same.

This task is best accomplished with the use of mini whiteboards to ensure ample feedback for pupils. The task is clearly about technical details rather than conceptual understanding. However, such details are important: experience has shown me that many pupils struggle with these more sophisticated technical details in calculus.

The task is rooted in the idea of doing and undoing. Once the grid is completed, pupils can go back and work in the opposite direction, integrating and differentiating their answers to get back to the initial questions. When I trialled this task with one pupil, he jotted down, 'power to front → one off power → multiply by derivative of bracket'. It was interesting to see him retrace his steps backwards along this journey when looking at integration. The doing and undoing allowed him to work independently, with self-directed feedback, as he worked through the task for the second time in reverse.

Of course, with integration, it is not the derivative of inside the brackets but the coefficient of x in the linear expression. The task deliberately includes two examples that can be differentiated but not integrated at this point in time. I want pupils to see that there is a need for more sophisticated techniques such as integration by substitution: I don't want them to overgeneralise the idea.

This would, by necessity, be only one task in a sequence. The cognitive demand comes from how I choose to use the task, not the nature of the task itself. The same task could be used with much lower cognitive demand as a review exercise at the end of teaching these ideas.

There are many other areas of the curriculum where related ideas could potentially be interleaved: area and perimeter, volumes of shapes, sine and cosine rules etc. One thing I frequently think about, in terms of research, is that we have to test ideas in our own experience. Much of the work from cognitive science is propositional when applied to mathematics teaching, which is to say it has been proposed or theorised by an academic but has not yet been shown to work in live classroom settings. We can learn from the ideas, of course, but we have no rigorously proven ways of making them work. The task above is a result of my own experiments with interleaving. When using such approaches to create 'desirable difficulties', I am aware of a tension: the balance between ensuring pupils have high levels of success and making the learning hard enough to secure their long-term performance.

7 Conceptual tasks

That pupils develop conceptual understanding is desirable for many reasons. Conceptual understanding has significant impacts on retention of procedural fluency.

> *As facts and methods learned with understanding are connected, they are easier to remember and use, and they can be reconstructed when forgotten.*
>
> (Hiebert and Carpenter, 1992)

Conceptual understanding includes, but is not limited to:

- understanding connections between ideas
- being able to discriminate between ideas
- appreciating underlying principles and relationships between attributes
- representational fluency – the ability to comprehend and translate between representations
- appreciating and making mathematical arguments related to the idea
- understanding 'why' and 'why not'.

Activity that might help to develop this includes:

- sorting and matching
- classifying
- using multiple representations – interpretation and generation
- exploring principles and deliberate interaction with attributes
- scaffolded proof
- guided discovery
- discussing mathematical statements
- combining ideas
- interpreting and creating stories.

As in the previous chapter, the tasks described below address more than one strand of mathematical understanding. Arguments could have been made for their inclusion in other chapters. However, conceptual understanding is the *primary* focus of these tasks.

Sorting and matching

On many occasions over the years, the topic of composite functions has lulled me into a false sense of security. At the time of initial teaching, it seems that pupils have grasped the ideas and can perform the substitutions correctly. At this point, I usually have a sense of 'job well done'. Nevertheless – and almost inevitably – in a homework exercise or class quiz a week later, a notable number of pupils will make significant errors on these questions. The most common error involves substituting functions the wrong way around (e.g. f into h instead of h into f). Most of the time, pupils are able to produce accurate composite functions based on these incorrect starting points. The issue is then having some way of re-focusing on the initial composition itself rather than on the subsequent algebra.

It would be inefficient to have pupils do more composite function questions in their entirety; they clearly don't need to practise the whole process since the algebraic manipulation after the substitution is usually fine. Instead, they need to re-attend to the idea of substitution. I say re-attend, as we will have discussed the concept at the time of initial teaching. The problem is that it is very difficult to tell somebody conceptual understanding. Previously I have found myself re-telling or re-exemplifying the ideas to pupils and giving them more practice, but this is problematic for two reasons. First, the whole process takes valuable time. Second, it takes agency away from pupils – they no longer 'own' the learning, and the responsibility for pupils' understanding moves back to the teacher. Pupils need to interact with the mathematics themselves and make sense of it. Can we achieve this with a different type of task? Here is an example:

$f(x) = 3x + 2$		$g(x) = x^2 + 1$	$h(x) = 5x - 4$
$f(g(x))$	$5(3x + 2) - 4$	$x \rightarrow \boxed{f(x)} \rightarrow \boxed{h(x)} \rightarrow$	Substitute f(x) into f(x)
$g(f(x))$	$(3x + 2)^2 + 1$	$x \rightarrow \boxed{g(x)} \rightarrow \boxed{g(x)} \rightarrow$	Substitute g(x) into f(x)
$h(f(x))$	$3(5x - 4) + 2$	$x \rightarrow \boxed{g(x)} \rightarrow \boxed{f(x)} \rightarrow$	Substitute f(x) into g(x)
$f(h(x))$	$(x^2 + 1)^2 + 1$	$x \rightarrow \boxed{f(x)} \rightarrow \boxed{f(x)} \rightarrow$	Substitute h(x) into f(x)
$f(f(x))$	$3(3x + 2) + 2$	$x \rightarrow \boxed{h(x)} \rightarrow \boxed{f(x)} \rightarrow$	Substitute g(x) into g(x)
$g(g(x))$	$3(x^2 + 1) + 2$	$x \rightarrow \boxed{f(x)} \rightarrow \boxed{g(x)} \rightarrow$	Substitute f(x) into h(x)

This task is designed to be used in a relatively short period of time to help pupils focus on the key idea. The inclusion of the different representations is intended to give pupils something on which to focus their thinking as they do the initial substitutions. Rather than making arbitrary decisions based on a sketchy understanding derived from procedural imitation, pupils' work will be based on conceptual thinking.

There is, of course, no guarantee that the task will work, but I have often found it to be an adequate intervention task – I would be interested to hear about the experiences you have in your own classroom should you choose to try this task with your pupils.

Classifying

Symmetry

Classification tasks are powerful. Here is an extract from a classic example from the Standards Unit (Swan, 2005):

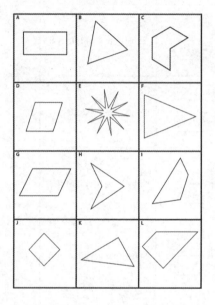

	No rotational symmetry	Rotational symmetry
No lines of symmetry		
One or two lines of symmetry		
More than two lines of symmetry		

This task involves pupils discriminating between line and rotational symmetry. Pupils encounter line symmetry early in primary school, yet it is not uncommon to see them working specifically on this idea, with little increased demand, at secondary level. This task increases the demand as pupils have to work with two ideas simultaneously. As such, it is a powerful assessment task: if pupils can handle this, one has to ask if there is much point in spending time on the basics of either idea.

There are also some generalisations that arise here, such as the fact that it is possible to have line symmetry but no rotational symmetry and vice versa. These generalisations can serve as the basis of a class discussion. A nice follow-up task is to ask pupils to create a shape of their own that belongs in each category.

Rational functions

Thomson shared the following task with me. The intention is for pupils to begin to perceive the information present in the algebraic representation of each rational function.

Match each rational function to its correct position in the table.

$$y = \frac{x^3 - 5}{6 - 5x - x^2}$$
$$y = \frac{10x^2 - 16x - 9}{2x^2 - 3x - 2}$$
$$y = \frac{x^3 - 2}{x^3 + x^2 - 9x + 12}$$

$$y = \frac{x + 5}{x^2 - 10x + 25}$$
$$y = \frac{x}{x^2 + 4}$$
$$y = \frac{x^4 + x - 2}{x^3 + 8}$$

$$y = \frac{x + 2}{x^2 + 2x - 3}$$
$$y = \frac{3x^3 - x + 2}{x^2 + 1}$$
$$y = \frac{4x - 3}{x^2 + x + 2}$$

	No vertical asymptote	One vertical asymptote	Two vertical asymptotes
Horizontal asymptote (x-axis)			
Horizontal asymptote (y = k)			
Oblique/ non-vertical asymptote			

For each type of asymptote, pupils have to be aware of certain conditions. This task keeps the focus on those conditions, which is an efficient use of time. Pupils may be told or shown the conditions when various types of asymptote are present, but they will only really begin to internalise this information after repeated engagement with function graphing tasks. Rather than embarking on such extended tasks immediately, this task allows pupils to practise examining the features of the algebraic representations. By narrowing the focus, pupils have a chance to attend to these important details. Having a secure understanding of this content will help pupils when they do move on to extended curve sketch tasks.

I asked Andy how we might use this task with pupils. He said:

> *I'd ask them to focus on the classification process and not to simply take each function on its own merits. I'd also ask them – for each function – to provide two reasons why they've assigned it to a particular location. I'd be looking for high quality explanations, for example, 'this function has no vertical asymptote because the denominator cannot be equal to zero. I know this because ...' As a follow-up 'testing' task, I'd challenge them to find and justify their own example for each of the nine slots in the table.*

Roots classification

Tom Carson created this classification task on evaluation of roots. This involves several layers of complexity, and includes some excellent opportunities for reflection. First, pupils have to determine the magnitude of the numbers. In some cases, this might mean evaluation, but generally, inspection and 'reasoning it out' should be sufficient. Pupils may want to convert the fractional powers to root form to interpret them.

Tom's use of 'Rational' and 'Irrational' as column headings is a good way of encouraging pupils to think meaningfully about the definitions. Rather than giving pupils definitions to remember, this task allows them to interact with the concept of rationality; it gives them some experience on which to hang the meaning. Pupils have to use the numbers given and repeatedly refine their understanding of rational numbers by reflecting on the examples.

$\sqrt{-(7)^2}$ is a curveball. Pupils at this stage are unlikely to have encountered imaginary numbers, so this question gives them a look at what lies ahead in their mathematical journey.

	Rational	Irrational			
>10			$\sqrt{100}$	$\sqrt{28}$	$\sqrt{\frac{3}{4} \times 160}$
			$\sqrt{25\pi}$	$\sqrt{7^2}$	$\sqrt{\frac{1}{4} \times \frac{1}{2}}$
			$\sqrt{\frac{4}{5}}$	$\sqrt{(-7)^2}$	$\sqrt{-(7)^2}$
<10			$\sqrt{100}+5$	$\frac{\sqrt{2}}{\sqrt{12}}$	$7^{\frac{1}{2}}$
			$9^{\frac{1}{4}}$	$9^{\frac{1}{2}}$	$12^{\frac{3}{4}}$

Multiple representations: interpretation and generation

Completing the square
David Wees was involved in the New Visions project, creating tasks and instructional materials and delivering CPD. One of the task structures he often used is that of 'connecting representations', as shown in the example below.

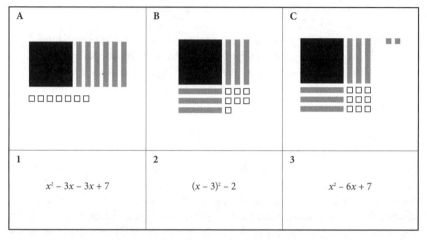

A	B	C
1	**2**	**3**
$x^2 - 3x - 3x + 7$	$(x - 3)^2 - 2$	$x^2 - 6x + 7$

This task is not simply about matching each algebra tiles representation with the correct algebraic expression. A key piece of thinking behind the task involves adding meaning to the steps of completing the square. David recalled using this task with a group of teachers. They made the initial matches successfully and, once they had achieved this, David told them, 'these are the steps to completing the square'. Interestingly, the teachers had not noticed this. The teachers then sequenced the cards and put them in order.

The task is multi-step. As well as matching the representations, the user has to think about the transformations that happen within the representations as the process of completing the square is carried out. The task supports their thinking around the procedural steps, by attaching the manipulations to the tangible concept of the tiles. Many of the teachers with whom David was working had non-mathematical backgrounds and hadn't seen completing the square since they were in high school – and many had not understood it even then. As David explained, after the matching activity, the teachers were comfortable with the visuals, and this meant the only thing they had left to think about was the sequencing. As a result, they found it very straightforward. These teachers were suddenly all much more confident about teaching completing the square. They loved the idea that the visuals made the concept much more obvious.

What these teachers experienced – developing understanding – is exactly what the task aims to help pupils do.

David employs variation theory in his task creation. In the example above, we have the area model at the top. All that changes between the models is the location of the bars – although the pupil is likely to be unsure of what these bars represent at the outset. Picture C is likely to require the most thought. David says this is a design decision when employing variation theory:

> you can't just give pupils a bunch of things that simply vary, you have to break the pattern at some point so they have to think about how to use what they've learnt from the patterns in order to extend it to the new object. After varying the pictorial representations, I think about how it will look if it were varied in the algebraic expressions.

All three of the algebraic expressions are equivalent but they vary in similar ways to the pictures. If a pupil looks at picture B, they'll see there are two groups of three bars, which could represent the two '$3x$' terms in expression 1; this might be an inroad for them. They might wonder what the squares mean. They will see that the large square is the same in all three pictures and a 'squared' term appears in all three expressions (this is the only thing that is the same in all three expressions). The task is deliberately trying to get pupils to notice these things.

David describes the 'connecting representations' task as part of an instruction sequence. It's not a card sort in the normal sense: when he uses it with teachers, they don't have the cards in front of them. Instead, the information is displayed on posters and the teachers don't get to write anything until quite late in the activity. The objective is to make the matches, as in a card sort, but without touching or moving the cards. This means the teachers have to describe the cards while talking to their partner about what the matches might be. There are no extra cards, as there might be in a card sort, because this would make things too difficult; the scope of the work is deliberately limited. The goal is to talk about the features of each representation that allow matches to be made, and to construct the mathematical argument.

Next comes the part of the routine where the whole room is involved. Two people present their work together, with one person pointing while the other talks; this, intentionally, slows down the presentation. David suggests that the presentation of mathematical procedures normally goes much too fast for most people. Slowing things down in some way, while keeping the attention required high, is important. As David says:

What we want is for people to restate what [their partner] has said and start to describe what the other person saw rather than adding a new idea. A huge flaw in many number talk routines is that [they only involve] sharing different things. In this discussion we're hammering on one particular idea until we get it. My role in this is to annotate and record the connections people have made and then press with questions. There's a bunch of rich pedagogy involved. People work with a partner to make a match and then we share the matches; everybody looks at it, everybody unpacks and understands it. And then they reflect on learning.

After this period, in workshops, David gets teachers to attempt a similar, related task. This is where the stark difference between using this routine as a worksheet and using it through the rich pedagogy described above becomes clear. Teachers are now working in isolation, without the support of their peers. They feel there is a certain time pressure, so they try to work through the task quickly. When they get stuck, they have nothing to do except ask David for help. It is powerful for teachers to recognise the differences between the situations, despite the fact that they involve the same kind of task.

Straight line

Straight line is one of the most pivotal topics in secondary mathematics. It is here that pupils first bring together algebra and geometry in a meaningful way. This topic is the basis of all later work on functional relationships, into quadratics and beyond. It is relatively straightforward to give pupils a formula for finding the gradient and tell them about $y = mx + c$, then claim the topic has been 'taught'. Being comfortable with those formulae is important, of course, but it barely scratches the surface in terms of effective teaching of straight line. There are multiple layers of ideas in this topic and they all need consideration. The intention of the task below is to help pupils develop a somewhat deeper understanding of straight lines, by sorting and matching different representations of various lines. Pupils are issued each of the cards below, cut up in advance by the teacher.

$y =$	equation	x / y values	graph	properties	description
$y =$	$\dfrac{-y}{3} = x + \dfrac{2}{3}$	x: −2, −1, 0, 1, 2 y: 4, 1, −2, −5, −8		Gradient = −3 y-intercept (0, −2)	For a given x coordinate, to find the corresponding y coordinate, multiply by −3 then subtract 2.
$y =$	$\dfrac{-y}{3} = x - \dfrac{2}{3}$	x: −2, −1, 0, 1, 2 y: (blank)		Gradient = −3 y-intercept (0, 2)	For a given x coordinate, to find the corresponding y coordinate, multiply by −3 then add 2.
$y =$	$y + x - 1 = 0$	x: −2, −1, 0, 1, 2 y: 3, 2, 1, 0, −1		Gradient = −1 y-intercept (0, 1)	
$y =$	$y - 3 = x$	x: −2, −1, 0, 1, 2 y: (blank)			For a given x coordinate, to find the corresponding y coordinate, add 3.
$y =$	$y - 3 = 2x$	x: −2, −1, 0, 1, 2 y: −1, 1, 3, 5, 7		Gradient = 2 y-intercept (0, 3)	For a given x coordinate, to find the corresponding y coordinate, multiply by 2 then add 3.

Some of the cards are deliberately left blank. The reason for this is two-fold. Firstly, I want pupils to perform some generation of representations: generation is harder than interpretation, so this raises the level of challenge in the task. Secondly, the blank cards ensure pupils can't quickly resolve the problem as they near the end. Previously, when I have created such tasks without blanks, I've heard pupils say, 'that one must go there!' This is not a result of mathematical thinking, but rather a simple process of elimination.

There are various aspects to this task. Rearranging the equation of a straight line so it is in the form $y = mx + c$ is an important skill, so practice of this is built in. The links between line equations, tables of values and graphical representations are also important. Finally, written representations (in words) are often under-emphasised in mathematical tasks, so I felt it important to include them, to draw pupils' attention to the *idea* of functions: the line equations relate an input x to an output y.

The first iteration of the task is shown here. I offer this to pupils to complete in pairs and, as they work, I move around the class, asking questions about their choices and probing their understanding. Most of all, I listen carefully to their conversations to hear what insights they are coming up with; I might ask them to share their ideas later in a whole-class discussion. Pupils do not usually complete this task quickly, but pace is not important here: the quality of the thought processes and the making of connections are the main focus.

Here is a complete pupil solution to the initial task.

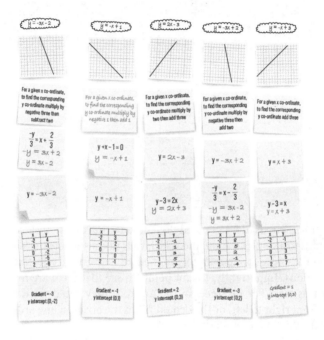

As pupils complete the task, I look at their work, pointing out where they might need to think again and make some corrections. If pupils finish early, I might ask them to produce six more cards for a line of their choosing. Once the majority of the class has finished the first task, I like to have a whole-class discussion about the ideas that have emerged; during this discussion, I highlight the key connections between these ideas. For instance, 'the *y*-intercept relates to 'add' in the verbal description of each line', or 'the coordinate of the *y*-intercept is always of the form $(0, y)$ and this is clearly identifiable in the table of values'. If any key ideas do not come out of the class discussion, I push the conversation further to bring these ideas to the fore.

I want to build on the connections pupils have made and give them the opportunity to act on the feedback they have had on their work and thinking. The second version of the task is a stripped-down version, with only one representation per row. Here is an example of a partially-completed attempt at this task:

This time, pupils do not need to cut out the cards; instead each row corresponds to a single straight line. The idea is to consolidate the learning from the first task and allow pupils to progress to converting effectively between representations. Importantly, I want pupils to see that there are multiple ways through this task. For instance, in the top row, they could work from left to right, or from right to left, or they could fill in the boxes in any order they like. I emphasise this in the pre-task discussion.

The sequencing of these tasks, in conjunction with other conceptual tasks, gives pupils a stronger grounding for work on straight line, rather than simply trying to remember steps for 'how to find...'. If pupils have representational fluency, they can use this to support their thinking in any problem, whether routine or problem-solving in nature.

Assessment of fractions

Multiple representations can be used effectively to assess pupil understanding of fractions. In the example below (from Thomson), pupils have to think about the principles of fraction multiplication. The procedure for multiplying two fractions together is trivial, but a rich layer of mathematics underpins this procedure.

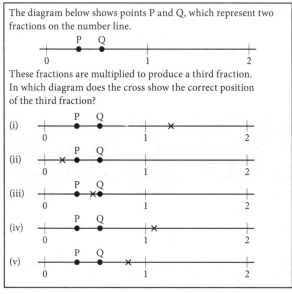

The diagram below shows points P and Q, which represent two fractions on the number line.

These fractions are multiplied to produce a third fraction. In which diagram does the cross show the correct position of the third fraction?

Conceptual tasks like this can help pupils to develop their thinking beyond the procedural imitative approach to drawing generalisations. This task can also be adapted easily, by varying the positions of P and Q and asking pupils to plot, roughly, where various products and quotients of these fractions may lie on the number line.

Another useful task for assessing pupils' understanding of fractions is proposed by Hodgen and Wiliam (2006), who offer the following simple diagram:

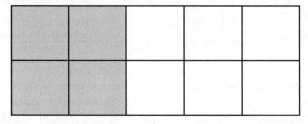

They propose asking pupils what fractions could be represented by the diagram.

> *The open-endedness of the problem provides an opportunity to suggest ways in which pupils could extend their understandings by asking them to find other diagrams or images to represent the different fractions.*

> (Hodgen and Wiliam, 2006)

Standard deviation

I am not a statistician. At school, I remembered formulae, applied them and usually struggled to interpret the results. When teaching, I recognised many of the same behaviours in my own pupils: they could apply the standard deviation formulae but struggled when asked to explain what standard deviation means or to interpret their results.

In this task, I present the first five data sets, one by one, to the whole class. I let pupils work in pairs to discuss, describe and do calculations. After each data set, I draw the class back together to discuss what they have established and to identify and correct any misconceptions.

The focus of the task is not on doing lots of standard deviation and mean calculations (although some such calculations are required). Instead, it is about attending to what standard deviation actually represents.

Data set 1	Data set 2	Data set 3
5 5 5 5	6 5 5 4	6 4 6 4
Mean Standard deviation	Mean Standard deviation	Mean Standard deviation
Data set 4	Data set 5	Data set 6
3 2 3 2	4 3 4 3	1 5 7 1
Mean Standard deviation	Mean Standard deviation	Mean Standard deviation

Pupils can find the mean by imagining a 'levelling' of the tower blocks: taking all the blocks and laying them out so each tower is an equal height. In the first data set, pupils should be able to write down that the mean is 5 and the standard deviation is 0, without any working. In the second data set the mean is 5 again. At this point, some pupils might assume the standard deviation will also be the same; this is an important moment in developing their understanding. In the third data set, the mean is still 5 but the standard deviation increases once more. Pupils may begin to articulate language around 'jaggedness' or 'spikes', which is informal but can be built on. The fourth data set halves the data set from question 3. Some pupils will correctly suggest that the mean and standard deviation will halve, before doing any calculations to check. Data set 5 adds one to every point in data set 4. This deliberate variation is to stop pupils over-generalising: some of them will incorrectly conjecture that both the mean and standard deviation will increase by 1. This erroneous thinking is a positive outcome, as it creates a cognitive dissonance and helps pupils to further appreciate standard deviation and how it differs from the mean.

After this sequence, I present pupils with the complete task and ask them to continue working from data set 6 onwards. Every pupil has to produce their own work, but they can discuss their thinking in pairs. The task moves on to generation of the visual representation, with a significant increase in cognitive demand in later questions.

Data set 7	Create a data set which works for the given values	Create a data set which works for the given values
2 2 8 2		
Mean Standard deviation	Mean 6 Standard deviation 0	Mean 4 Standard deviation $0 < s < 2$
Create a data set which works for the given values	Create a data set which works for the given values	Create a data set which works for the given values
	4 ? 4 3	
Mean 6 Standard deviation $3 < s < 5$	Mean 4 Standard deviation $\dfrac{1}{\sqrt{2}}$	Mean 4 Standard deviation $\dfrac{1}{\sqrt{2}}$

I do not necessarily expect all pupils to get the last couple of questions correct through a sophisticated strategy. If I see them using an informed version of trial and error, at this stage, I am content. These final tasks are there for extension and challenge, and they stretch pupil thinking beyond anything they are likely to encounter in a summative assessment.

Linear sequences

Helen Konstantine wrote the following excellent task sequence, designed with the aim of helping pupils to notice the shift in times tables and use this to find the nth term. She explains:

I was struck by the simplicity of '6n is 6, 12, 18, 24 so 6n + 1 is 7, 13, 19, 25'. I've shown this to students for years, but I felt that a visual representation might be more compelling. The colours are meant to help students see that term has been shifted.

| 1 | 2 | 3 | 4 | 5 | 6 | 7 | 8 | 9 | 10 | 11 | 12 | 13 | 14 | 15 | 16 | 17 | 18 | 19 | 20 | $4n$ |
| 1 | 2 | 3 | 4 | 5 | 6 | 7 | 8 | 9 | 10 | 11 | 12 | 13 | 14 | 15 | 16 | 17 | 18 | 19 | 20 | |

| 1 | 2 | 3 | 4 | 5 | 6 | 7 | 8 | 9 | 10 | 11 | 12 | 13 | 14 | 15 | 16 | 17 | 18 | 19 | 20 | $5n$ |
| 1 | 2 | 3 | 4 | 5 | 6 | 7 | 8 | 9 | 10 | 11 | 12 | 13 | 14 | 15 | 16 | 17 | 18 | 19 | 20 | |

| 1 | 2 | 3 | 4 | 5 | 6 | 7 | 8 | 9 | 10 | 11 | 12 | 13 | 14 | 15 | 16 | 17 | 18 | 19 | 20 | |
| 1 | 2 | 3 | 4 | 5 | 6 | 7 | 8 | 9 | 10 | 11 | 12 | 13 | 14 | 15 | 16 | 17 | 18 | 19 | 20 | |

| 1 | 2 | 3 | 4 | 5 | 6 | 7 | 8 | 9 | 10 | 11 | 12 | 13 | 14 | 15 | 16 | 17 | 18 | 19 | 20 | |
| 1 | 2 | 3 | 4 | 5 | 6 | 7 | 8 | 9 | 10 | 11 | 12 | 13 | 14 | 15 | 16 | 17 | 18 | 19 | 20 | $6n - 5$ |

Before this, Helen had started the lesson with the tasks below:

What do you notice?

1st term	2nd term	3rd term	4th term	5th term	6th term	nth term
						$5n$
6	12	18	24	30	36	
						$7n$
8	16	24	32	40	48	

If the highlighted row has an nth term '$3n$' what will the other rows be?

1st term	2nd term	3rd term	4th term	5th term	6th term	nth term
0	3	6	9	12	15	
1	4	7	10	13	16	
2	5	8	11	14	17	
3	6	9	12	15	18	$3n$
4	7	10	13	16	19	
5	8	11	14	17	20	
6	9	12	15	18	21	

Starting with these two tasks means pupils are comfortable with the nth term of the times tables. Helen explains:

Then we can move on to the idea that we can find a general rule for a times table that has been shifted. Every student I have ever taught has found it easy to continue a pattern such as 4, 7, 10, 13 (adding three from any starting point). I then like to look at connecting the ideas to other areas of maths.

Helen concludes with the following task, which links many related ideas and representations. This helps pupils not to view these ideas as discrete procedures but to make connections in how they link together.

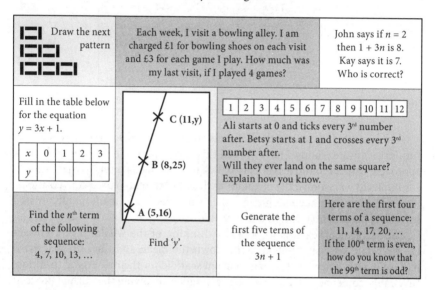

Exploring principles and deliberate interaction with attributes

Calculating the mean

Tom Carson sent me this task a couple of years ago. I've used it regularly ever since and found it helps pupils to develop real insight into the idea of the mean, beyond simply 'adding up the numbers and dividing by how many we have'. I find it particularly effective if pupils have some familiarity with the tower block representation of the mean (as described above), although this does not negate the requirement for some arithmetic when we encounter non-integer values.

Find the mean of each set.

(1)	4	4	4	4	4
(2)	6	6	6	6	6
(3)	6	6	6	6	
(4)	6	6	6	6	0
(5)	6	6	6	5	
(6)	5	6	6	6	
(7)	12	12	12	10	
(8)	1	2	3	4	5
(9)	1	2	3	4	50
(10)	1	2	3	4	4
(11)	1	2	3	4	2
(12)	1	2	3	4	−2

Tom has carefully varied the data sets so pupils can discern differences and similarities more readily. I have offered this task to pupils in two ways. The first approach, which I found less effective, was to issue the data sets to the class and ask pupils to write down the mean for each set. Even with paired conversations, the task seemed to become just another worksheet, and many pupils missed several of the potential insights that should have arisen.

The second approach is to pool the thinking of the whole class. I present the first data set, ask pupils to write down the mean and then draw a visual representation. The visual is an important scaffold for their emerging thinking. Inevitably, someone will do a written calculation involving the normal process. By allowing various pupils to share their thinking, I ensure everyone is exposed to the conceptual layer of this task. Generally, on the second question, all pupils realise that no calculation is needed and confidently write 6 as the mean.

The task then takes us on a journey, and I highlight a few particularly interesting points. For example:

- Data set 3 has the same mean as set 2, but the deliberate variation in the size of the data sets is important.
- The role of the zero in set 4 is also important, since 0 is non-trivial and needs to be considered when working with statistics, but is often left out of textbook exercises.
- Sets 5 and 6 reorder the data, leading to conversations around whether or not the order of data is relevant when finding the mean.

- Set 7 doubles each data element from sets 5 and 6, and pupils begin to discuss the impact on the mean when this happens.
- The visual model is especially helpful for pupils from data set 8 onwards.
- The impact of an extreme data value skewing the mean is illustrated in data set 9.

The essential idea here is that pupils, by working on different data sets, begin to understand the *meaning* of the mean beyond the surface level. I suggest that the basis of further, deeper learning around statistics is laid down here.

Reasoning chains

Mike Askew offers the question:

$5542 \div 17 = 326$
Explain how you could use this to work out 18×326

This question is from an assessment given to primary pupils in England; in the original assessment, 23% of pupils managed to answer the question successfully. Mike suspects many of the pupils tried to do some calculating rather than using reason.

Mike uses this question as the basis of some reasoning chains, to support the sort of thinking required of pupils. In the chain below, pupils are expected to discuss if each of the equations is true. Some whole-class discussion to share ideas and insights is useful here.

True or false?
A. $3 \times 5 = 5 \times 3$
$3 \times 5 = 3 \times 4 + 5$
$4 \times 6 = 3 \times 5 + 3$

Next, the following number chain is presented. Again, pupils discuss if each of the equations is true. The intention now is for pupils to observe that calculation is not required. The structure from part **A** has been developed: part **B** is deliberately not an exact replica of the structure from part **A**, since that could lead to a superficial level of engagement. The subtle introduction of subtraction means pupils need to think about the mathematics, rather than simply observing the pattern.

True or false?
B. $26 \times 39 = 39 \times 26$
$26 \times 39 = 26 \times 40 - 26$
$26 \times 40 = 26 \times 39 + 26$

The final task builds on the thinking in parts **A** and **B**. The numbers in this question might be uglier, but the reasoning is exactly the same. There is good evidence from research that suggests pupils can understand the structure of such calculations and use reasoning to find answers long before they could do the calculations in the conventional way (Nunes *et al.*, 2009). In this section of the task, Mike draws on the primary assessment question mentioned above. He gives one true equation and then presents five more equations for pupils to consider.

> **True**: $5542 \div 17 = 326$
> **True or false?**
> C. $326 \div 17 = 5542$
> $5542 \div 326 = 17$
> $17 \times 326 = 5542$
> $326 \times 16 = 5542 - 16$
> $18 \times 326 = 17 \times 326 + 326$

The task can be drawn together with an explicit highlighting of the underlying structure, shown below.

> $3 \times 6 = 3 \times 5 + 3$
> $26 \times 40 = 26 \times 39 + 26$
> $326 \times 18 = 326 \times 17 + 326$

If working with secondary-age pupils, we might capture this as $a \times b = a \times (b - 1) + a$

More, Same, Less

John Mason developed this task template based on an idea from Dina Tirosh and Pessia Tsamir. Such tasks provide excellent opportunities for pupils to reason about and, in doing so, deepen their understanding of mathematical concepts. Typically, there is some given mathematical object in the centre cell, with attributes on the outside axes. Pupils have to vary the given object in relation to these attributes.

The example below, produced by John Mason (2015) is the original task of this type. In the cell immediately to the right of the centre, pupils are expected to create a shape with the same area as the centre shape, but a greater perimeter. In the cell immediately above the centre, pupils are expected to create a shape with the same perimeter but a greater area. Similar actions are then repeated for the various requirements around the grid.

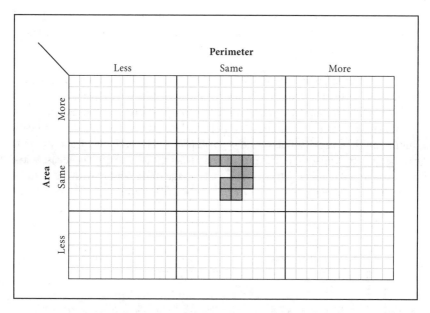

Most pupils can solve simple area or perimeter problems presented as blocked practice on a worksheet with the title 'area' or 'perimeter' given at the top of the page. However, when pupils have to find *both* area *and* perimeter, it is not unusual to hear them ask, 'is this a times or an add?' This question suggests the pupil has reduced the ideas of area and perimeter to multiplication and addition respectively. While it is true that those are the operations involved, it is possible that – in their desire to 'make sense of' things – the pupil has lost sight of the concepts of area and perimeter. This task removes the focus from applying procedures and instead focuses thinking directly on the conceptual understanding –on the fundamental ideas of what area and perimeter are. If pupils are already secure in solving perimeter and area problems, this task serves as the basis for an inquiry into the relationships between area and perimeter and how these attributes of a shape interrelate. John suggests the task can serve as a basis for rich mathematical thinking; he offers the following questions that might be useful in whole-class discussion or as prompts to individual pupils:

- For which part of the grid is it hardest to find an example?
- How can we do this task, making the smallest possible change in each cell (in the case above, perhaps repositioning a single block)?
- What principles emerged for altering area without altering perimeter, and vice versa?

- Are there any central shapes for which not all of the grid can be filled in?
- What other shapes can you put in the centre which have the same shape and the same perimeter as the one chosen?

The first time pupils attempt a more, same, less task, some exemplification by the teacher may be required. However, once the format has been understood and is familiar to pupils, it can be used for many different mathematical ideas. From experience, it is useful to print out and laminate a class set of these tasks. Pupils can then use dry-marker pens to fill in the grid. Knowing their attempts can be quickly wiped out and altered encourages pupils to try out ideas, make more attempts, not fear getting stuck and engage more readily with the task.

A generic task template is shown below (NCETM, 2016).

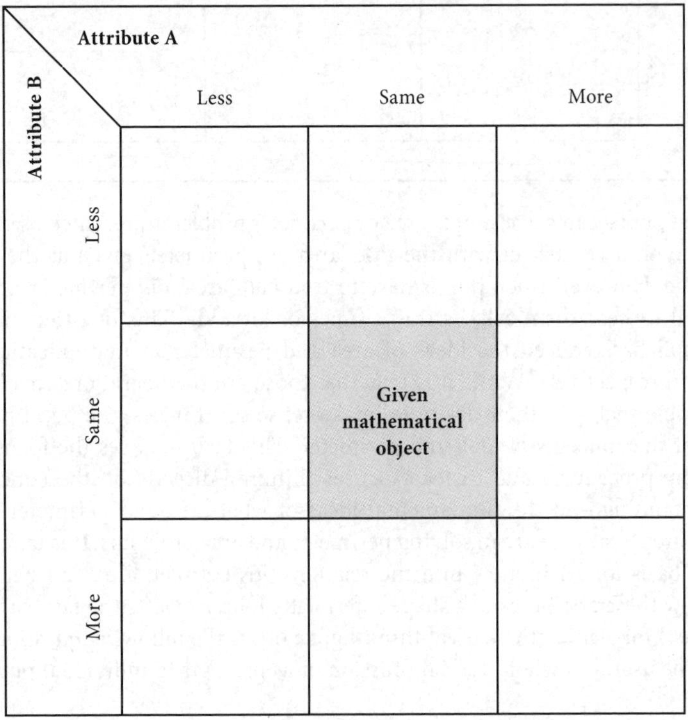

Attribute B \ Attribute A	Less	Same	More
Less			
Same		Given mathematical object	
More			

Drawing on this, I have created several such tasks. Perhaps the most useful one has been the example shown below, which was inspired by an idea from a delegate at a CPD session I was running. Pupils know the terms gradient and y-intercept and can usually find what they are algebraically. This task involves no algebra whatsoever. It simply asks pupils to create examples of lines relative to the one in the centre. I have found this to be a useful moment of formative assessment, which helps me to determine whether or not pupils truly understand the meaning of gradient and *y*-intercept.

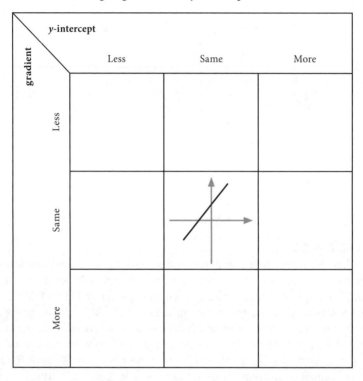

Another example of this sort of task can be found rooted in statistics, with pupils required to calculate the mean and standard deviation of the data set in the middle cell. They then have to create their own data sets, which satisfy the conditions on the other cells. Pupils have to think hard about the meaning of each measure and how the two measures relate to one another. A process of trial and error may be a useful starting point for some, before more informed conjectures begin to emerge. Pupils are likely to have more success with this task if they have previously encountered multiple representations of the mean and standard deviation (as in the towers task above). Here is an example:

Mean \ Std. dev	Less	Same	More
Less			
Same		1 2 3 4 5 $\bar{x} =$ $\quad$ $s =$	
More			

Area of triangles

A further idea for developing an understanding of the attributes of a mathematical object is to present several related instances. When using the task below, I ask pupils to find the area of each triangle and tell them that I do not know the answers. Once pupils have worked on the task, I will ask for the area of the first triangle. I will then immediately write up the answers for the second and third triangles. The reaction of the pupils is usually, 'Sir, you must have known the answers!' I like to ask pupils to consider how I might have done this so quickly, emphasising that I am not very good at long multiplication mentally!

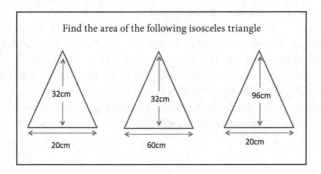

Find the area of the following isosceles triangle

I then follow up with some questions, such as those suggested below.

- What do you notice about the answers for the second and third triangles?
- How do those answers compare with the original triangle?
- Can you create another triangle with the same area as the first triangle?
- Can you create another triangle with the same area as the second and third triangles?
- Can you predict the area of a triangle with base 60 cm and height 96 cm? Calculate the answer. Were you correct?
- Can you create your own set of three triangles which have the same relationship as those shown?
- Can you create a set of three triangles where the original triangle has base x and height y? (Can we generalise?).

I do not present these questions as a worksheet; instead, I ask them verbally. For the rich follow-up questions, I like pupils to reply on mini-whiteboards so I can quickly evaluate the mathematical thinking in the room. The purpose of the task is to consider the multiplicative relationship between base and perpendicular height and the impact of these attributes on the triangular area. Moreover, this is a task where pupils get to make predictions, test conjectures and generate their own examples, which adds a level of richness compared with working through a normal worksheet, finding the areas of various triangles.

Scaffolded proof

When encountering new identities for the first time, many pupils find it challenging to appreciate the associated proof. All too often, I have written up mathematically-rigorous proofs on the board, which pupils have copied down meticulously while appreciating almost none of what I have said or written. I have found it beneficial to give pupils some experience of working with specific instances, before trying to engage them in proof. Depending on the complexity of the proof, I think it is sometimes useful for pupils to use a result before considering the proof.

Trigonometric addition formulae

Susan Whitehouse likes pupils to be involved in the formulation of the proofs, rather than being mere passive recipients. Below is a task she created which carries pupils through the journey of proving the compound angle formula. In her own words:

I think mathematical proof is hugely important but is something that pupils (and sometimes teachers) struggle with. My aim is to give the pupils an active role in the process. I'm aware it's a compromise. It could be argued that by breaking down the proof to this extent, I've done all the thinking for them and they're not doing the proof at all. I don't disagree, but my answer is that it's not instead of the pupils doing the proofs in full for themselves, it's instead of them not doing them at all.

I agree with Susan. It is better for pupils to experience proof in some form than not at all. It is rare that pupils, without some form of scaffolding, are able to produce proofs from scratch for such sophisticated mathematical ideas. Getting a feel for the proof helps to develop pupils' conceptual understanding.

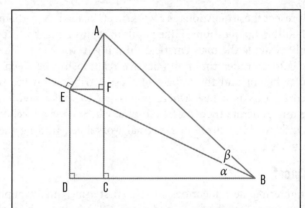

For simplicity, let's scale the diagram so length AB = 1.
Now work out the following in terms of α and β
1. Angle EAF
2. Side BE using triangle ABE
3. Side AE using triangle ABE
4. Side ED using triangle BDE
5. Side AF using triangle AFE

Use triangle ABC to find a formula for $\sin(\alpha + \beta)$

Now work out the following
1. Side BD using triangle BDE
2. Side EF using triangle AFE

Use triangle ABC to find a formula for $\cos(\alpha + \beta)$

Differentiation from first principles

With differentiation from first principles, I like to use an approach similar to Susan's method for scaffolding a proof. In the past, I might have written up the proof at the start of the work on differentiation; now, I prefer to come to the proof once pupils have got to grips with some basic processes and have heard me repeatedly say, 'the derivative is the gradient'. I will do lots of conceptual teaching at the start of the topic, but it is incredibly difficult to tell pupils conceptual understanding: it is much easier to teach the processes and rules. With differentiation, I set up a task like the one below, where pupils work on first principles numerically.

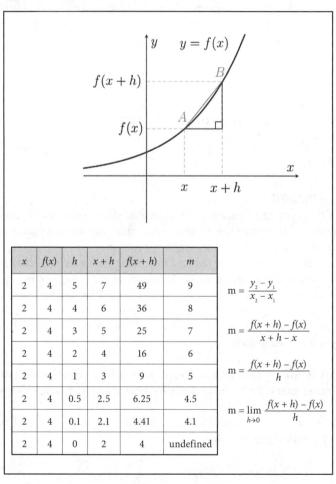

x	$f(x)$	h	$x + h$	$f(x+h)$	m
2	4	5	7	49	9
2	4	4	6	36	8
2	4	3	5	25	7
2	4	2	4	16	6
2	4	1	3	9	5
2	4	0.5	2.5	6.25	4.5
2	4	0.1	2.1	4.41	4.1
2	4	0	2	4	undefined

$$m = \frac{y_2 - y_1}{x_2 - x_1}$$

$$m = \frac{f(x+h) - f(x)}{x + h - x}$$

$$m = \frac{f(x+h) - f(x)}{h}$$

$$m = \lim_{h \to 0} \frac{f(x+h) - f(x)}{h}$$

I use this task once pupils can securely find the gradient of the curve at a specific point. This task is based on $y = x^2$. I ask pupils to find the gradient when $x = 2$. Once we have agreed that the gradient is 4, I give pupils a blank version of the table above and work through the first two rows with them. At this point, we are simply using the gradient formula. As the h value gets smaller, pupils begin to notice that we are tending towards our gradient value of 4. At this point, there are often gasps and exclamations of, 'that makes so much sense now!' This is a result of pupils having some experience of differentiation. The significance of the result is not lost on them, as it might have been if we had considered first principles at the outset of teaching differentiation. I have been saying, 'the derivative is the gradient' for a couple of weeks now, but actually seeing the result manifest in front of them is infinitely more powerful. The technique pupils have learned is now connected to their existing knowledge about gradient.

Like Susan, I appreciate this is scaffolded. In my case, it also isn't a robust proof. However, a formal study of limits and the associated ideas is beyond the scope of school mathematics. This task gives pupils a first look at mathematics they will hopefully go on to encounter at university, without becoming mired in notation.

Guided discovery

Division of fractions
Tasks of this type can be used to develop procedural fluency and conceptual understanding simultaneously. These tasks often lead to some generalisation regarding the most efficient way of solving problems.

Division by fractions can be reduced to phrases such as 'keep – change – flip' or 'turn it upside down and multiply'. While these phrases might help pupils to produce correct answers, they are not rooted in understanding. I have tried to scaffold this task so pupils can work through it independently or in pairs.

As a prerequisite, pupils need to be familiar with both models of division: partitioning and measurement.

- **Partitioning:** 6 divided by 2 means 'share 6 into 2 equal groups of 3'
- **Measurement:** 6 divided by 2 means 'how many times does 2 go into 6?'

Pupils need to have flexibility in their thinking and be able to switch between these metaphors as appropriate.

$2 \div \dfrac{1}{4} = 8$		**Top row:** 2 wholes **Second row:** 1 quarter goes into 2 wholes 8 times
$1 \div \dfrac{1}{3} =$		**Top row:** **Second row:**
$1 \div \dfrac{1}{2} =$		**Top row:** **Second row:**
$2 \div \dfrac{1}{5} =$		**Top row:** **Second row:**
$3 \div \dfrac{1}{3} =$		**Top row:** **Second row:**
$3 \div \dfrac{1}{2} =$		**Top row:** **Second row:**

$2 \div \dfrac{2}{3} = 3$		**Top row:** 2 wholes **Second row:** $\dfrac{2}{3}$ goes into 2 wholes 3 times
$4 \div \dfrac{2}{5} =$		**Top row:** **Second row:**
$3 \div \dfrac{3}{5} =$		**Top row:** **Second row:**
$2 \div \dfrac{2}{5} =$		**Top row:** **Second row:**
$4 \div \dfrac{4}{3} =$		**Top row:** **Second row:**
$5 \div \dfrac{5}{2} =$		**Top row:** **Second row:**

$\frac{1}{2} \div 2 = \frac{1}{4}$		**Middle bar:** One half of top bar **Bottom bar:** One half divided by 2 equals $\frac{1}{4}$ of the top bar
$\frac{1}{2} \div 3 =$		**Middle bar:** **Bottom bar:**
$\frac{1}{3} \div 2 =$		**Middle bar:** **Bottom bar:**
$\frac{1}{3} \div 4 =$		**Middle bar:** **Bottom bar:**
$\frac{1}{4} \div 2 =$		**Middle bar:** **Bottom bar:**
$\frac{1}{4} \div 3 =$		**Middle bar:** **Bottom bar:**

$\frac{1}{2} \div \frac{1}{5} = \frac{5}{2}$		**Middle bar:** One half of top bar **Bottom bar:** $\frac{1}{5}$ of the whole fits into $\frac{1}{2}$ of the whole $2\frac{1}{2}$ or $\frac{5}{2}$ times
$\frac{1}{2} \div \frac{1}{4} =$		**Middle bar:** **Bottom bar:**
$\frac{1}{3} \div \frac{1}{4} =$		**Middle bar:** **Bottom bar:**
$\frac{2}{3} \div \frac{3}{4} = \frac{8}{9}$		**Middle bar:** Two thirds of top bar **Bottom bar:** $\frac{8}{9}$ of $\frac{3}{4}$ of the whole fits into $\frac{2}{3}$
$\frac{1}{5} \div \frac{1}{3} =$		**Middle bar:** **Bottom bar:**
$\frac{2}{5} \div \frac{2}{3} =$		**Middle bar:** **Bottom bar:**

In these tasks, pupils have to work with three representations: numerical, pictorial and language. The sequencing of the questions is designed to allow pupils to begin making generalisations. I suggest pausing after each section to reflect on the principles pupils have discerned. A nice follow-up task, to help with the process of drawing generalisations, is to ask pupils to create another row that would belong on each page. Presenting a couple of questions, written numerically, after each section, will allow us to establish whether pupils have extrapolated the principles involved.

As I wrote this task, it occurred to me that division of fractions might be better taught using common denominators, as it sometimes is in southeast Asian countries. In setting up the questions, I had to define the whole as being the lowest common multiple of the denominators of the two fractions. So, in the case of $\frac{3}{4} \div \frac{2}{5}$, we could write $\frac{15}{20} \div \frac{8}{20}$, resulting in $\frac{15}{8}$. This is, of course, the same answer as would result from multiplication by the reciprocal.

Discussing mathematical statements

Deliberately addressing misconceptions is a characteristic of effective mathematics teaching. Airing these misconceptions and discussing why they are not correct can help pupils to become aware of, and understand, potential pitfalls.

Always, sometimes or never true

Presenting a mathematical statement and then asking pupils to decide if it is always, sometimes or never true has sparked many heated debates in my classroom. The inclusion of 'sometimes' adds a level of nuance to the debates that means pupils have to think hard about any exceptions to the statement presented.

An example of such a statement is:

$$5x^2 = (5x)^2$$

Many pupils decide quickly whether the statement is true or false. However, I have found it prudent to allow more time: I like to leave an almost awkward silence in the room, leaving pupils to ponder silently for a minute or so. There can be a sense of, 'we have the answer, why are you waiting?' After some time has passed, I allow pupils to discuss their thinking with a partner. Then I take a vote to get a sense of the popular opinion: 20 votes for never, 3 for sometimes, 7 for always, etc. Next I give pupils time to think again and change their minds if they wish to do so, before asking some pupils from each 'camp' to present an argument for their choice.

The evidence for layers of understanding is quite clear here. Some pupils, who believe the statement is always true, have significant misunderstandings of the idea. Those who believe it is never true are likely recalling the fact I have emphasised repeatedly: $(ax)^2 = a^2x^2$. I might ask a pupil to come to the board to explain their thinking using a diagram or other aid. The point of these tasks is to train pupils to be critical in their thinking; to look for exceptions to rules. The argument for sometimes true is, of course, rooted in the substitution of $x = 0$.

In these types of task, I am less concerned with getting the correct answer; the aim is to develop mathematical language and create opportunities for pupils to dig deeper and draw on their conceptual understanding.

Another classic task of this type can be found in the Standards Unit (Swan, 2005). Some of the most heated mathematical arguments I have ever witnessed have arisen from this prompt:

In a sale, every price was reduced by 25%.
After the sale, every price was increased by 25%.
So prices went back to where they started.

Is this always, sometimes, or never true?

Algebraic identities

Jo Morgan created this wonderful task on evaluating mathematical statements. It is notable that she has used 'true or false' rather than 'always, sometimes or never true'. However, given the large number of statements to be classified, I agree with Jo's choice in restricting the task to a binary true or false. If there are three options, the complexity of the task increases – 'sometimes' suggests there may be a twist to be considered. In this particular task, the aim is to take the identities at face value, rather than considering substitution of specific values.

True or false?
Cut out the identities and sort them into two groups: True or False.

$a + a = a^2$	$a^3 = a + a + a$	$2a \times a = 2a^2$
$a + a = 2a$	$3b - b = 2b$	$3a = 2a + a$
$a \times a = a^2$	$3a = 2a \times a$	$a + b = ab$
$a \times a = 2a$	$3b - 2 = b$	$3a \times 4b = 7ab$
$a \times b = ab$	$a \div 2 = \dfrac{a}{2}$	$3a + 4b = 7ab$
$2a + 1 = 3a$	$b \times 3 \times a = 3ab$	$3a \times 4b = 12ab$
$2a + b = 2ab$	$2 \times a \times a \times b = 2ab^2$	$a + b + 2a = 3a + b$
$2a \times b = 2ab$	$3b - 3b = b$	$3 \times a \times a = 6a$

In my experience of using this task, pupils confidently categorise some cards as true or false but often have some cards left over that they are unsure about. This is the point at which we want to encourage deep thinking and productive dialogue: it is important to discourage guessing. A conjecture which is reasoned is far preferable to a guess – even if the wrong conclusion is reached.

Once pupils have worked individually on the initial groupings, they can work in pairs to discuss the cards they are unsure about. If pairs of pupils have cards left uncategorised, they can join together in groups of four. In this way, pupils can become resources for each other: the progression from individual activity to collaborative discussion ensures everyone has time to think about the ideas for themselves, but also provides opportunities for pupils to verbalise their understanding and address misconceptions.

When using this type of task, I have often found my role is simply to get out of the way. If it was enough to *tell* a pupil that $2a + 1 \neq 3a$, no one would ever make that mistake! Instead, layers of experience, over time, help them to make sense of mathematics. This task, with pupils making arguments together and convincing each other, can play a part in that succession of experiences.

Combining ideas

Conceptual understanding involves making connections between related ideas. Dave Hewitt recalls that, throughout his career, teachers have said to him, 'there's never enough time, there's not enough time, etc'. He disagrees: in secondary school, we have five (or even six) years with pupils – this is loads of time! Dave argues:

> *If you stop thinking about the curriculum as a list of individual items, you start realising that some tasks can bring this, that and this into it all at once. You can work on two or three things at once.*

Percentages, fractions, decimals and division

Percentages, fractions, decimals and division are intrinsically linked but many textbooks treat them as discrete ideas to be covered separately. We can develop pupil understanding of the relationships between these ideas by using connective tasks. The task below was written to consolidate pupils' work on each of these topics, but also to make connections across them: an understanding of these connections helps pupils to select the most appropriate format for a given question. Some representations can be more intuitive than others, depending on the numbers in use. The table format is easily adaptable and can serve as the basis for many similar tasks.

As a division	Multiplication by a decimal	Multiplication by a fraction	As a percentage calculation	Solution
400 ÷ 10	400 × 0.1	$400 \times \dfrac{1}{10}$	10% of 400	40
300 ÷ 1000				
	0.3 × 0.01			
		$4.5 \times \dfrac{1}{5}$		
			25% of 6.4	
0.6 ÷ 0.06				
	3.14 × 0.005			
		$350 \times \dfrac{7}{10\,000}$		
			3.6% of 270	

Trigonometry

Trigonometry involves a rich web of related ideas, with many underpinning connections. The following tasks are designed to help pupils make connections between trigonometric graphs (and the unit circle) and the application of trigonometry in finding areas of triangles. The task is scaffolded to stimulate activity wherein pupils might notice patterns and begin to think about underlying principles. The role of the teacher here is not to tell pupils, but to ensure the level of mathematical activity remains high. If a pair of pupils is struggling to make headway, simply suggesting they look at the graphs is often enough to help them move forward. The level of pupils' success with this task also provides evidence about the extent to which they have understood trigonometric graphs and incorporated these ideas into their thinking.

The second part of the task aims to deepen pupils' understanding of what is happening. A unit circle representation and the obtuse associated rotation are much more intuitive here.

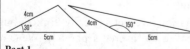

Part 1
1. Consider the areas of the triangles.
2. Create another pair of triangles that have this same property … and another … and another…
3. Why is this true?
4. Can you break your 'rule'?

Part 2
Paul writes this:
$$A = \frac{1}{2}(3)(4)sin(210)$$

1. What does this look like?
2. Can you find another angle that creates the same value?
3. Can you find another pair of triangles that share this property?
4. Why is the answer negative?

Interpreting and creating stories

Problems

Mike Askew drew my attention to the potential of stories as powerful vehicles for mathematics learning. Too often, I have used word problems towards the end of a conventional exercise, to add an element of 'real life' to the abstract mathematics. Mike suggests starting with a problem context that is meaningful to pupils. This will allow them to generate improvised solutions through which formalised mathematical understanding can be developed.

Mike describes his thinking as follows:

> *When developing conceptual understanding rather than just skills, kids should be involved in some sort of productive struggle. If you give them something they can already do, they are just practising something they have already learned. You can't give them something way beyond what they can already do as they'll just fall apart. I am an advocate of learning through problem-solving rather than learning to solve problems.*

> *Also, one of the things that trips us up is trying to think of things in 'lesson terms' rather than sequence of task terms. I want pupils to be involved in thinking, having a bit of a struggle, which the teacher supports. It is through the talk that they do around these tasks that the mathematics learning comes about.*

Mike went on to describe working with a group of pupils on the following problem:

> Anna and Josh took some friends for pizzas to celebrate their birthday. The boys and girls sat at separate tables: 6 boys altogether at one table and 9 girls at the other. Mark, their dad, knew the pizzas were too big for one each, so he ordered 4 for the boys' table and 6 for the girls' table.
> On the way home, Anna said, 'we girls got more pizza each because we shared 6 pizzas on our table'. Josh disagreed: 'No, there were only 6 boys but there were 9 girls. So, the boys got more to eat.'
> Who do you agree with? Why?

Mike suggests taking time at the start of the lesson to talk, generally, about such contexts – going out for pizza with friends. Rather than rushing to introduce the problem, the teacher can set up an atmosphere that says he/she wants to listen to what the pupils have to say. Then, when the problem is posed, it can seem to pupils to be a seamless continuation of the conversation.

This task is about equivalent fractions. Mike states, 'there is a key difference in starting with a problem. Improvised knowledge is used to support emergent mathematical understanding. This stands in contrast with the teach-the-content-first-then-apply-it approach that assumes pupils can easily access and use abstract mathematics to make sense of everyday situations' (Askew, 2015). The arguments pupils create – through diagrams, rough working and words – are the basis on which the teacher can move pupils' thinking towards the abstract.

Describing the rationale for the task further, Mike says:

> I would get rid of the word 'recognise' from the curriculum, in relation to fractions – 'Be able to recognise half' etc. We don't do enough establishing where fractions come from. There are two main approaches to this. First, solving equal sharing problems, where a fraction is the result of a division situation. If pupils can divide 4 by 2 and 2 by 2 then there is no reason why they can't move to dividing 1 by 2 and 3 by 2. Fractions arise by needing a non-integer value. The other route into fractions is measurement. If the unit is longer than the thing I am measuring, then I need fractional parts of the unit. This particular task is about establishing where fractions come from. In this task, we have 4 divided by 6 and 6 divided by 9. It is about having a conversation around where those fractions come from and establishing how we know they are the same. However, the conversation is also focused around 'why do we need fractions?' Rather than teaching fractions in isolation, this task allows us to have the conversation around requiring fractions to make comparisons.

Using a task such as this at the beginning of the teaching allows the teaching to be responsive to pupils' existing understanding. The teacher can draw on pupils' invented strategies and develop from there, rather than simply 'telling' them what they 'need' to know.

To connect the representations pupils come up with, an important aspect of the conversation should consider 'what is the same and what is different?' Further, the teacher should help pupils to agree on which representation is the most effective. It is not about the teacher saying, 'we now have all of these ways of doing things, so you can choose whichever way you like best'.

A related, but different, approach to using stories – also suggested by Mike Askew – is to take a mathematical expression and put it into a story. He recalls asking a group of teachers to take the calculation $1\frac{1}{4} - \frac{1}{3}$ and put it into a little story. The first story was:

> I got home from work and there was $1\frac{1}{4}$ pizza in the fridge. I ate $\frac{1}{3}$.

Of course, the issue here is $\frac{1}{3}$ of what? The teachers took it to mean they ate $\frac{1}{3}$ of what was in the fridge (i.e. $1\frac{1}{4} \times \frac{1}{3}$). In fact, it means they ate $\frac{1}{3}$ of a pizza – so they need to subtract that from what was in the fridge to start with. The teachers could do the calculation but they couldn't actually contextualise it. Similarly, there is no point in pupils being able to do a calculation if they have no idea what it is about! The distinction between fraction as a measure ($\frac{1}{3}$ of a pizza) and fraction as an operator ($\frac{1}{3}$ of what is in the fridge) is blurred here. In the same way, the stories pupils create can be powerful formative assessment tools. From these stories might emerge the basis of something the teacher can use to develop conceptual understanding.

8 Problem-solving tasks

Maths lessons in secondary schools are very often not about anything. You collect like terms, or learn the laws of indices, with no perception of why anyone needs to do such things. There is an excessive pre-occupation with a sequence of skills and quite inadequate opportunity to see the skills emerging from the solution of problems.

(Cockcroft, 1982)

There is perhaps no greater challenge in mathematics teaching than enabling pupils to become capable problem solvers. Yet, there is no more pressing concern: problem-solving *is* mathematics. A mathematics education that fails in this respect can be said to have failed overall.

Colin Foster captures much of the difficulty here:

I have seen problem-solving lessons where the rationale seems to be to give the pupils an interesting problem to solve and then just stand back and let them struggle with it. I think I have taught lessons like that myself, but I am now unconvinced that that is an effective way of teaching pupils to solve problems. If the pupils end up solving the problem without help, then I worry that it was not challenging enough. If they do not, then I worry that they have not learned anything.

Procedural fluency and conceptual understanding, together, can support pupils in becoming efficient problem solvers. However, while necessary, they are not in themselves sufficient for pupils to become problem solvers. Pupils also need to develop their habits of mind, have a positive disposition towards mathematics and develop their range of mathematical behaviours. Opportunities to behave mathematically occur in all lessons but, at times, specific focus and attention should be placed on this.

In this chapter, I will briefly outline some thinking on problem solving before considering some activity types which will support the development of mathematical behaviours. I suggest that development of these behaviours, in conjunction with conceptual understanding and procedural fluency, will enable pupils to become confident problem solvers.

Initially, we explore the following ideas:

- What matters in successful problem solving?
- Expertise reversal effect
- Novel versus familiar work
- Maturation and varying demands
- Heuristics.

What matters in successful problem solving?

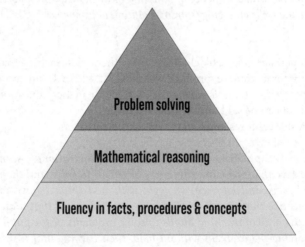

(Foster, 2019)

This model from Colin Foster attempts to capture the factors on which problem solving depends. The previous two chapters focused on tasks to help pupils become fluent in procedures and to develop conceptual understanding. Some of those tasks, if used collaboratively, also give pupils opportunities to articulate their own thinking. This is important in the development of mathematical reasoning but not sufficient in itself. Sometimes, the focus in lessons has to be on the mathematical behaviours (reasoning being a part of this) that underpin problem solving. This chapter suggests task sequences and pedagogical choices that can help pupils to develop their reasoning and, in turn, become more proficient at problem solving.

Alan Schoenfeld (2014) lists attributes on which success with problem solving depends. This list complements the model from Foster and includes:

- mathematical knowledge and resources
- access to productive 'heuristic' strategies for making progress with challenging problems
- monitoring and self-regulation (metacognition)
- belief systems regarding mathematics and one's sense of self as a thinker in general and a doer of mathematics in particular (mathematical identity).

Knowledge and resources have been addressed in previous chapters. We will discuss some heuristics below. Clearly, metacognition has a domain-specific component (that is, the more knowledge one has, the more effective one can be in monitoring and self-regulation), but aspects of it are domain-general (Brown, 1987). We need to support pupils to step back and observe their thinking about their work, rather than just doing the work. The sense of what mathematics is, and each pupil's identity as a doer of mathematics, will be wrapped up in their experience of mathematics. As I have argued throughout this book, the sorts of task in which pupils engage play a significant role in determining their perspective of mathematics. Pupils whose experience is largely limited to drill worksheets are less likely to develop the attitudes and beliefs about mathematics, and of themselves, that will enable them to embrace problem solving effectively – no matter how successfully they complete these worksheets. Danny Brown suggests an additional point to add to Schoenfeld's list: motivation. The set-up of a task can pique the pupils' interest or completely disenfranchise them. Further, pupils' prior experience is an important determinant of the level of motivation: if a pupil has previously experienced success, they are more likely to engage purposefully with a task (Garon-Carrier *et al.*, 2016).

A significant factor in developing pupils' problem-solving competencies is the degree to which they are 'let off the leash'. If lessons are tightly-scripted, with pupils engaging in routine tasks only, the mathematical behaviours required to support problem solving have no opportunity to flourish. There is a significant role for tasks whose primary goal extends beyond developing procedural fluency or conceptual understanding. It is my view that tasks such as investigative work, mathematical inquiries and modelling activities can all help pupils to develop the mathematical dispositions and attitudes that can support thinking in problem solving. Pupils do not necessarily improve at problem solving by solving problems alone.

Expertise reversal effect

There are significant arguments from the field of cognitive science that suggest allowing pupils the chance to explore unfamiliar problems independently is important. The expertise reversal effect is an idea from cognitive load theory (CLT); CLT takes into consideration a pupil's working memory and the limitations this presents in terms of their ability to learn new material. When engaging with new ideas, with little prior knowledge, pupils need scaffolding. However, when pupils have existing knowledge, it is beneficial to step away from examples and reduce scaffolding.

> *Learners would have to relate and reconcile the related components of available long-term memory base and externally provided guidance. Such integration processes may impose an additional working memory load and reduce resources available for learning new knowledge.*
>
> (Kalyuga, 2007)

Essentially, some pupils already have a well-developed understanding of a particular mathematical idea. These pupils will learn better by engaging directly with the idea for themselves, rather than having to interpret their teacher's understanding of the idea. Low-knowledge pupils benefit more from studying structured worked examples than from solving problems on their own. As knowledge increases, open-ended exploration becomes the more effective learning activity (Renkl and Atkinson, 2003).

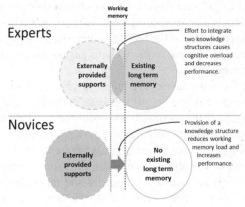

(Wikipedia, 2020)

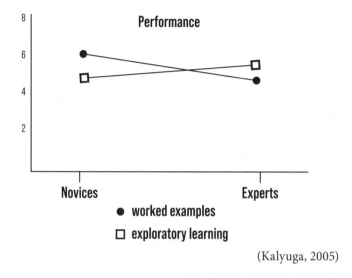

(Kalyuga, 2005)

Consider, for example, the teaching of equations. A class will typically encounter a sequence of examples and practice exercises over consecutive lessons, learning the principles of solving linear equations. Initially, there is an argument for a high level of teacher-guided instruction; as the unit progresses, however, the amount of guidance can be reduced. The next type of equation to be learned might be only a small step from the previous type encountered. For instance, pupils might have been working on equations of the form $ax + b = cx$, and the focus in the next lesson might be $ax + b = cx + d$. At this point, rather than teaching explicitly, it can be more effective to simply pose the question as a problem at the outset. Most pupils will have enough experience and a reasonable sense of the principles involved in solving equations, so they can tackle this sort of problem unaided. Starting the lesson by asking them to solve the problem – rather than by exemplifying it – allows pupils to develop their self-image as mathematicians: they have the opportunity to make this small cognitive leap for themselves and develop a sense of being able to solve mathematical problems. These little moments of success are important in creating a disposition for more involved problem solving. Of course, not every pupil will succeed in solving the problem correctly, but effective peer discussion followed by sharing, contrasting and critique of strategies through whole-class discussion, can mitigate any negative impacts of this.

Generally, in my experience, reducing the amount of direct instruction and increasing the problem-solving dimension as you progress through a topic can have a significant impact on how pupils view themselves as mathematicians. It is important for pupils to become used to – and comfortable with – 'having a go' even when they don't know exactly what to do: they develop self-reliance and the ability to trust their own thinking, rather than waiting to be told what to do by the teacher. This is a simple pedagogical step, but one which can support pupils in becoming mathematical thinkers rather than passive recipients of procedures.

Novel versus familiar work

We can consider two broad categories of task: familiar and novel. Familiar work involves little ambiguity about what to do and how to do it. Doyle estimates that, in most classrooms, familiar work accounts for more than two thirds of the tasks pupils complete. Novel work requires pupils to 'assemble information and operations from several sources in ways that have not been laid out explicitly in advance by the teacher' (Doyle, 1985). In novel tasks, pupils are responsible for deciding what to do and how to do it.

Problem-solving tasks are unpredictable as they place specific cognitive and emotional demands on pupils. Doyle uses the term 'work flow' to describe the classroom activity arising from different tasks. Familiar work typically results in a smooth, well-ordered lesson with high levels of productivity and involvement. Novel tasks, on the other hand, can result in slow, messy activity sequences, with low levels of productivity. Novel tasks increase the complexity of the classroom environment and bring classroom management challenges for the teacher.

It would be easier to avoid problem-solving lessons, particularly as the 'learning' is not straightforward to infer: typically, with genuine problem solving, many pupils will not produce a correct solution, so the teacher must turn these problem-solving attempts into opportunities for learning (see the discussion around Japanese teaching in the pedagogy chapter). However, there are very real and important reasons for pupils to engage in problem solving and related activities. Firstly, this is what mathematics is about – problem solving *is* mathematics. Secondly (as discussed above), as pupils develop expertise, the activity in which they engage needs to change. From an educational perspective and in terms of beliefs, arguments can be made for the inclusion of problem solving in every classroom.

Maturation and varying demands

An interesting idea to emerge from the Shell Centre at Nottingham University is that of the maturation gap. Hugh Burkhardt explains:

You cannot solve genuine non-routine problems with mathematics you have just recently learned (recently means the last year or so). There is a tendency to criticise non-routine problems as not being 'up to grade'. It is actually quite unrealistic to expect most secondary pupils to use algebra to solve problems, never mind calculus! We did a study on pupils learning to model mathematically. We had a test with three tasks, each of which cried out for algebraic modelling. The cohort was 120 pupils, all of whom were expected to achieve two As at double A-Level Maths; very high attainers. They had never been taught modelling explicitly though. The pupils were effective at solving the problems but not one of them used algebra. Instead they used arithmetic. Some of them made tables of values and others created graphs. But their modelling failed to utilise algebra, despite five years' successful experience of formal algebra! The pupils' knowledge of algebra was procedural.

Colin Foster also supports the maturation gap idea, saying:

If you want to see pupils being creative and solving problems, you need to use content they're already quite secure with so they can apply it flexibly and so on. Otherwise the cognitive load is just too much. I think the other advantage of this is that problem solving doesn't become just what we've been doing in class. For me, part of problem solving is selecting the mathematics that you're going to use. You can't really do that if you're using what you've just been taught. If you're being asked to draw on something you know quite well but haven't thought about for a while – perhaps something you did a year ago or two years ago – that gives you the opportunity to really think 'well, what have I got in my toolbox that might be useful here?' rather than 'what have we done recently?' The focus is on considering what matches the demands of this problem, what can be brought out to help solve the problem.

The analogy we used in Nottingham was learning a language: if you're going to use words in conversation, they can't be the words you just learnt yesterday. You can use those in a very tightly structured exercise, but in a more wide-ranging conversation the vocabulary you will use is actually the vocabulary you have embedded and developed some time ago. It's the same feeling with problem solving, if you want pupils to be thinking about 'how do I formulate the problem, what assumptions should I make, how can I estimate...' all that sort of high-difficulty stuff. They need to be doing it with things that are a bit more secure.

Hugh describes how the difficulty of a task can come from many different sources. If a task is procedural, then all of the difficulty is technical. But if you have a non-routine complex task, which requires the pupil to construct a substantial chain of reasoning in solving the problem, other dimensions come in, including:

- the complexity of the task
- the non-routineness (familiarity)
- technical demand
- the length of the chain of reasoning.

So, if a task is non-routine and complex then the technical demand must be low. If the task is more routine, but technical demands are high, you might need to decrease the task complexity and the length of the chain of reasoning required. Often, this is a cause of problems: when engaging with problem-solving, one really should start with easy, non-routine tasks.

I am not suggesting pupils should not solve non-routine problems using what they have just learned. However, we need to be aware that even successful performance on these tasks may not transfer to future problem-solving ability on the topic.

Teachers may have encountered the idea of maturation without recognising it as such. The UK Mathematics Trust (UKMT) issues sets of challenge questions to pupils each year. The Junior problem sets are for early secondary pupils and the pupils entered for the challenge have generally covered much of the mathematics involved. However, a large number of these pupils fail to perform. This could be due to a number of factors, but significant among them is the idea of maturation: the pupils have some comprehension of the mathematics, but have not yet fully assimilated it. Thus, they do not recognise it and/or cannot draw upon it without recency or cue. If you issue those same Junior problems to pupils a couple of years later, they do much better. The problems are still non-routine but the more experienced pupils have two advantages. First, the mathematics involved has had a period of maturation. Second, it is likely that pupils will have called on this mathematics in engaging with subsequent learning and used the ideas as sub-skills in more sophisticated chains of reasoning. Both of these factors support the reduction in challenge of the Junior problems when encountered later. Experience counts for a lot in problem solving.

Heuristics

Thus far, I have suggested we take several factors into consideration when teaching problem solving:

- Fluency in procedures and conceptual understanding
- An appropriate maturation period
- Reducing direct teaching as appropriate once a degree of expertise has been reached.

The next significant element is heuristics – the strategies derived from experience of similar problems. These strategies give pupils a framework for thinking about their thinking (metacognition).

Schoenfeld (1985) offers some generic questions to ask pupils whenever they are stuck on a problem:

- What exactly are you doing? Can you describe it precisely?
- Why are you doing it? How does it fit into the solution?
- How does it help you? What will you do with the outcome when you obtain it?

By using these questions regularly and repeatedly, teachers can help to focus pupil thinking. Over time, pupils can begin to internalise these questions and pose them spontaneously to themselves, thus supporting metacognition. The questions contain no mathematical content and can be used at any curricular level. The goal of the problem-solving lesson is to apply, in creative ways, pupils' existing mathematical knowledge: Schoenfeld's questions focus on what pupils are doing or intend to do with the mathematics they already know. Colin Foster emphasises the importance of stepping back, both during and after the lesson, to reflect on what is working and what is not – in terms of both the mathematics itself and the problem-solving strategies used.

The most famous heuristics are from George Pólya (Pólya, 1957). David Watkins composed an excellent visual summary, which is shown in an adapted form overleaf.

How to solve it

Teacher scaffolding of problem solving:
an adaptation of George Pólya's method

Always aim for general questions like those below. Only move to task-specific questions when general ones don't elicit a response.

Understand
- Do you understand the **words**?
- What are you being asked to **find/show**? (*the 'unknown'*)
- What **information** are you given? (*the 'data'*)
- What **conditions** must you take account of?

Set up
- **Make** a diagram, table or model if appropriate.
- **Introduce** notation.

Plan
There are no rules, but these questions might help in some order. Practising solving problems helps to develop instinct for when each strategy might work.
- **Think** of similar problems you've seen with a similar unknown.
- **Remember** relevant formulae/facts/definitions.
- **Restate** the problem in an equivalent way.
- **Split** the problem to try an easier part first.
- **Find** a simpler special case that you could try first.
- **Check** for any data or conditions you haven't used yet.
- **Add** in something that might help. (an *'auxiliary'*)
- **Ask** your teacher to suggest a problem or method that you've solved before that will help.

Complete
- **Carry out** your plan carefully.
- **Monitor** *what* you're doing; *why*; and whether it's helping.
- **Use** these answers to decide whether to persevere or re-plan.
- **Check** each step is correct.

Reflect
- **Check** the answer.
- **Prove** your logic is valid.
- **See** another way of getting the answer.
- **Create** another problem you can now solve.
- **Learn** from which plans worked and did not work.

Source: D Watkins, 2020 (@mrwatkinsmaths). Adapted from Pólya, 1990.

These heuristics serve as ways of working. The role of the teacher is to bring attention and focus back to whichever heuristic is being used. This needs to happen regularly, over the medium to long term, so pupils begin to internalise these ways of thinking and recognise where, in their own thought process, they currently find themselves.

Colin Foster describes the important role of reflection in Japanese problem-solving lessons.

In Japan it is often said that 'the lesson begins when the problem is solved'. This means that most of the learning is seen to take place in what Pólya called the 'looking back' phase, reflecting on the choices made, the paths taken, and the advantages and disadvantages of different approaches. The purpose of time spent solving the problem, or attempting to, is to get pupils into a position where they have enough relevant experience to contribute to and learn from this critical discussion. I think that that is an interesting way of thinking about the structure of the lesson. The plenary is not an afterthought to tie things together at the end, if there happens to be time. It is the main part of the lesson. What happens before the plenary is seen as preparing pupils for that discussion.

(Foster, 2019)

Activity types

While this chapter is about problem solving, I stated at the outset that the role of mathematical behaviours is important. I suggest that a variety of activity types, in addition to non-routine problem-solving tasks, can be used to help pupils develop their mathematical thinking and actions. The layering of experiences gained from procedural and conceptual tasks should equip pupils with relevant skills and knowledge, but also with positive attitudes towards the subject. If pupils have a range of experiences, their impressions of mathematics will be different to (more positive than) those of pupils who have predominantly encountered drill worksheets. Further, the messy nature of mathematics learning and 'doing' mathematics will not be completely alien to pupils. Some of the tasks in the conceptual chapter are quite demanding and require significant amounts of independent pupil thinking. If pupils have had this sort of experience, they will be more equipped to deal with problem solving, both mathematically and emotionally.

Some activity types which can be used to develop problem-solving actions and thinking include:

- mathematical investigations
- mathematical inquiry
- contextual modelling
- non-routine problem-solving tasks.

The Cockroft report (Cockroft, 1982) recommended that mathematics teaching should include opportunities for:

- exposition by the teacher
- discussion between teacher and pupils and between pupils themselves
- appropriate practical work
- consolidation and practice of fundamental skills and routines
- problem solving, including the application of maths to everyday situations
- investigational work.

Mathematical investigations

Laurinda Brown explains:

> Investigations are fundamental both to the study of maths and also to the way in which maths is used to solve problems in many fields. The processes involved are essentially creative – more like those of a mathematician – rather than recollecting an appropriate technique. Investigations need to be neither lengthy nor difficult and the best investigations arise from pupils' own questions.

The topic of the investigation could arise from real life or from a mathematically designed problem (e.g. investigate the sum of angles in polygons). Again, an investigation can be a very open exploration or it can take the form of a more structured task that guides the learner into discovering mathematics (Yeo and Yeap, 2010).

Laurinda suggests there is great value in teachers writing up investigative lessons afterwards. Such write-ups allow teachers to see how things 'might go' in their classroom, which in turn enables them to see the potential of investigative tasks. The teacher should be able to focus pupils' thinking on the principles or ways of working he/she is trying to encourage, rather than being caught up in thinking about the specific task. Write-ups might suggest common issues or pupil actions and identify questions or prompts that effectively addressed them.

Laurinda describes the idea of finding the 'middle questions'. This involves presenting a series of tasks until encountering something the pupils can't do, at which point they begin to ask these 'middle questions'. Rather than beginning with a challenge or an open question, Laurinda starts with something like, 'find me a square of area ten'. The pupils work on dotted paper and can be heard to say things like, 'one', 'four', 'nine'. As they struggle to create a square of area ten, they encounter other areas that are possible – the middle question arises from the pupils asking, 'I wonder which numbers *are* possible?' No pupil at the start of their secondary education is going to do that straight away because it involves Pythagoras, but what they are doing is working out areas of squares and thinking about constraints that might apply. The task has a closed beginning so the pupils can open it out for themselves; from their activity, the middle questions can emerge.

Using investigative tasks such as this is about creating a space where you know things are going to arise. This same starting point can have different outcomes depending on the age and stage of the class; for example, when working with older pupils, Pythagoras will jump out. Investigations are about giving pupils a large space in which to play and to apply things – that is, a safe space in which to be mathematically creative and expressive.

Sums to 22

Laurinda contributed to *An addendum to Cockroft* (Brown and Waddingham, 1982). An investigational task from this resource is shown below.

A. Choose any 3 numbers less than 10.
Make all the possible 2-digit numbers with them.
$$6, 7, 3$$
$$67, 63, 76, 73, 36, 37$$
Add all the 2-digit numbers together:
$$67 + 63 + 76 + 73 + 36 + 37 = 352$$
Divide by the sum of your original three numbers:
$$6 + 7 + 3 = 16$$
$$\frac{352}{16} = 22$$
What is your answer?

(Brown and Waddingham, 1982)

This task has the lovely result that, no matter which numbers you start with, the result will be 22. I have to admit, here, that earlier in my career I might have shared a task like this with a class, concluded 'wow, isn't that cool!' and then moved on with the core curriculum. I would have treated the task as an interesting distraction but completely missed the pedagogical potential.

Once the element of surprise and intrigue has been generated, by engagement with the task, there are opportunities both to develop understanding of curriculum areas and also to develop pupils' patterns of mathematical behaviour. We want pupils to pose their own questions and observations about the task, rather than all questions coming from the teacher; we might prepare some questions to facilitate a flagging lesson but should encourage pupils to share their thinking first and foremost.

Pupils generally ask questions such as, 'does it always work?', 'can we pick numbers that break it?' or 'what if all the numbers are the same?' They can then be given space to explore these ideas. With some classes, we might want to move towards generality – for example, we might ask pupils to prove the result is **always** 22. The majority of pupils will not succeed with this but that's fine: as Burkhardt says, it is unrealistic to expect secondary pupils to use algebra to engage with problems. I offer the prompt, 'what if the numbers we choose are a, b and c?' Depending on the age and stage of the class, pupils will make varying degrees of progress. When they have had some time to work individually, I follow up with a whole-class discussion to compare and contrast pupils' attempts, with some presentation of my own solution if required. This isn't specifically about teaching pupils how to prove using algebra; rather, the aim is to sensitise them to the fact that algebra might be useful beyond those boring textbook exercises, and to remind them that it is a tool they have at their disposal in future problems or investigations.

The next opportunity to give pupils freedom to play is to ask them to experiment with variations on the original phenomenon. This is something we might want to do in problem solving: to get a sense of a problem, it is useful to modify it in some way or to try different cases. The layering of experience of different available actions is important. For example, we can ask, 'what could we change about this situation?' Pupils might say things such as, 'make three-digit numbers' or 'choose numbers under one hundred'. Depending on the classroom culture and the pupils' confidence, I might let them explore a range of different situations in groups (one situation per group). In other circumstances, it might be better to choose a single point of inquiry for all pupils to work on.

Some follow up prompts are included with the original task. I have found it helpful to use Prompt B some days after the first part of the task. When asking pupils to prove the answer is always 202, I am curious to see if anyone, of their own accord, uses algebra to do this. Has some learning resulted from the previous experience?

B. *Choose any 3 2-digit numbers.* 27, 34, 28
Make all the possible 4-digit numbers. 2734, 2728, 3428, 3427, 2827, 2834
Add them up.
Divide by the sum of the 2-digit numbers: 27 + 34 + 28 = 89

$$\frac{17978}{89} = 202$$

<u>What do you get?</u>
C. *What happens if I use different starting numbers?*
What if I change the number of digits?
Try out your own ideas?

(Brown and Waddingham, 1982)

It might be easy to dismiss this task and the activity sequences as a diversion from the curriculum with no 'impact on attainment'. However, this is about developing a classroom culture, mathematical habits of mind and pupil agency – allowing pupils to see themselves as mathematicians. These elements are important in supporting problem solving even though it is hard, or even impossible, to measure the outcomes. In using this task, my main focus is on developing ways of working, rather than having procedural fluency or conceptual understanding as the core focus. Of course, there are investigations that can be used with a focus on developing these other aspects of mathematical understanding – for example, many teachers use investigations on the laws of indices to allow pupils to generalise the laws for themselves.

Classroom footprints

This practical task from Anne Watson acts as a basis for significant amounts of rich mathematical activity. The priority here is development of multiplicative reasoning and, while one of the intentions of this task is the development of conceptual understanding, this is inherently an investigative task. A class of secondary pupils was given the prompt:

Find out which of your primary schools had the biggest / smallest 'footprint'.

Keep notes of all your thinking and calculating.

Start by finding the footprint of your own primary school.

The class consisted of a diverse group of pupils for whom low prior attainment was the common characteristic for a variety of reasons: chaotic home lives, migration, frequent changes of school, trauma, illness, and various kinds of cognitive delay. The lessons in that school term were nearly all about some aspect of multiplicative reasoning. Anne had taken a medium-term view that her task as teacher was to give a range of shared experiences of multiplicative situations that pupils could refer back to (depending on episodic memory) to develop an expanded notion of multiplication and division as tools for understanding quantity. This overall principle means that one sometimes prioritises social and emotional aspects of participation in mathematics lessons over cognitive aspects; this task – as Anne taught it and reported it – demonstrates the weight given to that priority. Of course, no lesson or task is isolated, and this was one in a sequence of scaling tasks.

Before this task, the pupils had had the following shared experiences:

- Several lessons about powers of ten (as a vehicle for revisiting place value and the decimal system).
- Area of rectangles (extending from an array model of multiplication to an area model).
- A lesson in which non-standard units, i.e. tenths on a wall-length number line, had been used to measure distances in the number line (to understand measure as a repeated unit of a fixed size).
- Some experience of using scale on maps (from geography lessons).

The furniture and seating arrangements during each lesson had been flexible according to task and expected learning.

For this task, pupils were given Google Satellite views of their primary schools with a metric scale; these views had been scaled by Anne so that each school footprint filled an A4 sheet. Pupils were grouped according to their primary schools and worked around blocks of tables, with enough copies of the satellite images for every pair of pupils to have one.

Anne recalls the activity in the room:

Working with the whole class, I asked what 'footprint' might mean and made sure they understood it meant total floor area. I asked for suggestions of methods to find area, using what they knew already. A plan emerged in orchestrated whole-class discussion: the school outlines would be carved up into rectangles whose dimensions would be measured and multiplied to get the areas, then the pieces would be added to get the whole area of the footprint. Some pupils knew about finding areas of triangles but I decided that for this task, so long as there was someone on each table who knew, it was not important for everyone to know. The key idea in the task was going to be about scaling by multiplying and dividing.

The task was tackled with enthusiasm. I had depended on emotional attachment, familiarity and ownership to get them engaged, plus the bonus of remembering where they had been the oldest and most experienced pupils as a contrast to being the youngest in their new school. There was some competitiveness between schools, and there was some off-task chat about memories – fair enough.

Note that the scale was different for most tables, since small schools and big schools had all been scaled to fit A4 paper, but pupils did not worry about scale: mostly they measured in centimetres and multiplied and added what they found. After a while, we therefore had several calculations of footprints in square centimetres. When pupils had finished their calculations, I gave each school a 'mystery number' by which they had to multiply their final value to get the real footprint area and answer the questions. So far, the lesson had been about applying rectangle (and sometimes triangle) area rules to find a compound area – valuable practice with a purpose but not yet about scale.

Next, I asked the whole class to think about the mystery numbers I had given them. One by one, the groups said what their mystery number had been. One school had a larger 'mystery number' than another and someone shouted out, in a taunting fashion, 'your school must have been very small then!' What a delightful comment! To avoid more shouting, I asked them to be silent for a while and think about what had been said. Was it true that a school with a large mystery number to get back to real measurements must be a small school? This, for me, was absolutely the key point of the task. After the silence I asked for comments using hands-up. Some contributions were about assumptions or local knowledge and I would say, 'but I want a mathematical answer'. One contribution included gestures that suggested shrinking and expanding. Eventually someone gave an answer that paraphrased: 'if you have something big you have to shrink it a lot to fit it onto the page, and then you have to multiply it a lot to get it back to full size'. I used her answer and the gestures someone else had used to get the whole class to act out and talk about shrinking a small thing to fit the page and re-sizing it, and shrinking a big thing to fit the page and re-sizing it. That took us to the end of the lesson.

The follow-up lesson involved guided reflection on where the mystery numbers had come from – namely, reversing the shrinking, including changing square centimetres to square metres. This lesson used the actual numbers pupils had found and reminded them about powers of ten in metric, constructing 'doing and undoing' rules and ending up with an estimate of the actual footprint of each school, using calculators so the main focus was on the meaning rather than the arithmetic.

Some tables finished their footprint calculations before others; these groups were given print-outs of other buildings they wanted to know about so they could repeat the process until all tables completed the main task. The lesson was necessarily noisy, with movement between tables as people wanted to compare their work. The end of the lesson was quiet, ordered and contemplative after the shouted remark. The follow-up lesson mainly involved individual work with reminders about the scaling gestures.

What strikes me most about Anne's lesson is that it recognises the complex dynamic of classrooms. This is particularly true at the time of transition from primary to secondary. In my opinion, we should never be apologetic for focusing on the mathematics; that is our role as teachers. However, the most gifted teachers I have ever worked with all had one thing in common: an ability to build positive working relationships with even the most challenging groups of pupils. This task is mathematically robust and can be used to support learning, while at the same time advancing the social fabric of the mathematics classroom community. Earlier in my career, I sometimes fell into the trap of using 'fun' activities, which were light on mathematics, to provide positive classroom experiences and build such relationships. Anne's task, in contrast, has the potential to serve as the basis for a rich trail of mathematical learning in subsequent lessons. Anne says she might use the follow-up lesson to lay the foundations for later discussion about ratios of areas, and this would include the following algebraic structure:

$$\frac{\text{image length} \times \text{scale factor}}{\times \text{image width} \times \text{scale factor}} = \frac{\text{image length} \times \text{image width}}{\times \text{scale factor}^2}$$

and its inverse using real lengths and reciprocals of scale factors.

The first n^2 odd numbers

Chris Smith shared this lovely mathematical phenomenon:

Pick a positive integer "n".
I'll go for 7.

Arrange the first n^2 odd numbers in a square. Here $n^2 = 49...$

1	3	5	7	9	11	13
15	17	19	21	23	25	27
29	31	33	35	37	39	41
43	45	47	49	51	53	55
57	59	61	63	65	67	69
71	73	75	77	79	81	83
85	87	89	91	93	95	97

1. Add up the numbers in the first row. I get 49. You'll get n^2.

2. Add up the numbers along either diagonal. I get 343. You'll get n^3.

3. Add up all the numbers in the square. I get 2401. You'll get n^4.

The investigation is not explicitly stated here. A whole range of mathematical ideas can emerge from activity on this task, including but not limited to:

- integers
- odd
- even
- consecutive numbers
- square numbers
- cube numbers
- fourth powers
- summation formulae.

Can we imagine building the first n^3 odd numbers in three dimensions? What about the first n^2 even numbers, or the first n^2 prime numbers. The task provides an opportunity for pupils to spot patterns and make conjectures. Proofs can arise, either formally or informally, and the resultant activity can move towards algebra including generating formulae.

The only limitation on this task is our imagination. I would suggest, as teachers, we sit down and play with tasks such as the one above, to create possible lines of inquiry of our own and see where they lead us. There is also value in having pupils generate their own problems, although at other times we might want to work with the task in such a way as to focus the pupils' attention on a specific curricular idea. Indeed, this task could be used several times, each time focusing on a different mathematical concept.

Mathematical inquiry

Andrew Blair is an advocate of teaching through inquiry prompts. While I suggest investigations can be used to develop mathematical thinking, Andrew uses prompts as the basis for teaching new concepts. On his website, Inquiry Maths, Andrew suggests such prompts should meet the following criteria:

- A prompt must promote curiosity and questioning in pupils, of the sort, 'Is it true that ...?' or 'I've noticed ...'. Prompts should be intriguing and ripe for speculation or conjecture.
- A prompt must be aimed at pupils' *developing* mathematical knowledge, challenging them to decide whether new concepts are required to understand it fully. It must be accessible yet should stand just beyond the recognition of a class. It should not be designed to intimidate a class; rather, pupils must feel confident enough to be able to manipulate and change the prompt. In short, a prompt should encourage pupils to *reach up* to acquire new knowledge.
- A prompt must be open enough to offer pupils the opportunity to regulate their own activity. Ideally, it will offer a number of pathways and incorporate different areas from the curriculum, at both abstract and concrete levels.
- A prompt should provide opportunities for different forms of thinking as part of the inductive and deductive processes of mathematics.

Andrew explains that:

> a prompt is designed to initiate mathematical inquiry. The 'task' forms an integral part of the pedagogy. Indeed, the prompt can only

function as a 'prompt' if it leads to classroom inquiry. It is, therefore, the case that the same prompt might work for one class but not another. If the prompt is not intriguing, then it will not lead to inquiry. The skill of the inquiry teacher is to select or devise a prompt that sits just above the current understanding of her class.

An example prompt on right-angled triangles is shown below:

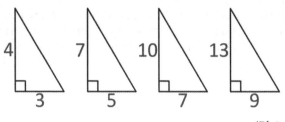

(Blair, 2020)

This prompt is designed to link a number of concepts and act as a way into trigonometry. Typically, pupils notice the sequences on the short sides and speculate about the length of the third side (the hypotenuse). Progress on this line of inquiry requires a knowledge of Pythagoras' theorem, which might be introduced by the teacher. Pupils might also speculate (or be invited to speculate) about the angles. Progress on this line of inquiry requires a knowledge of the tangent ratio, which could lead to a formal introduction to trigonometry. The inquiry, which the teacher might structure or guide, can occupy many lessons.

This prompt can spark an open, exciting and multi-faceted inquiry that combines Pythagoras' theorem and trigonometry with algebraic expressions for sequences and area. Sometimes it does this too well and the teacher has to guide the inquiry to ensure pupils have access to necessary mathematical concepts. The prompt can develop along different pathways, based on the pupils' questions or observations:

- *The sides of the triangles form ascending linear sequences.* What is happening to the hypotenuse? Does its length also increase in a linear sequence? Can its length be made to increase linearly?
- *The angles in each triangle are (not) the same.* Is the angle in the bottom right-hand (or top) corner getting bigger or smaller? If bigger (smaller), can you make it go smaller (bigger) with ascending sequences? What happens with descending sequences? Can you find two sequences that keep the angles the same? What happens when you use other types of sequence?

- *The area increases in a quadratic sequence.* How would you find an expression for the nth term of the sequence? Is there another set of triangles that has the same expression for the nth term of the area sequence?

The inquiry can be used to develop pupils' conceptual understanding of the tangent ratio and, by calculating the length of the hypotenuse, the sine and cosine ratios as well. Pupils come to appreciate that the size of an angle is determined by the ratio of the lengths of two sides of the triangle. This explains how both sides can get longer, yet the angle gets smaller. Indeed, it is possible in the initial stages to use a unit ratio before introducing trigonometry in a formal way. The bottom right-hand angle in the prompt, for example, increases because the length of the opposite side increases at a faster rate than the length of the adjacent side (as shown in the working below).

The questions and observations below come from a year 10 class at Haverstock School (Camden, UK). The pupils suggested a variety of pathways, which were to generate five one-hour lessons of inquiry under the teacher's direction. The first pathway involved the pupils using Pythagoras' theorem, which they had studied before, to find the length of the hypotenuse of each triangle.

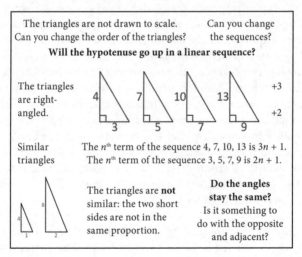

(Adapted from Blair, 2020)

The main inquiry pathway related to the angles. To determine if the angles stayed the same, the class needed to use the trigonometric ratios, which the teacher introduced one-by-one, starting with the tangent ratio. After calculating the size of the angles, pupils began to reason that the bottom right-hand angle in the prompt was increasing because the length of the opposite side was increasing at a faster rate than the length of the adjacent side. The class then started to change the linear sequences to see what would happen to the angle (having calculated the length of the hypotenuse, the teacher introduced the sine and cosine ratios in subsequent lessons). Pupils posed further questions as the inquiry developed:

- Can we use descending sequences?
- Does the angle always get bigger if the sequences ascend?
- Does the angle always get smaller if the sequences descend?
- Will we get different answers for the size of the angle depending on the ratio we use (sine, cosine or tangent)?
- What happens if I calculate the size of the top angle instead?

The teacher used the final question as the basis for a teaching phase on identifying the opposite and adjacent sides and the hypotenuse. Below are some of the pupils' responses to their supplementary questions.

SEQUENCES ASCEND, SIZE OF ANGLE INCREASES

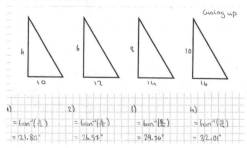

(Blair, 2020)

SEQUENCES ASCEND, SIZE OF ANGLE STAYS THE SAME

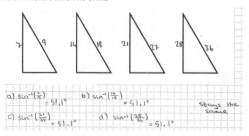

(Blair, 2020)

205

ONE SEQUENCE DESCENDS, SIZE OF ANGLE DECREASES

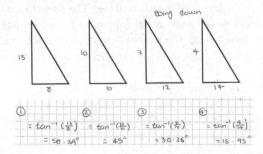

(Blair, 2020)

SEQUENCES ASCEND, SIZE OF ANGLE DECREASES

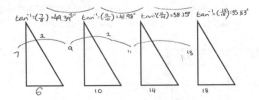

(Blair, 2020)

These inquiry prompts give pupils the experience of being mathematicians, but also allow them to develop some of the thought patterns and behaviours required in problem solving. Pupil self-image is important in problem solving. Used appropriately, these prompts give pupils a space in which to voice their own questions and thinking. Andrew emphasises that the prompts are not about 'discovery lessons in which pupils are expected to discover a concept independently. If pupils identify a need for new conceptual or procedural knowledge to make progress during an inquiry, the teacher should give instruction. Moreover, if pupils request an explanation, they are more likely to be motivated to listen and engage actively with what the teacher says.'

Contextual modelling
In this section, we look at tasks that involve applying mathematical ideas to model real-world situations and to solve some problem.

Outbreak

> **The task: Outbreak!**
> The situation is getting extremely serious.
> A disease has started to spread around the city.
> If you get the disease you have only hours to live.
> Our city has been put under quarantine; no one in or out.
> The good news is you are able to help.
> The scientists from the Research and Development
> Department have worked flat out and have managed to put
> together two vaccines.
> - Vaccination A is 95% effective and costs £8.00 per dose.
> - Vaccination B is 70% effective and costs £6.50 per dose.
> We have a budget of £5 000 000 maximum.
>
> **Your task is to recommend:**
> - how many of each vaccine we should make
> - who will get those vaccines.

(Adapted from Wake, Swan and Foster, 2015.)

Pupils were also given additional data relating to the population of 946 000, broken down into occupations such as 'medical workers' and 'farmers and food producers', with the numbers in each category given.

The task above was part of a study by Geoff Wake, Malcolm Swan and Colin Foster. The task was designed using principles from Japanese problem-solving lessons, which typically include the following steps:

- The teacher gives the class a problem, to initiate discussion.
- The pupils tackle the problem in groups or individually.
- The teacher moderates a whole-class discussion in which alternative strategies are compared and contrasted and consensus is sought.
- The key points of the lesson are summarised.

The focus of this task was not percentages, as might seem to be the case on first reading. Instead, the teacher focused on two problem-solving processes – strategic planning and communication.

The task began with a 20-minute 'pre-lesson phase' of pupils working on the task alone, after which the teacher collected the pupils' work to analyse with colleagues before the next lesson. This analysis was used to inform the planning of later stages, such as determining pupil groups for the second part of the task in the next lesson. The teacher also used these responses to tabulate some anticipated issues, along with questions and prompts that could be used to scaffold pupils' work without easing the problem (see below).

Anticipated issues	Suggested questions and prompts
Students start detailed calculations before planning an approach. For example, they start at the top of the list and calculate the cost of vaccinating medical workers, then move to the next row, etc.	<ul><li>Describe in words a plan for tackling this problem. What are the key decisions you have to make?</li><li>Which information are you going to focus on at the start? What information will you ignore?</li></ul>
Students ignore one or more constraints. For example, they forget that they only have £5 million budget, or that they only need 946 000 vaccines.	<ul><li>Do you have enough resources for your solution? Have you made enough vaccine for everyone?</li><li>Have you wasted any money? Have you wasted any vaccine?</li></ul>
Students do not justify decisions made. For example, they state a solution with no explanation.	<ul><li>Why have you chosen to allocate the vaccines in this way?</li><li>How can you be sure this is the best solution?</li></ul>
Students leap to conclusions. For example, they quickly assume that only vaccine A should be used because it is more effective; or that only vaccine B should be used because it is cheaper.	<ul><li>Have you taken all the issues into account?</li><li>Could you vaccinate more people if you used some of vaccine B?</li><li>Could you save more lives if you used more of vaccine A?</li></ul>
Students do not understand the concept of a budget. For example, they assume a good solution will be a cheap solution and do not realise they need to spend the whole budget to save the most lives.	<ul><li>What is your main objective when trying to solve the problem?</li><li>Are there any more lives that you could possibly save?</li></ul>
Students are overwhelmed by the large numbers. For example, if they spend £4.8 million of the budget, they might believe this is close enough to their maximum and not appreciate that with £200 000 they could save many more lives.	<ul><li>How much money do you have remaining in your budget?</li><li>How many more vaccines would you be able to purchase with this amount of money?</li></ul>
Students do not grasp the meaning of their calculations. For example, students might perform a sensible calculation but not understand what their answer represents.	<ul><li>What does this figure represent? Is it how much money is left over or how much money has been spent? Does it represent a number of people?</li></ul>

Anticipated issues	Suggested questions and prompts
Students only write numbers with no justifications.	• Where have these figures come from? Do you know what they represent? • Are you able to justify why you have used these numbers?
Students do not understand the effectiveness of each vaccination. For example, students might not be able to grasp the idea of something being 70% effective.	• If 1000 people were given vaccination B, how many would be likely to survive?
Students are confused between numbers representing money and people. For example, students might perform a calculation and get the solution 12 500, but not know whether this is people or money.	• Can you think of a way of distinguishing between numbers that represent different values? • How can you distinguish between values that represent people or money?

(Adapted from Wake, Swan and Foster, 2015)

This table was used to write some questions based on each pupils' work; these questions were designed to help individual pupils reflect more deeply on the approach they were taking. At this stage, pupils were given no evaluation of their work, only the questions.

The second lesson involved the following steps:

- Pupils discussed the task in pairs, with prompts from the teacher: 'Talk to the person next to you about the task from last lesson. What was the task? Can you remember any of the facts and figures?'
- The teacher then gave out the task and returned the pupils' initial responses. For the next five minutes, pupils read their individual feedback questions and responded in writing.
- Next, the teacher instructed the pupils to work in pairs: 'Explain your thoughts to your partner: what you've done, how you've done it and how far you've got.' At this stage, the teacher felt the pupils could justify their decisions more carefully, so he prompted them to do this. He had anticipated this issue when preparing for the lesson and had prepared suitable questions to ask.

As discussed previously, one of the issues with problem-solving tasks, generally, is that it is difficult to make inferences about pupil learning. The teacher involved in this study had similar concerns. To identify the extent to which pupils were developing the chosen aims (strategic planning and communication), he decided in advance to change the constraints of the task at this point, to see whether this change would encourage pupils to adapt their existing strategies or whether they would simply start again. The teacher believed that this approach might give new insight into the problem and encourage greater discussion and collaboration.

The proposed changes, for partway through, are shown here:

Two possible vaccines:
A. Effectiveness of 90%, cost £8 per person
B. Effectiveness of 70%, cost £6.50 per person

Changes to:
A. Effectiveness of 100%, cost £12 per person
B. Effectiveness of 70%, cost £5.20 per person

The pupils were asked to discuss with their partner what had changed and how this changed the overall picture. They were encouraged to discuss the extent to which this modification would change the problem and affect the solution. There was an objection from one of the pupils that all the previous work had been for no reason, but the teacher responded by pointing out that such a change in circumstances was entirely realistic.

Pupils were allowed to work uninterrupted for 20 minutes. Some began the problem again, others adjusted their initial solution by looking at the changes in cost. The teacher identified several pairs of pupils who had decided to vaccinate 50% of the people in each category and asked them to explain their reasoning; for example, had they considered how much money would be left? He used this moment to remind the whole class to clearly record all of their thinking in their solution.

As the lesson neared its end, the teacher held a five-minute whole-class discussion, pointing out a range of approaches and selecting two solutions to discuss with the class.

- First, he presented a tabular approach that one pair had started and suggested that others might benefit from using a similar approach.
- Next, he asked a second pair of pupils to describe their approach. They explained how they had allocated money in the ratio 1 : 4 to vaccines A and B and calculated how many people would be saved. They then tried to vaccinate more people using the same approach and realised everyone could be vaccinated.

The teacher commended the second pair on keeping in mind both the goal (maximising the number of survivors) and the budget. Others, he pointed out, had lost sight of the budget.

In advance of this second lesson, the teacher and researchers had also compiled a table to describe progression of communication and strategic thinking skills:

	Strategic approach	Communication
Little progress	Pupil attempts to work towards a solution by carrying out operations with figures but shows little strategic awareness that will lead to a solution.	Pupil begins to represent the problem using only numbers, without indication of what these represent. Pupil does not offer any explanation of what is happening.
Questions for progression	Can you write down an action plan as to how you are going to complete the task effectively? What are the other pieces of information you need to consider?	What does each of these numbers represent? Can you think of a way of making it clearer for someone else who looks at your work to understand what you are doing?
Some progress	Pupil carries out appropriate and correct calculations but does not take constraints into account.	Calculations are clear, giving correct units (e.g. £), but fail to communicate the reasons behind the calculations.
Questions for progression	Are there other pieces of information you have not thought about?	What are the reasons behind the decisions and calculations you have made?
Substantial progress	Pupil works towards a solution logically, reaching a viable solution.	Pupil uses inefficient methods to communicate ideas (e.g. long essay answers, rather than a two-way table).
Questions for progression	Can you think of an alternative approach to solving this problem? What would be the effect on the outcome?	Can you think of a more efficient way of displaying this information that will make your thoughts easier to follow?
Task accomplished	Pupil arrives at a solution having considered alternatives.	Pupil communicates clearly their solution in a variety of formats, selecting the most appropriate format for what is aiming to be achieved (e.g. a two-way table, a letter). All reasons are clearly explained and justified, using logical arguments.

(Wake, Swan and Foster, 2015)

The creation of these two tables (listing anticipated issues and progression routes) played a key role in supporting the pedagogical actions of the teacher. These tables also acted as excellent professional learning devices.

The collaborative planning of both tables in anticipation of pupil actions and progression developed professional knowledge of how to maintain productive mathematical activity on such tasks. The tables were also a catalyst for meaningful post-lesson discussion.

While production of such tables for every problem-solving lesson is unrealistic for busy teachers, occasionally spending time collaboratively planning such tables can be valuable in increasing teacher confidence and ability in facilitating problem-solving/modelling lessons. This corresponds with what Laurinda Brown described in writing up investigative tasks. Building a bank of such write-ups or tables over time can only serve to support the quality of learning and assessment of mathematical behaviours.

City populations

I have used the data below as the starting point for many lessons, with the intention of creating an activity which is focused on pupils developing their own mathematical models and using these models to make predictions. I also have at least one curriculum content aim in mind whenever I use this task: I may want to ensure pupils engage with a specific target area (such as percentages, graphing, exponential decay or statistics) or I may be aiming to bring various ideas together. Depending on the experiences of the class and their confidence in working independently to 'inquire into' ideas, I will use the data in various ways.

Shown below is the population of the largest cities in Germany.
Complete the table:

Rank	City	Population	Population as a percentage of the largest city
1	Berlin	3 520 000	100
2	Hamburg	1 787 000	
3	Munich	1 450 000	
4	Cologne	1 060 000	
5	Frankfurt	732 000	
6	Stuttgart	633 000	

Plot a graph of city rank versus population.

With some groups, I show the populations only and ask pupils to discuss what they see and then come up with some questions to explore; this often results in a discussion about arithmetic versus geometric sequences. With other groups, I display the full table: the table and resultant percentages help to focus attention. Generally, I encourage pupils to create graphs to illustrate the trend in the data. With more advanced pupils, we might – later in the task – attempt to find equations of these graphs.

Pupils begin to articulate that the rank 2 city has a population that is half that of the rank 1 city, while the rank 3 city has a population roughly one third of that of the rank 1 city. This pattern continues down the list and is a result of the remarkable regularity in the population ranking of the cities in many countries. If one ranks the population size of cities in a given country and calculates the natural logarithm of the rank and of the city population, the resulting graph will show a log-linear pattern.

Spain is another country which shows a rough manifestation of this phenomenon. Even when I have scaffolded the data for the Germany task, I have found it is not necessary to do so for Spain. Pupils are inherently interested and want to see if 'it works' again.

Rank	City	Population
1	Madrid	3,255,000
2	Barcelona	1,622,000
3	Valencia	814,000
4	Servillie	703,000
5	Zaragoza	674,000
6	Malaga	568,000

I then present the following table and ask pupils to apply whatever model they think they have established.

Rank	City	Population
1	Zurich	341,000
2	Geneva	
3	Basel	
4	Bern	
5	Lausanne	
6	Winterthur	

Next, I might give pupils a graph for another country (Vietnam works well), with the largest city already plotted, and ask them to plot the positions of the other cities. I tend to do this if graphical representations and curve fitting are a key focus. If pupils have access to digital devices, I then ask them to 'check' their predictions by looking up the populations of the cities in Switzerland and Vietnam.

After considering several countries, I like to ask pupils, 'do you think your model works for all countries?' and suggest that we investigate the United Kingdom. I often show the population of London and ask pupils to predict the populations of the other cities shown. Some pupils have prior knowledge about some of these cities, which adds to the richness of the conversations.

Rank	City	Population
1	London	7,566,000
2	Birmingham	984,000
3	Liverpool	864,000
4	Nottingham	730,000
5	Sheffield	685,000
6	Glasgow	620,000

Once we establish that the UK fails to follow the model, the most common question is, 'which other countries are like this?'

Throughout this task, I use the data to stimulate conversation and mathematical activity and, depending on the curriculum area(s) I want to focus on, I will nudge the activity in a certain direction. In all cases, I want pupils to have opportunities to pose questions, pursue answers to those questions and develop models of the data for themselves to inquire into the scenario. The task can be used to help establish ways of working and give pupils confidence to make conjectures and explore ideas.

Depending on previous experiences, I will alter the level of prompting and support. With one class, with whom I had worked for a long time, the presentation of the first data set was enough to sustain a whole lesson of meaningful activity. Partway through, I asked pupils to share what they had investigated so far, which prompted other groups to pursue similar lines of thinking. These investigations were captured in the form of a poster. However, this level of independence would have worked less well with pupils who were not used to such a way of working.

The development of self-reliance is an important aspect of pupils beginning to see themselves as mathematicians and problem solvers. They need to gain confidence in themselves, rather than always looking to the teacher for an explanation of what to do. This way of thinking and ownership of learning can be carried over into non-routine problem-solving tasks. This task is 'authentic' in that the data has not been assembled for the purpose of learning mathematics. As such, the utility of mathematics, and its value in other fields, is an important point which emerges from the task.

Tower of pennies

Dan Meyer uses the structure of 'three-act tasks' in his lessons. He likes to root the mathematical activity in some captivating situation (read more about Dan's design principles in the following chapter). For example, Dan saw the image below and found himself wondering, 'how many pennies is that?'. It is likely that the majority of pupils would have the same question – they are mathematising the situation for themselves.

In this task, pupils are presented with a video (sped up) showing a man building the tower of pennies shown below.

The task begins with pupils making a series of estimations, since there is good evidence that making estimations can support the effective teaching of subsequent formal strategies (Thomsen, 2017). The teacher guides this part of the task by asking questions such as:

- How many pennies are there?
- Guess as closely as you can.
- Give an answer you know is too high.
- Give an answer you know is too low.

In contrast to a textbook problem, where all required information is given, Dan likes to ask pupils, 'what information would be valuable here?' He will then record their responses on the board. There is space for pupils to use their own contextual knowledge and to work together on co-construction of the problem.

Some pupils might make a suggestion such as, 'we need to know the weight of the pyramid and the weight of one penny.' Other questions might relate to the number of stacks, or the number of layers. This language arises from the pupils, to support the conversation, and Dan will ask pupils to clarify what they mean by those terms, to ensure everyone is using the terms consistently. Dan allows pupils to be the mathematical authorities in the room by giving them this space to articulate their own explanations of the key ideas.

After some gathering of these suggestions, Dan will tell pupils which information he is able to give them. The pupil who asked for the weight of the pyramid, for example, will be acknowledged as having contributed a good mathematical idea, but Dan might say, 'I would need a massive scale to lift the pyramid, which I don't have, so I can't give you that information.' He would then offer some alternative information, such as dimensions of a penny, the number of layers and the number of coins in each stack.

At this point, Dan will give pupils five minutes to begin working on the task. This approach comes close to what might be regarded as 'discovery learning', but Dan does not anticipate that pupils will produce a solution. Instead, his intention is to observe the ways in which pupils are thinking about the structure, which he can then use in his teaching.

Pupils quickly realise that to do the calculations for the entire pyramid would be laborious – they identify the need for efficient calculation methods. This gives Dan the opportunity to introduce the summation formula for square pyramidal numbers.

$$P_n = \sum_{k=1}^{n} k^2 = \frac{n(n+1)(2n+1)}{6} = \frac{2n^3 + 3n^2 + n}{6} = \frac{n^3}{3} + \frac{n^2}{2} + \frac{n}{6}$$

At this point, Dan shows pupils the following newspaper article, which gives a figure for the number of pennies. He asks pupils to check this figure using the formula.

A penny saved? Ha! He has 300,000

A South Florida man is going for the Guinness record and trying to raise cancer awareness.

April 16, 2006 | By Robert Nolin, South Florida Sun-Sentinel

MIRAMAR — This is no penny-ante endeavour. Dominating the living room of Marcel Bezos' home is nearly a ton of copper slowly taking shape as a massive pyramid of pennies — about 300,000 of them.

(Nolin, 2006)

Dan compares the task to a movie, which has a clear beginning, middle and end. Just as with real movies, there should be the potential for a good sequel. In the context of this task, some potential paths for sequel tasks are laid out below:

- I have £1 000 000 in pennies. How large a pyramid can I make?
- Each stack has 13 pennies, which is a strange number to choose. Why do you think Marcelo Bezos chose it? [Hint: not out of an abundance of superstition!]
- Bezos says he can tell you the number of pennies in a pyramid using this equation:

$$p = s \left(\frac{1}{3} b^3 + \frac{1}{2} b^2 + \frac{1}{6} b \right)$$

where s is the number of pennies in a stack and b is the number of pennies on one side of the square base of the pyramid. Does this equation work? If so, prove it.

Non-routine problem-solving tasks

Lockers problem

There is a school with 100 pupils and, correspondingly, 100 lockers. All the lockers are closed.

The first pupil opens every locker, starting with the first. The second pupil closes every other locker, starting with the second. The third pupil changes the state of every third locker, starting with the third. That is, if the locker is open, she closes it, and if it is closed, she opens it.

This continues similarly until all 100 pupils have passed along the row of lockers.

This is a classic problem, which has appeared in many different places and with many variations to the context. I have found the problem to be both accessible and challenging for pupils. Undertaking the task serves also as an excellent reinforcement for the ideas of factors and primes.

I like pupils to work in groups of two or three on this problem. Some groups begin by writing out the numbers from 1 to 100, to represent the lockers, and attempt to simulate the problem by marking the lockers as closed or open. This is generally difficult to track, and pupils quickly realise some other approach is necessary; for example, some groups choose to use coloured counters to model the problem. Most pupils acknowledge early on that trying to look at all 100 lockers will be overwhelming, so they need to refine their strategies.

Patrick Kimani, Dana Olanoff and Joanna Masingila explored this problem in depth, recording examples of pupil actions and responses, some of which I include here to exemplify the type of work pupils can produce using coloured counters.

This student work example illustrates the status of the first 16 lockers after student 16 has gone through the lockers.

(Adapted from Kimani, Olanoff and Masingila, 2016)

Sometimes, pupils struggle to establish the insights required to extend the problem from this reduced case back to the case for 100. Encouraging them to use another representation where the numbers are visible can help with this.

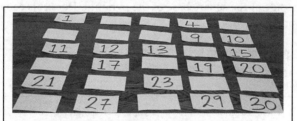

Students using numbered cards to show points in time – in this case, how the first 30 lockers appear after student 9 has gone through them.

(Kimani, Olanoff and Masingila, 2016)

A nice twist on the problem is to ask pupils to keep track of which pupils touch each door. By tabulating these results and looking at the corresponding representations pupils have worked with (counters or paper), the key focus begins to come together.

Locker number	Students who touch it	Final status
1	1	open
2	1, 2	closed
3	1, 3	closed
4	1, 2, 4	open
5	1, 5	closed
6	1, 2, 3, 6	closed
7	1, 7	closed
...	...	...

(Kimani, Olanoff and Masingila, 2016)

It is clear from the working above that the doors which are open are square numbers. The teacher can also prompt conversations about primes by asking pupils to consider which doors are touched twice only. The task can be extended by asking, 'can your solution be extended to 1000 lockers, 1 000 000 lockers or *n* lockers?'

The effectiveness of the task will likely be determined by the actions of the teacher and the extent to which we intervene or not. The task serves as an opportunity for pupils to develop confidence in trying unfamiliar problems but retains the support of working with classmates. The entry threshold for beginning the work is sufficiently low that all pupils can begin.

Set ratios

> Given 17 counters, in how many different ways can you place them in two sets *A* and *B* (which may overlap), so there is the same number of counters in *A* as in B? Generalise.
> In how many different ways can the counters be placed so that the ratio of the number of counters in *A* to the number of counters in *B* is 3 : 2?

When John Mason sent me this task, I was immediately drawn by the fact it is accessible at so many different levels. I ended up using an adaptation of this task, focusing on the first part, with my own 6-year-old children, by drawing overlapping circles and giving them counters to use. The task is quite sophisticated and requires a significant amount of mathematical thinking.

John recalls that, when he uses this task with teachers, one of the things that tends to emerge is that there is a structural or systematic way of working. Some people work out a way of grouping the counters so the condition is satisfied, then stop: for example, when John used the task with teachers in South America, they stopped after finding one possible solution, and he had to encourage them to continue to find all possible sets. However, the idea of finding the number of different ways in which you can do something is very common in mathematics teaching in Japan.

In answering this type of question, pupils are likely to stumble on a systematic way of working. With this task, the systematic way involves doing the same thing to both sets or both sides. It is very helpful to do this with plastic counters – the physical actions are entwined with the abstract ideas here. After some time, John might say, 'in fact there has been a mistake. One of the counters got lost, so there are actually 18 counters.' Pupils then have to adapt their answer. John might go on to suggest other numbers of counters to be considered, leading to opportunities to generalise. Even very young children can make generalisations here because they have the physical counters and are therefore able to describe the patterns.

John pondered what might happen with three sets, so that, instead of balancing two sides, pupils have to balance three sets. In this way, the task can quickly develop into something much more challenging:

> In the past, I have written down a general formula such that, if you want to have n counters in the ratio p : q, I can tell you the number of ways you can do that. If you give me three sets, I can still do this, but only using ugly mathematics. I cannot find a closed formula for p : q : r in three sets, as there are many overlaps between the sets. I worked on this quite hard, but I've got a bunch of summation signs I can't get rid of. The point is, you can be on the boundary of quite difficult mathematics by doing something which is quite elementary.

That final sentence captures the essence of the task. This problem is accessible and useful for pupils in early primary yet, with some slight tweaks, becomes something a university student could meaningfully engage with.

9 Task design

Introduction

In the previous chapters, I have shared a view of mathematics learning and suggested various task types that are required for pupils to fully develop their mathematical skills, understanding and behaviours. This chapter addresses the questions around where new tasks might emerge.

I argue that we can consider five professional actions related to tasks:

- Selecting tasks and appreciating the possible pupil activity.
- Sequencing tasks.
- Using templates to create new tasks.
- Tweaking and adapting tasks written by others.
- Writing new tasks from scratch.

I hope that the discussion in the preceding three chapters will have supported your thinking around task selection; being a critical consumer of tasks is an essential skill for any mathematics teacher. Creating good tasks of our own is difficult, so we often need to rely on tasks created by others, but we must be thoughtful in selecting tasks. For instance, if a scheme of work states that the class should be working on adding decimals, the teacher might trawl the internet to find some worksheets that 'cover' the objective. However, if we want something meaningful to issue to the class, we as teachers need to think about how the task meets the needs of the pupils, rather than how it meets our requirements. We need to ask questions such as:

- What are pupils going to think about in completing the task?
- To what extent does the task provide procedural practice, opportunities to think deeply about the idea, or some element of problem solving?
- What new understanding of decimals might a pupil take from engagement with this task?

Hugh Burkhardt argues that learning to adapt and tweak tasks is important, but that teachers should not be required to create tasks from scratch on a regular basis. There is sometimes a belief that teachers should create all of their own tasks and lessons etc. This is simply too demanding a definition of a good teacher, and not something which is replicable system-wide.

Hugh makes an interesting point and sets a challenge to teachers, saying:

> *Great teachers don't have to be great designers, just as great actors don't have to be great playwrights. It is quite healthy to think of the classroom as a theatre. A good English or history teacher, their lessons are often mini-dramas. They raise an issue; they talk about something and they get the pupils engaged in disputation. The traditional maths lesson is a soliloquy followed by pupils doing imitative exercises. I believe that teachers should, sometimes, stop being the star of the show and instead become the director. I want teachers to give pupils good tasks which are worth investing a lot of time in.*

Building such high-quality tasks can be expensive. For example, owing to the level of research, classroom trials and refinement required, the materials available on the Mathematics Assessment Resource Service (MARS) website cost around $30 000 each to create (although, of course, those tasks are world class). This is not to discourage teachers from writing tasks: as Mark McCourt highlights, task-writing can be a powerful professional learning experience:

> *designing, doing, testing and iterating mathematical questions, prompts, activities and problems increases a teacher's awareness of the characteristics of tasks most likely to bring about effective learning in the classroom.*

> (McCourt, 2019)

Collaborative planning

A possible problem in task design is that we may provide an experience which unintentionally encourages pupils to believe something that is not true. Consider the task below, which I used a few years ago. All of the numbers are in ascending order, which is clearly unnecessary when finding the mean or the standard deviation; however, it is something a pupil might 'learn' from this task. This was an oversight on my part: I was too focused on what I wanted the pupils to do and failed to consider what they might think about in doing the task. It would have been much better if I had recognised this before using the task with the class. This process could have been aided by collaborative working.

Standard deviation and mean For each set of data, find the mean and standard deviation.						
5	5	5	5	5	$\bar{x} =$	$s =$
4	4	4	4	4	$\bar{x} =$	$s =$
8	8	8	8	8	$\bar{x} =$	$s =$
3	4	5	6	7	$\bar{x} =$	$s =$
4	5	6	7	8	$\bar{x} =$	$s =$
6	8	10	12	14	$\bar{x} =$	$s =$

In the previous chapter, I described the development of work on the task about a virus outbreak – the teachers worked collaboratively to list anticipated issues and to create prompts to help address these issues as they arose. Similarly, Laurinda Brown describes writing up summaries of investigative tasks, so teachers can see where the tasks might go and how they might be used. For teachers, time working together in a group to share, adapt and create tasks is time well spent, but department collegiate time is very limited, with many competing priorities. Thankfully we now have another powerful collaborative tool which can help with task design: Twitter. I, and many others, have benefited from the insights of colleagues on this platform. I regularly share tasks on which I am working and enter into discussions with other teachers and educationalists about the task design process.

For example, when thinking about addition of integers, I shared the following exercise.

Do the following mentally, then check your answers using algebra tiles.			
(a) $5 + (-5)$	(b) $(-7) + 7$	(c) $5 + (-4)$	(d) $6 + (-7)$
(e) $(-7) + 8$	(f) $(-3) + 2$	(g) $(-5) + 7$	(h) $(-5) + 3$
(i) $6 + (-4)$	(j) $6 + (-8)$	(k) $(-4) + (-4)$	(l) $(-2) + (-2)$
(m) $(-4) + (-3)$	(n) $(-2) + (-1)$	(o) $(-6) + (-4)$	

This task is designed to be more than routine practice. The questions are grouped such that certain generalities can be discerned, either during the task or through discussion afterwards. I was confident these generalities would arise in my own classroom, because I knew the intention; however, I was concerned they might be missed by another teacher using the task, since it looks like any other addition worksheet that doesn't require significant principles-based mathematical thinking.

Richard Perring proposed the following task which captured my purposes much more clearly.

	Sum is positive	Sum is zero	Sum is negative
positive + positive			
negative + negative			
positive + negative			
negative + positive			

A teacher using this task is more likely to understand the purpose, compared with using my original task. In addition, for pupils, the categories draw attention to the different cases of adding integers, in a more explicit way than the original task. Richard's task increases the likelihood that pupils will spot the patterns, and thus supports their progress toward making generalisations. As I was beginning to think I should throw my task in the bin, Richard suggested pupils could use their answers to the original questions to generate examples that fit in the table; that is, my exercise and the table become components of a single larger task. Richard also suggested we could ask pupils if any boxes cannot be filled and, if so, how they know this?

While I was thinking about integers and ways to provoke generalisation, I also wrote the following task.

Some numbers exist such that $-d < -c < 0 < c < d$.
Complete the empty number line to show possible positions of the numbers.

Using these same numbers, state if each of the following is positive, negative or zero.

(a) $d + c$ (b) $c + d$ (c) $d - c$ (d) $c - d$

(e) $(-c) + c$ (f) $c + (-d)$ (g) $d + (-c)$ (h) $(-d) + (-c)$

(i) $d - (-d)$ (j) $d - (-c)$ (k) $(-c) - c$ (l) $(-d) - (-c)$

(m) $(-d) - d$ (n) $(-d) - (-d)$ (o) $d + (-d)$ (o) $c - (-c)$

Neil Tilston asked if the full inequality was necessary. It was interesting that he picked up on this, as I had debated it myself when writing the task. I started off with a < b < 0 < c < d but realised this wasn't very helpful as the absolute values of a and c, for instance, were incomparable. Neil suggested the following alternative opening prompt:

$$0 < c < d$$
Show $-c$, $-d$, 0, c and d on the number line.

This alteration might increase the initial demand of the task, as pupils have to draw on their knowledge of the symmetry of the number line around the origin and use this to order the numbers themselves. In the original task, most of the thinking has been done for pupils; with this new prompt, there is more to consider.

Some people raised concerns about the algebraic nature of the task; they felt this might disenfranchise some pupils. I accept this point but suggest they key is to know the pupils who will be working on the task and to consider their previous experiences. I would anticipate using this task sometime after the two above, and after we had worked on some integer subtraction.

However, the idea that there might be a better representation to use in this task lingered in my mind. A few weeks later, I stumbled upon the following image on Don Steward's website (https://donsteward.blogspot.com/):

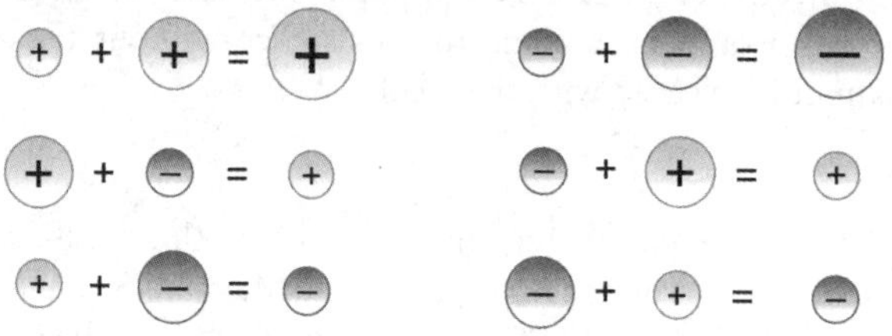

(Steward, 2011)

This was just the inspiration I had been looking for! The following task – a remodelling of my algebraic version using Don's visual – was the result.

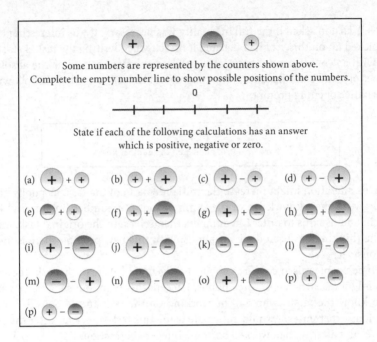

I have had countless similar Twitter exchanges regarding task design. I find that sharing tasks and actively seeking comments and constructive criticism is a great way to develop my craft and to expand my thinking to new possibilities. The perspectives of remote colleagues have been tremendously beneficial to my task design work and, in turn, to the pupils who use my tasks. It is highly unlikely this task would have come into existence without the professional dialogue – I am quite pleased with the result.

Creative process

I interviewed many people during my research for this book. Every single person I spoke to brought up the name of the late Malcolm Swan. Malcolm was a truly world-class task designer. The esteem in which he is held, by so many leading experts in mathematics education, is testament to his unique talents. I asked Hugh Burkhardt, who worked closely with Malcolm for many years at the SHELL centre in Nottingham, about Malcolm's design process.

> *One of the things Malcolm did a lot is that he redrafted things again and again and again. Often, he didn't start with a blank sheet of paper. Instead, he very often started with something he'd devised previously, sometimes years ago. His first thought when you mentioned a topic*

was, 'well, what have I done before on this?' and he would go back and dig out stuff, sometimes from 10 years previously. He very much had the idea that design often starts with something you did yourself or someone else did, which we try to improve upon. He made no apology about not always coming up with a brand new, never-before-thought-of idea. Instead he liked to take an idea everybody knows and try to make it just a tiny bit better. That can be a really good contribution to what we have.

Another thing he did was to look at a task that's out there and exists in six different versions on six different websites. He would take it and consider the pros and cons of some of those different changes. He would then make a really high-quality version of it. He's famous for a lot of the wonderful tasks he did but I think people don't always know how many iterations those went through – how many times he drafted and redrafted.

Of course, in many of the projects there was expensive trialling in classrooms. He had amazing ideas and an amazing instinct for what pupils would do and often the main way he helped people was that he would look at something they had drafted and say, 'I think pupils might do this, what would you do then?' and you might think, 'ah, I never thought of that, of course they would do that, wouldn't they?' So you could save several iterations of the trialling by simply thinking through those things first. It's efficient if you've already thought of three possible things pupils might do and built them into your plan. Then you go and trial the task and get so much more out of it than if you'd trialled the initial version, without considering those possible pupil actions.

He was also amazing at coming back to things; he never seemed to tire of looking at the same things and making them better still. I think that's why so much of his stuff is of such immense quality – because it went through those multiple iterations.

If a world-class task designer didn't feel it necessary to start from scratch every time, then neither should we. As teachers, we can go through iterations of tasks as well. However, it may be a whole year before we use a task again. I asked Hugh to what extent the team at the SHELL centre worked collaboratively.

We used to work together a lot, but we also worked separately a lot. You'd want to make something as good as you possibly could and then you'd take it to Malcolm and he would move it to the next level. If we'd started with a blank sheet of paper, working together probably wouldn't have been as productive. If you work and spend time on a task until you're actually quite proud of it and you think it is really good, that's when you're ready to share it and get someone else to pull it to pieces. It's not that they necessarily think it's bad or that it wouldn't work or it's problematic. It's that they're looking really hard for ways to tweak and improve it.

One of the things Malcolm did quite well was just thinking about all the dimensions you could change. So, if you had made a card sorting task, he might ask questions like, 'How many cards is it best to have? Is it better to have 6? 8? What are the pros and cons if you have two extra cards? What would you put on them?' You might decide not to act on some of the possibilities raised, but he would go through all the things you could change. You might end up coming back to your original idea, thinking that it is the best way to proceed, but you would have considered all the possible options. The main idea, I always felt, was not to just go with the first or second thing you came up with. You had to iterate systematically through the different possibilities and choose one with a good reason. Of course, that could change after trialling with a class, but it meant you were less likely to be surprised.

This iterative process is fundamental to high-quality task design, which is why I so strongly advocate teachers do this, either with colleagues or on Twitter. There's a saying that the best way to have a good idea is to have a lot of ideas. Hugh said of the team at the SHELL centre, 'I'm sure all of us have loads of folders of stuff that didn't make it. We ran into problems or we thought at the end it was quite good but not that good, so it just sat in a folder. I think the ratio of junk to what you actually use is quite high.' Personally, I have a notebook where I capture task design ideas in their earliest stages. Sometimes, these ideas turn into tasks; at other times, they remain in the notebook as 'problems' I have yet to find a satisfactory resolution for. For instance, at the time of writing, I am thinking about changing the subject of a formula and how to give pupils a deeper understanding of this, by using something other than a drill exercise. So far, I haven't come up with a task I'd even be prepared to discuss with a colleague!

It is interesting that Malcolm also saw value in anticipating pupil responses. Colin Foster describes a project he was involved in with some colleagues from Tokyo. Colin says the Japanese researchers spent a great deal of time anticipating pupil responses in great detail –to the level of writing out six possible things they expected pupils to do in response to a prompt. They would then analyse the responses in detail. This is well beyond simply asking, 'what are the common misconceptions?' For a specific task, the researchers would ask how pupils might solve it. Interestingly, Colin says, they would be quite definite that there were, for example, six different ways you could solve a particular task. Colin says he felt that sounded a bit rigid, but when he thought about it more he realised, 'well, actually I can't think of a seventh'. The Japanese researchers really thought in depth, which appears to be the key to strong task design. They thought so carefully and in so much detail about what pupils might do and then planned how they would respond to these different actions.

When I asked Colin about creating tasks, he replied:

> I suppose one of the things that strikes me is, with task design, there's a highly creative aspect to it. It is very hard to capture that – to say to someone, 'here's how to make a good task'. Even then, the question is: what is a good task? As John Mason says, 'There's no such thing as a rich task, only a task used richly'. Even the most dull exercises can be used richly, if you treat them as discussion points and use prompts such as, 'what's the same, what's different', 'can you make up another one like that?', 'can you make an easy one or a hard one?'

Colin doesn't think this means that every task is as good as every other task, or that every task is equally rich. Most of us probably need as much help as we can get from the setting up of the task, so it's worth building the best tasks we can.

John Mason is another master of task design. I asked John if there are some ways in which he comes up with tasks. He replied:

> The answer to that, in a sense, is yes, but you won't like the detail! The detail is that I sleep on it. I walk on it. I put it in the back of my mind and think about it while I'm waiting for a bus. This is because most of the tasks I like to use have arisen in some context other than preparing to teach something. In fact, I keep working on mathematical problems. Few of them are of any interest to mathematicians as such, because they are not at the boundary of mathematics, but I work on mathematical problems that occur to me. Sometimes I notice something which makes me think, 'gosh yes! That shows me some aspect of ratio or fractions or graphing functions or thinking about

slopes of curves in some way I haven't considered before.' When I get some insight into an aspect of mathematics, I ask myself if I can convert that into a task.

I asked John for some example of this. He continued:

Several years ago, I came across a film showing different numbers of blobs for numbers. 1 is a single circle, 2 is two circles, 3 is three circles in a triangle, 4 is four circles in a square, 5 is five circles in a pentagon – but then it starts to get interesting. I loved the film but it went by too fast, so I spent a lot of time converting it into PowerPoints so I could move around between numbers. Fairly recently I came across something else – I can't recall what it was – but I thought 'ah yes! The blobs!'. Then, I really began to come to grips with what was involved in the multiplicative structure of numbers. In this particular situation, I thought the blobs showed the idea beautifully! So, I've spent a long time developing a sequence of tasks, which I'm now calling 'Lots of'. This is a good example of how a possible task arises from my own mathematical thinking. I then tinker with the task and modify it according to various principles and try it out on people. Next I modify it and modify it again. In fact, I almost always modify a task before using It, even if I've used it a hundred times before.

This is quite a compelling argument for us, as mathematics teachers, to be doing our own recreational mathematics. It is particularly valuable for teachers who are interested in task design. John agreed with this sentiment, saying:

If you were hiring an art teacher for a school, would you hire somebody who did not actually do art? If you were hiring a music teacher, would you hire somebody who didn't play music? If you were hiring a history teacher, would you hire somebody who had no interest in history outside school? I would try not to, if I possibly could! The same is true for mathematics. To keep myself alert to the sort of situations pupils are going through, I've got to be experiencing these things: struggling, making mistakes, making conjectures, modifying those conjectures and then re-modifying them.

As well as experiencing these same frustrations, there is a positive offshoot – we may gain for ourselves new insight into fundamental mathematics or awareness of some new representation. This new insight can serve as the basis for task design. John also says that, when he is developing a sequence of tasks, he likes to push the tasks beyond what the intended audience will actually work with.

At this point in the chapter, some key ideas to reflect on are as follows:

- Anticipating pupil responses means the task is more likely to 'work'.
- Collaborative planning helps to improve task quality.
- Refinement and iteration are essential in task design.
- Doing our own mathematics can lead to insights for task design.

Instructional design versus task design

An important distinction to draw is between the design of instruction and the design of tasks. In teacher training, much of the practical focus is on how to design and plan instruction, with little focus on planning the task that goes with the lesson. In designing tasks, the focus is on the object that will go 'in front of' pupils – for example, a problem spoken by the teacher, which is never visually shown to pupils, or a problem on a poster, or a situation created in Cuisenaire rods, or a worksheet, a card sort or something else. Instructional design focuses on the actions of the teacher and how the teacher is going to interact with pupils. In school schemes of work, we see lists of tasks but often little indication of the instructional routines to support effective use of these tasks. In world-class materials – such as those from the Standards Unit (Swan, 2005) and MARS resources, the instruction and task design have been considered together. Task design focuses on the minutiae, such as the decision to use a specific template (e.g. a matching task), whereas instructional design involves thinking about the wider context of the lesson. For instance, instructional design would include thinking about how the lesson might start with some formative assessment to ensure pupils are ready for the main task sequence.

Pedagogical insight from writing tasks

In working on, writing and adapting tasks, we open ourselves to the possibility of gaining pedagogical insight. For example, Richard Perring shared a task on simultaneous equations (shown below), saying:

> *Tactiles were being talked about a lot at the time, as a way of modelling collecting like terms and that sort of thing. I felt a little uncomfortable about that (as I do now with algebra tiles) as it felt like it was just a rebranding of 'fruit salad algebra'[a is for apples, b for bananas, etc.] – there was no mention of the tiles representing a value.*

Below are eight compound shapes and two shapes with areas of x and y.

Students may work in groups. Mini whiteboards would be useful to help with jottings.

Starter

Starting activity could be to find the area of each of the compound shapes in terms of x and y.

Initial questions might be:

- Draw a shape with an area of $2x$.
- Draw a shape with an area of $4y$.
- Draw a shape with an area of $x - y$ (this is fundamental to continuing with the task).

The compound shapes have the following areas.

A: $2x$ B: $2x + 3y$ C: $6x + 3y$ D: $7x + y$

E: $2x + 7y$ F: $4x - y$ G: $4x + 9y$ H: $4x + 6y$

Main activity

Students could work individually or in groups to answer questions such as:

- Which shape has half the area of H?
- What's the difference in area between A and B? Between B and C?
- If you know that B has an area of 9 cm² and C has an area of 21 cm², what other areas can you work out?
- Shape P's area is written $3x + 2y$ and shape Q's area is written $3x - 2y$.
    - Which is the bigger shape and by how much?
    - If shape P has an area of 7 cm² and shape Q has an area of 5 cm², what is the area of shape x and shape y?

Plenary

- Which two shapes would you want to know the area of to make it easiest to find the areas of the others? Why?
- Why can't you work out the other areas if B has an area of 7 cm² and H has an area of 14 cm²?
- What is the smallest number of areas you need to know to be able to work out all of the other areas?

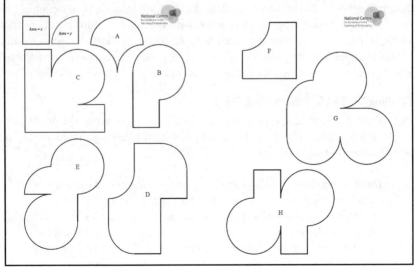

Richard continued:

> *I was mucking about with the idea of the areas of tiles representing values and I realised I could repeat different patterns of tiles. I connected this to scaling up equations when solving simultaneous equations and I was away!*
>
> *My intention was to find a representation that cut straight to the maths. What I liked here was that I could get the class to work on the task without too much instruction, then I could record what they'd done with symbols.*

Richard's intention here was to allow pupils to gain an understanding of what was happening, before worrying about how to record it symbolically. He mentioned hearing Pete Griffin talk about 'manipulating the symbols versus symbolising the manipulation'.

On reflection, Richard says he would now write the task differently: he suggests there are shapes that don't need to be there and he has reservations about the representation of area, saying, 'if I were to do it now, I'd use a bar model approach'. Thus, Richard gained significant pedagogical insights from writing this task. He explains:

> *The thing that shifted in me as a result, was that I started to approach simultaneous equations using comparison. For example, if I presented the class with $2x + 3y = 8$ and $2x + y = 3$, my intention would be for students to realise the 'number of' xs is the same but the 'number of' ys is different in each equation, and for them to use that comparison to continue. I allow plenty of time for students to play around with this sort of equation – comparing the coefficients and deciding what could be done.*
>
> *This leads me to consider other topics. If I could adapt my approach so significantly with this topic – something I'd previously taught almost entirely procedurally – I could surely do the same with other topics too. Developing this resource shifted my pedagogy quite significantly.*

Creating tasks from templates

David Wees suggests that teachers' understanding of mathematics is a key determinant in their ability to design tasks. If the teacher is not completely fluent with the mathematics, this is an additional thing they have to think about a lot when trying to design a task. This leaves them less mental space to focus on the structure of the task. Without a strong understanding of the mathematics being taught (and, I might argue, some experience of teaching it to pupils), the teacher will find task design challenging. Teachers designing tasks have a lot to contend with. They have to consider:

- the maths
- the task purposes
- the design features of the task
- the pupils' interaction with the task
- the classroom instruction.

Asking teachers to focus on both instructional design and task design is a significant demand. David points out that most truly expert task designers are in the later stages of their careers; he suggests this is because they have mastered earlier things and can choose to attend to each element as required, without being overwhelmed.

It might be that a set of principles for task design would be useful. Indeed, when I started writing this book I hoped to achieve this. However, even if I could pull together such a list, it would be incredibly difficult to use it to design tasks. In academic writing, there are 'style guides'. David says, 'I've never seen a style guide that's fewer than 10 pages long. It has a lot of information in it. It's actually impossible to use a style guide proactively. You almost always end up using the style guide to check your work.' The same is true of task design. Essentially, you need something in front of you to modify even if you have established task design principles.

I argue that templates are an effective starting point for teachers to begin to explore task design. Many websites provide structures for tasks:

- 'Visual Patterns' from Fawn Nguyen.
- 'Which One Doesn't Belong?' from Mary Bourassa.
- 'Open Middle®' from Robert Kaplinsky and Nannette Johnson.
- 'Maths Venns' and 'SSDD Problems' from Craig Barton.
- 'More, Same, Less' from Ashton Coward and Peter Mattock.

Using a template from a site like this means the burden on the teacher is somewhat reduced. The structural similarities between all Open Middle problems, for example, mean the teacher can become confident with the instructional routines around this type of problem. Initially, the teacher can use some Open Middle problems created by other people, becoming comfortable using the tasks and gaining insight into what makes a 'good' version of a task. From here, the teacher can begin to create and experiment with their own versions of Open Middle problems.

In the following section, I will examine Open Middle problems in more depth, as a basis for task design. I recommend investigating all of the websites above – I could have chosen any of these templates for the following deep dive (and SSDD and More, Same, Less templates have been discussed in some depth in Chapters 6 and 7 respectively).

Using templates: Open Middle

Open Middle problems are relatively simple to create, yet have the potential to enable pupils to do some fantastic mathematics. Nanette Johnson and Robert Kaplinsky have created the website http://www.openmiddle.com, which is a compendium of these sorts of problem.

Nanette and Robert describe the key features of these tasks:

- **A closed beginning:** This means they all start with the same initial problem.
- **A closed end:** This means they all end with the same answer.
- **An open middle:** This means there are multiple ways to approach and ultimately solve the problem.

Thus, almost any routine question can be turned into an Open Middle problem, simply by removing the numbers.

Open Middle problems give pupils opportunities for productive struggle. The nature of the problems means there are many possible ways of solving them. It is easy to create an 'instance' that satisfies the majority of the criteria laid out. However, there is often some 'constraint' which means that, while a problem initially appears to be simple, it can turn out to be challenging and complex! The tasks are inherently low threshold, so all pupils can begin, but have a high ceiling – they can be taken along different tangents.

Open Middle example 1

Choose five different digits

What combination gives the biggest product?

☐ ☐ × ☐ ☐ ☐

Is there a strategy for any five digits?

(Hewitt and Francome, 2017)

235

Tom Francome shared this task with me, from the book he wrote with Dave Hewitt, Practising Mathematics. This task is an example of purposeful practice. That is, it provides plenty of opportunities for multiplication practice but this happens in the context of problem solving: there is a reason for doing the multiplication, rather than aimlessly working through a page of multiplication questions.

A theme permeating all open-middle problems is that of freedom and constraint. The task allows some element of pupil choice in the five digits. However, three observable constraints are present:

1. The five digits have to be different.
2. The multiplication must be a three-digit number by a two-digit number.
3. The target is to generate the biggest product.

These constraints help to direct pupils' mathematical activity. Pupils' choices may be random at first but will become increasingly informed as more cases are tried.

Hewitt and Francome outline how these tasks can give pupils opportunities to behave mathematically:

- Pupils may notice patterns and relationships (the position of the digits and how this affects the result).
- Pupils have opportunities to make conjectures, e.g. 'if I put the two biggest digits in the unit boxes, the answer will be small'.
- Pupils have opportunities to test and refine their conjectures.
- Pupils may generalise or be encouraged to do so, after repeated specialisation.
- Pupils will have scope to prove and justify *why* a conjecture is true.

The task can also be extended or simplified. For some groups, the problem could be to multiply a two-digit number by a one-digit number. For others, pupils might be asked to include a decimal point in one or both of the numbers.

Open Middle example 2

Closest to One
Directions:

Using the digits 1 to 9 at most one time each, fill in the boxes to create a fraction as close to one as possible.

(Morris, 2016)

This second example also demonstrates the key characteristics discussed above. There is an element of freedom, but with some constraints. The task is low threshold, so all pupils will be able to begin, but can easily be extended or eased as required.

A key learning point in this specific task is to focus on the question, 'how do we know how close to one our fraction is?' Pupils need some way of interpreting their answers. This requires flexibility in thinking and pupils may use different representations such as number lines, bar models or decimal approximations.

The author Peter Morris offers some prompts which might be useful with pupils who are struggling to engage:

- When you change the denominator, what happens to the size of the parts?
- Name a fraction that you know is pretty close to 1. How do you know it is close to 1?
- Which is closer to 1, $\frac{2}{3}$ or $\frac{5}{6}$?

These prompts hint at the key relationship involved in the task – the ratio between the numerator and denominator. They describe the instructional thinking required to use the task.

Using templates: Geometric templates

Other templates which can be used as the basis or inspiration for task design include those I categorise as 'geometric templates'. There are many examples, but my two favourites are pyramids and spiders. Both types of template can be used flexibly and creatively to generate practice for pupils, while incorporating some element of 'working backwards' and problem solving.

Pyramids

Pyramids are a highly flexible geometric template. The most common approach is to consider each building block as the sum of the two blocks immediately below, but there are many possible variations on this theme (including changing the operation to subtraction, multiplication or division). For example, pyramid 3 below is designed to be completed using multiplication rather than addition.

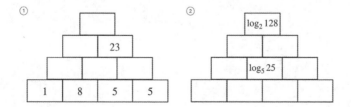

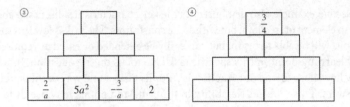

The pyramid template is powerful as it can be used at all levels, depending on the contents of each block and the operation required. A significant element of challenge arises when pupils are given a block higher up the pyramid, while the blocks directly below are left blank. In this situation, pupils need to work backwards to find out what could add (or multiply or whatever) to give the known block. Giving pupils the top block only and asking them to create a pyramid that works is a stimulating challenge, which results in a lot of purposeful practice as pupils try various combinations of terms to find a solution.

Spider diagrams

Dave Hewitt has written about spider diagrams, calling them 'Polypedes' (Hewitt, 1998). As with pyramids, there is a multitude of ways to use spiders and pupils can be encouraged to work backwards if only an end node is given. Two examples from Don Steward are shown below.

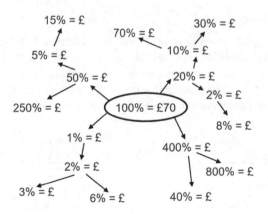

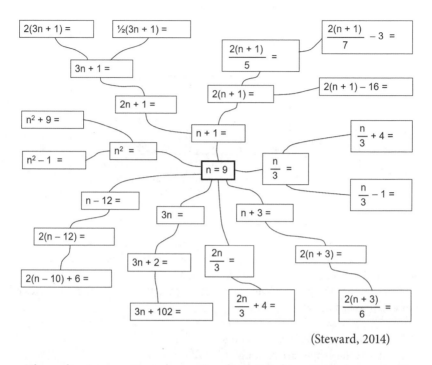

(Steward, 2014)

These diagrams capture proportional relationships in a clear way. For example, pupils can reason their way towards finding 250% of a quantity using the associated knowledge of 50%. Thus, the spiders can become a device that pupils use to scaffold their own working. The algebraic example includes sequences of nodes, which signify operations being applied to the preceding node; this approach would also work with numerical values. A further example could present a graph of a function in the middle of the page, with each branch showing a succession of transformations.

Adapting tasks

Much of the discussion in this chapter thus far has focused on the idea of adapting and tweaking tasks created by others. In the following section, I intend to explore this in more depth.

What-if-not

Brown and Walter (2005) describe a strategy for generating new problems, which involves starting with some mathematical phenomenon (a diagram, a relationship, etc.) or some existing problem.

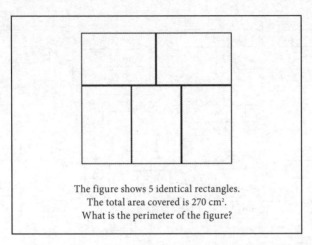

The figure shows 5 identical rectangles.
The total area covered is 270 cm².
What is the perimeter of the figure?

Before reading further, it is worth attempting to solve this problem, to ensure you have a firm grasp of the mathematics involved. It is not a trivial question. Take the time to do some recreational mathematics.

To exemplify the problem-generating strategy, let's consider the attributes of our existing problem:

1. The problem deals with rectangles.
2. All of the shapes are rectangles.
3. There are five rectangles.
4. All of the rectangles are identical.
5. Two of the rectangles are placed horizontally on top of three laid vertically.
6. The problem deals with the total area.
7. The total area is 270 cm².
8. The problem asks for the perimeter.
9. The rectangles are arranged so there are no enclosed gaps.
10. The problem starts with area and moves towards perimeter.

It took me a few minutes to generate all of the attributes listed above, and they did not arise in the order shown. Some were immediately obvious – such as the fact that the problem deals with rectangles. Others only came to me when I asked myself, what else is significant about this attribute?

The next step is to consider 'What-If-Not' for each of these attributes – that is, to take each attribute and consider it being something else. For instance, what if the shapes were triangles, not rectangles? What if the problem started with total perimeter, not total area? We might decide to change more than one attribute at a time, or we might have to do so, due to the nature of the mathematical relationship. For example, asking 'what if the shapes were a mix of pentagons and triangles?' (as shown below) affects attributes 1, 2, 3, 4 and 5.

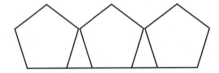

I will pursue each change as the starting point for creating a new task. I will maintain some element of attribute 4 as we proceed, by keeping the shapes of each type identical to each other. However, by changing the component shapes, I immediately have to consider several other attributes, because they are linked together.

Without looking to change anything else, I wondered to what extent the new problem (using pentagons and triangles) was different to the original one. I started thinking about the area and how I might work out the constituent areas. I quickly realised that my choice of pentagons would create significant issues for pupils – the problem would grow arms and legs! At this stage, I offered the problem on Twitter to maths teaching colleagues instead.

Then I asked myself, 'what if not pentagons?' I quickly settled on regular hexagons instead, since they have a host of mathematical features that are 'nicer' to work with (not least the fact that the triangles between them will now be equilateral). I also know that six of these equilateral triangles combined will create one of the hexagons. At this stage, I made the decision to tweak the layout of the triangles, as I felt the version below was more aesthetically pleasing – 'taste' is entirely subjective, but likely has some role in the level to which others will find the problem enticing to solve.

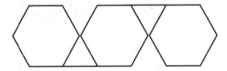

Thinking about this problem algebraically, I realised that a total area of 270 cm^2 (as in the original question) would mean the numbers quickly became messy. With this in mind, I decided to make the total area 320 cm^2, as this divides nicely. However, when attempting to find the perimeter, I found an answer which was deeply unsatisfying. Purely in terms of taste, I had really hoped for a nice exact value. Therefore, I decided to rework the question from the end point. I decided I would like each edge to be of length 2 and, as a result, changed the starting area to 20√3 cm^2.

I discussed this task generation with Siobhan McKenna, who sent me an image made up of dodecagons and triangles. I immediately felt this looked nice, both mathematically and on the surface.

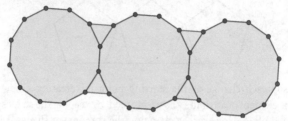

Siobhan explained that she chose this approach by working back from shapes with exact values for angles: the interior angle of a regular dodecagon is 150°, which implies the triangles are equilateral.

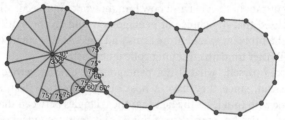

I was hopeful that Siobhan was onto something here, but the she sent me several photos of her working that looked like this:

$$P = 19y$$
$$P^2 = 361y^2$$
$$P^2 = 361(2x^2 - \sqrt{3}x^2)$$
$$P^2 = 722x^2 - 361\sqrt{3}x^2$$

$$P^2 = 722\left(\frac{405 - 135\sqrt{3}}{6}\right) - 361\sqrt{3}\left(\frac{405 - 135\sqrt{3}}{6}\right)$$

$$P^2 = \frac{292410 - 97470\sqrt{3} - 146205\sqrt{3} - 146205}{6}$$

$$P^2 = \frac{146205 - 243675\sqrt{3}}{6}$$

$$P^2 = \frac{48735 - 81225\sqrt{3}}{2} \qquad P = \sqrt{\frac{48735 - 81225\sqrt{3}}{2}}$$

This resonated with me so much. Task design is really hard. The constraint Siobhan and I had imposed upon ourselves was to create a problem with a 'nice' solution. In pursuit of such a goal, there will be a lot of scribbling and many dead ends. It is essential to work through any task you are writing, but when there are chains of reasoning it is almost impossible to create the task without becoming entrenched in screeds of scrappy working!

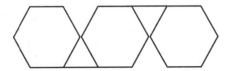

Returning to the image above, I considered the next step in the problem generation process, which is to ask questions (even if they make no sense with the current problem). Here, the sorts of questions that serve as a basis for thinking include:

- Is there a generalised formula?
- What is the maximum or minimum?
- Can the problem be extended?
- Can we make a table?
- How do the attributes relate to each other?
- What does it remind you of?
- Is it relevant?

The excellent book from the ATM, 'Thinkers' would also serve as a useful tool here.

At this point, we might completely change the question type, to direct or guide pupils' thinking in ways that did not seem plausible with the original diagram/question. For example, looking at the diagram above, a host of other potential tasks began to emerge in my thinking, such as:

- Generalisation – are there formulae that can be constructed not just for this problem, but for this *class* of problem?
- Potential trigonometry problems related to the interior angle of the pentagons.
- Tabulation of perimeters versus areas when considering various polygons with number of sides > 4.
- Potential for a calculus problem considering the maximum value of one attribute with respect to some other attribute.
- A task focused on volume and *surface area*, which gave rise to the following diagram.

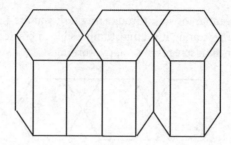

The 3D variation of the task leads to many new potential problem stems. Having started with one task, I now have a goldmine of tasks to create, play with and (maybe) solve. By modifying, creating and attempting to solve problems, I may generate mathematical tasks that could be of use in my teaching. This approach can be used to create new geometry problems from existing ones, or to take a geometry problem and turn it into something completely different. Even if, through such activity, I do not manage to create a task I wish to use with a class, I am still keeping myself fresh mathematically – I am doing mathematics and frequently getting stuck, just like the pupils in my classes.

Tom Carson shared some thinking with me which reminded me of the what-if-not approach. He saw the following exam question and began to consider what problems were related to it.

> Show that the line with equation $y = 3x - 5$ is a tangent to the circle with equation $x^2 + y^2 + 2x - 4y - 5 = 0$ and find the coordinates of the point of contact.

Highlighting some key attributes demonstrates the range of possible changes we could make to this routine problem. Also changing the structure of the question in some way could result in a much more challenging task.

> Show that the <u>line</u> with equation $y = 3x - 5$ is a <u>tangent</u> to the <u>circle</u> with equation $x^2 + y^2 + 2x - 4y - 5 = 0$ and find the coordinates of the <u>point of contact</u>.

Tom's thinking resulted in the table below. My first thought, as a teacher, is to wonder why I had not considered intersections as an explicit teaching theme before. I teach children how to find the intersection of two lines, of a line and a circle, of a quadratic and a cubic, etc. Is this a complete waste of time? Could we, instead, spend a couple of lessons thinking about intersections generally? This could result in pupils having the skills to apply whenever required, whatever the situation. My second thought, as a mathematician, is – do I know how to find the intersection of each of these functions?

	Line	Quadratic	Circle	Trigonometric	Exponential
Line					
Quadratic					
Circle					
Trigonometric					
Exponential					

As in the geometry example, there are potential insights or new tasks which can emerge for learning and teaching, but also opportunities for me to engage in some mathematics of my own. For instance, in school mathematics, how often do you routinely have to consider the intersection of an exponential and a quadratic? In Scotland, where I teach, the answer is never. Encountering this unusual situation will allow pupils to develop a sense of the range of their knowledge and to realise where future learning might take them. The necessity of iterative methods comes to the fore, while dynamic geometry software could be used to enable exploration of these intersections before more formal approaches are considered.

More strategies for adaptation

Several factors determine the difficulty of a problem, including:

- **complexity** – from simple calculation up to complex synthesis
- **length of reasoning** – the amount of work required between prompts in the task
- **degree of unfamiliarity** – how much the problem differs from the task types pupils normally encounter
- **openness** – the number of possible solution methods available.

We may choose to alter combinations of these factors. However, it is important to be aware that the factors can interact in unpredictable ways, so it is not always possible to determine how difficult a problem will be for pupils in practice.

Swan and Burkhardt present some strategies for turning routine problems into non-routine problems. For example, considering a racetrack of the sort shown below, Malcolm and Hugh set out a table of deliberate variations, which the teacher can use to alter the level of cognitive demand.

1.	Routine task	A running track is made up of two semicircles with radius 20 metres and two straight sections with length 100 metres. Find the distance round one lap of the track.
2.	Reversing what is known and unknown	The distance round a running track is 400 metres. The straight sections have a length of 100 metres. What is the radius of the bends?
3.	Removing constraints	A running track must have two semicircular ends joined by two straight sections. The distance round the track is to be 400 metres. Design two different tracks that satisfy these constraints. Label your drawings to show the relevant dimensions.
4.	Linking with other content	A running track must have two semicircular ends joined by two straight sections. The distance round the track is to be 400 metres. Using a graph, describe how the radius of the bends will depend on the length of the straights you choose.

(Swan and Burkhardt, 2012; Figure 5)

Task reversal

Mathematics problems tend to follow the pattern:

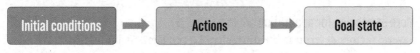

Consider the following question: $\frac{2}{5} + \frac{1}{4}$

The initial situation and the prescribed actions are clear. To reverse the task, we would ask the solver to give a pair of fractions which sum to $\frac{13}{20}$. This opens the task to more creative thinking. Once pupils have created one pair of possible fractions, we might use the prompt '…and another…' repeatedly to ask them to generate more interesting pairs. We could also ask more challenging questions, or add a constraint – for example, 'come up with a pair of fractions nobody else will have thought of' or 'come up with a pair of fractions that include a negative'. In addition, we could change the action and ask pupils to create pairs of fractions with the product $\frac{13}{20}$.

Task reversal is linked with the theme of doing and undoing, which permeates mathematics. Frequently the undoing operation is harder to perform and requires more thinking. It is possible to teach procedures for undoing but, in my opinion, it is better to use pupils' existing knowledge as the basis for developing undoing. A nice introduction to the techniques of basic integration is to ask pupils the following question:

$$\text{If } \frac{dy}{dx} = 5x^4, \text{ what was } y?$$

Despite not having the notation for integration, pupils have to begin to construct the process for themselves, drawing on their existing knowledge, rather than being told some rule to apply. It is common for pupils to draw a flowchart to summarise the steps in differentiation and then work through it in reverse, applying inverse operations. The teacher can scaffold from this thinking. I ask several pupils to share their solution and many classes will agree, unanimously, that $y = x^5$ is the correct solution. When I tell them I was actually thinking of $y = x^5 + 3$, the pupils often exclaim, 'how were we meant to get that?' This is a great starting point for a discussion about the inclusion of the constant of integration. It is always difficult to see learning happen in real time, but these moments of incoherence or tension are the best examples of when I see pupils make sense of something. Harnessing the emotion of surprise is powerful. If I had told pupils about the constant at the outset, much of this energy would have been lost.

Removing or adding constraints – level of scaffolding

The level of scaffolding provided within a task is a major design consideration. Scaffolding refers to the extent to which pupils are led through a task step-by-step. For example, in many exam questions, problems are split into several parts to support pupils and to ease the assessment process. However, if the scaffolding provides too much support, we cannot truly assess pupils' problem-solving skills; we can only assess the knowledge for each part of the question. Pupils tend to perform less well when such problems are not broken up into constituent parts: handling long chains of reasoning is difficult. However, it is a fundamental part of genuine problem solving. As Swan and Burkhardt explain, 'there is often a tension between the degree of scaffolding and transparency in the purpose of the task'.

With open tasks, pupils may actually be engaged in different tasks! That is, they may interpret the initial prompt in different ways, make different assumptions and use different mathematical techniques. As a result, such tasks are of limited use for assessment purposes, because it is difficult to make inferences from pupil performance. For instance, did a pupil make a deliberate choice not to use Pythagoras' theorem, or did they simply not realise it could be used here? Swan and Burkhardt summarise the dilemma thus: 'How can we assess whether or not a pupil can generalise a pattern or validate a solution unless we ask them to?'

Here are two versions of the same problem, with and without scaffolding.

Unstructured version	Structured version
Design a tent	**Design a tent**
Your task is to design a tent like the one in the picture. These ends should zip together at night	Your task is to design a tent like the one in the picture. These ends should zip together at night Your design must satisfy these conditions:
It must be big enough for two adults to sleep in. Draw a diagram to show how you will cut the material to make the tent. Show all the measurements clearly.	• It must be big enough for two adults to sleep in (with their baggage). • It must be big enough for someone to move around in while kneeling down. • The bottom of the tent will be made from a thick rectangle of plastic. • The sloping sides and the two ends will be made from a single, large sheet of canvas. • Two vertical tent poles will hold the whole tent up. 1. Estimate the relevant dimensions of a typical adult and write these down. 2. Estimate the dimensions you will need for the rectangular plastic base. Estimate the length of the vertical tent poles you will need. Explain how you get these measurements. 3. Draw a sketch to show how you will cut the canvas from a single piece. Show all the measurements clearly. Calculate any lengths or angles you don't know. Explain how you figured out these lengths and angles.

(Swan and Burkhardt, 2012)

More information is given to pupils in the task on the right. This information forms a series of constraints, which will direct the activity of all pupils to be based on similar assumptions. There are also instructions to estimate, calculate and explain. The task can still diverge from this point, as pupils are not explicitly told which mathematics to use to solve the problem. Thus, a significant degree of problem solving is retained but the range of structural differences in pupils' solutions is likely to be lower in the scaffolded task.

In the example above, the success of the task was determined by adding layers of scaffolding. In contrast, Fawn Nguyen describes the removal of scaffolding from the following textbook question (Nguyen, 2013):

24. GOLF Jessica is playing miniature golf on a hole like the one shown at the right. She wants to putt her ball U so that it will bank at T and travel into the hole at R. Use similar triangles to find where Jessica's ball should strike the wall.

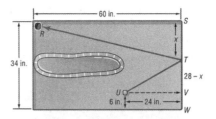

On reading this question, Fawn's initial reaction was that there is essentially nothing left for pupils to explore and figure out on their own. She argues that all the labels with numbers and variables conspire to turn pupils off from mathematics. Ironically, even though the problem tells pupils what to do (use similar triangles), the initial reaction of many was, 'I don't get it.' Fawn argues that this is because pupils have no opportunity to 'own' the problem.

Fawn deleted the entire question and, instead, gave each pupil this mostly blank piece of paper.

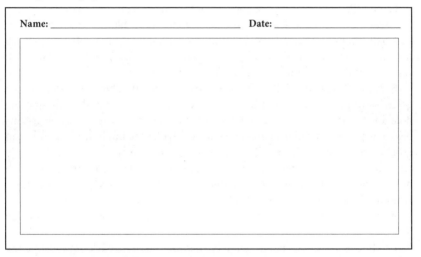

She then issued the following verbal instructions:

1. Make sure you have a sharpened pencil. Write your name and the date.
2. Inside the large rectangular border, draw a blob – yes, blob – with an area that's approximately one fifth of the rectangle's area. No one will die if it's not quite one fifth.
3. Next, draw a dot anywhere inside the rectangle but outside the blob. Label this dot H.

4. Now draw another dot – but listen carefully! – so there's no direct path from this dot to the first dot, H. Label the second dot B.

Here are some of the pupils' drawings:

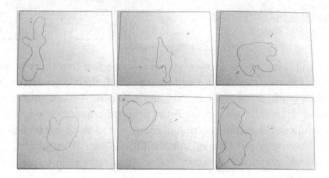

Fawn asked the class if they knew what they had just drawn. After a few silly guesses, she told them it was a miniature golf course: blob = water, point B = golf ball, point H = hole location. It is interesting how the relationships with her pupils and the task design are interwoven here – relaxed, informal language serves to maintain pupils' engagement.

Fawn then explained the scenario in more detail. The challenge, for the golfer, is to get the ball into the hole. They can't putt the ball directly into the hole due to the water hazard, so they need to make a bank shot. The discussions began as pupils started drawing paths for the ball. One pupil drew her solution quickly, then asked, 'is this right?' Fawn replied, 'I'm not sure, but that's my challenge to you. You need to convince me and your classmates that, if the ball hitting the edge right there will bounce out and travel straight into the hole. Does it? What can you draw to find out? What calculations are involved?'

As pupils embarked on the task, Fawn heard some of the following comments:

- The angle that the ball hits the border and bounces back out must be the same.
- Because we're talking about angles, something about triangles.
- This is like shooting pool.
- Right triangles.
- Similar right triangles.
- Do we need to consider the velocity of the ball?
- This is hard.
- I can't figure out how to use the right triangles.

- Similar right triangles because that'll make things easier.
- Even though it's more than one bounce off the edges, I'm still just hitting the ball one time.
- Happy Gilmore!

Pupils were engaged in significant amounts of struggle, but Fawn resisted the urge to help too much, recalling that she personally had struggled with some of the diagrams! Making an attempt herself, based on a pupil's diagram, allowed her to show the class that even she didn't find the task easy. I like this approach, as it strengthens the idea of a classroom community doing mathematics together – none of us has all the answers and ideas immediately, even if the teacher has more experience.

With this problem, pupils need to realise that the angle of incidence is equal to the angle of reflection. Some pupils may bring this knowledge with them and, if so, we can allow them to share it with the rest of the class.

In Fawn's lesson, pupils used many different approaches to address the problem; some measured the sides and found proportions to create similar triangles, others simply tried to 'eyeball' an angle that might work and then tried having the ball bounce off the borders at paired angles until it went into the hole. One pupil had angles of 90°, 33° and 63° inside a triangle (shown below)! Was this due to misuse of the protractor or not knowing the sum of angles in a triangle? This is a good example of a situation where probing questions can be used in the moment to support learning. Another pupil solved the entire problem using constructions with a straight edge and compasses. Towards the end of the lesson, Fawn made space for pupils to share their strategies and make comparisons between ideas and approaches.

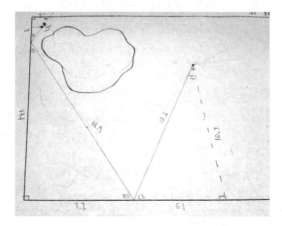

I agree with Fawn that none of this thinking and sharing would have occurred if she had given pupils the original 'problem'. Instead of doing a routine question on similar triangles, pupils had a genuine opportunity to behave mathematically and devise their own strategies.

Fawn acknowledged that some of her pupils were still struggling and working to find the correct bank shot(s) as the lesson drew to a close, but they were given the chance to struggle. Not one of them said, 'I don't get it'.

Linking with other activity - bringing topics together

Gerry McNally shared the following task, which brings together ideas of perimeter, ratio and fraction.

> The diagram below shows a composite shape created by joining a regular pentagon and a regular hexagon along a common side.
>
>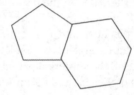
>
> Let the perimeter of the pentagon be P, the perimeter of the hexagon be H, and the perimeter of the composite figure be C.
>
> Some questions:
>
> Set 1:   If P = 15, what are the values of H and C?
> If H = 9, what are the values of P and C?
> If C = 3, what are the values of P and H?
>
> Set 2:   If P = 6, what are the values of H and C?
> If H = 5, what are the values of P and C?
> If C = 5, what are the values of P and H?
>
> Set 3:   If P = 1, what are the values of H and C?
> If H = 1, what are the values of P and C?
> If C = 1, what are the values of P and H?
>
> Set 4:   If P = p, what are the values of H and C?
> If H = h, what are the values of P and C?
> If C = c, what are the values of P and H?
>
> Set 5:   If $P = \dfrac{5}{6}$, what are the values of H and C?
>
> If $H = \dfrac{9}{5}$, what are the values of P and C?
>
> If $C = \dfrac{6}{5}$, what are the values of P and H?

Before reading on, have a go at this task – there is a lot going on.

At the outset, there is thinking to be done around the properties of the shapes and the idea of perimeter. I found myself coming back to those ideas repeatedly as I progressed through the task. I told Gerry that, when I tried the task, I knew I had P, H and C as well as the side lengths $\frac{P}{5}$ and $\frac{H}{6}$, so I created a table working with this information. Depending on the value I started with, I could identify the other values using the columns in my table.

Gerry replied that he used a different process: he established the ratio as being 5 : 6 : 10, then used whichever value he had to work out the other two, repeating this process for each of the questions. When he said this, I realised I had paid no attention to the ratio 5 : 6 : 10 in my work: I had simply stepped around my table, thinking about proportional relationships but not making direct links with my thinking about ratio. Gerry explained that he was quite content for me to do that, at least initially:

> *That is what I want a task to be. I want you to be able to do it. I want you to ask what you learned in doing it, but then also ask if there is a different way you could do it. Is there a more economical way of doing it? Is there a way that makes more sense?*

This is where discussion, and not working in isolation, are important. I took a lot from the task but could perhaps have got there more easily.

In Set 3, there are questions where each variable (P, H and C) is 1. Gerry explained that, for him, this is a general way of showing a ratio and helping pupils to understand the corresponding values, based on one of the variables being unitary.

Gerry advises against using a worksheet that looks like the one above. Instead, he prefers to reveal each set of questions in turn. The later sets can then be used to stretch pupils who have completed the other tasks, allowing them to explore the problem in more depth.

Gerry makes the following wonderful point:

> *I forget a lot. I can do a task and forget how I did it. As such, this influences my thinking about mathematics not being something that you have to remember. I hear a lot of talk about retention, but my question is, what is it that you want pupils to retain? Is it every single detail of what they have done? Maybe you want them to retain a sense of, 'I can't remember how I did that before, but I can remember I did it and therefore I would be able to do it again.' That would be a success to me. That is, it is about generating ideas. It's not always about reproducing.*

Planning rich activity from a routine starting point

Stein *et al.* (2009) describe an excellent example of changing a task to encourage more mathematical activity. The original task, typical of many found in textbooks, is as follows:

> Martha is re-carpeting her bedroom, which is 15 feet long and 10 feet wide.
>
> How many square feet of carpeting will she need to purchase?

This is a single-step procedural task with some language around it for context. Little depth of thought is required and the pupil is unlikely to gain any new insights into area from working on this task. Consider the contrasting problem below:

> Ms Brown's class will raise rabbits for their spring science fair. They have 24 feet of fencing with which to build a rectangular rabbit pen to keep the rabbits.
> - If Ms Brown's pupils want their rabbits to have as much room as possible, how long would each of the sides of the pen be?
> - How long would each of the sides of the pen be if they had only 16 feet of fencing?
>
> How would you go about determining the pen with the most room for any amount of fencing? Organise your work so that someone else who reads it will understand it.

(Stein, Smith, Henningsen and Silver, 2009)

This second task requires significantly more thought at a problem-solving and conceptual level, while incorporating significant opportunities for pupils to practise procedures. The task uses some of the ideas of task reversal discussed previously.

I have used this task several times with classes and found it to be an excellent basis for much rich activity. At first glance, there is significantly more text to process. I suggest giving pupils time to read the problem, before discussing in pairs or as a whole class to clarify the expectations of the task and to share ideas.

In attempting the original task, about Martha's carpet, I can predict fairly confidently that pupils will simply tell me the answer, having done a simple mental calculation, or will produce some working as follows:

$$A = l \times w$$
$$A = 15 \times 10$$
$$A = 150 \; square \; feet$$

With the second task, however, the solution strategies are more varied and pupils often generate different examples to get a sense of the problem. Immediately, they have to think hard about the underlying principles of area and perimeter. Some pupils are confused by the idea that the perimeter of 24 feet is shared between four sides, but we use only two of these sides to calculate the area. It is a great moment of cognitive tension.

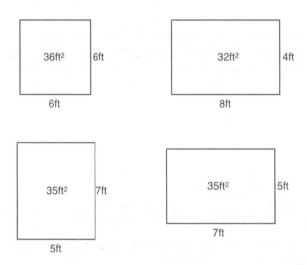

With some classes, this task is rich enough in itself – pupils work flexibly with both area and perimeter, thinking about them conceptually and practising the associated calculations. This is a nice example of purposeful practice as the calculations themselves are secondary to the principal aim of finding the largest possible area. Pupils need to start thinking systematically as they work on this task. I encourage this by asking them to continue to discuss their approaches with each other. It is common to see pupils try 'boundary examples' such as the 11 × 1 rectangle. This is a useful approach in many problem-solving activities, as I will highlight later when summing up. Walking around the room, I will offer prompts suitable to the particular class, which might include questions like:

- Do the sides need to have whole number lengths?
- Can they be something point something?

There will come a point in the lesson where I ask pupils if we can be more organised in our work and encourage them to consider how we might record our work systematically. Inevitably the idea of using a table arises.

Length	Width	Perimeter	Area
1	11	24	11
2	10	24	20
3	9	24	27
4	8	24	32
5	7	24	35
6	6	24	36
7	5	24	35

This is the basis for all sorts of discussion – for example, there is the invariance of the perimeter but the changing area. Depending on the class, I might allow pupils to agree that we have reached a conclusion about the maximum area. With other classes, this might be the start of an investigation into patterns with 'second differences' such as the area.

11		20		27		35		36		35
	+9		+7		+5		+3		+1	
		−2		−2		−2		−2		

A powerful follow-up task is to ask pupils to illustrate the areas in a graph, as shown below.

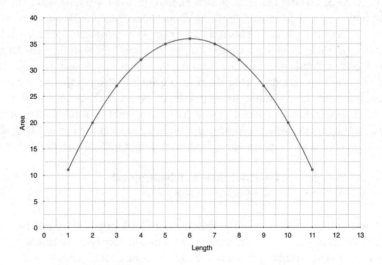

When working with younger pupils, this adds weight to the argument that we have found our maximum. With older pupils, the links to quadratics will hopefully be apparent. As such, this can be used as a pre-quadratics task to sensitise pupils to this sort of function. Alternatively, if used after pupils have learned about quadratics, there is likely to be a moment of 'wow! It's a parabola!' The task can then veer off towards finding the equation of the curve, finding roots, axes of symmetry and turning points, etc. For more advanced pupils, the problem can be reposed in terms of algebra and turned into a calculus maximisation problem.

I share this sequence here to make the point that we can start lessons with relatively low threshold problems and then move on to a variety of paths, all the while maintaining a narrative around some problem. This task is excellent for teaching functional relationships and helping pupils to see the reasons why we learn about tabulation, formulation and graphing. Of course, there is potential to go off-piste and we may not wish to do this regularly within the constraints of the curriculum. More scaffolding in the instruction can direct pupils towards the activities in which we want them to engage.

Contrasting the two tasks, it is clear that:

- the first problem can be solved by knowing and using the area formula, while this formula alone is not sufficient to solve the fencing task
- the first task does not lead to a generalisation, while the fencing task does – we can express the generality about the relationships in words or we can move to a symbolic representation
- the first task cannot be started by a pupil who does not know the formula for area, while there are many ways of entering the fencing task, such as sketches on squared paper.

Standing on the shoulders of giants

The most common source of tasks is my work with pupils. Typically, some error or lack of understanding will motivate me to create a resource to support learning. In the example below, however, the motivation was a desire for efficiency. It is often difficult to come up with a novel task layout or template, but we should remember there is no requirement to do this. Learning from Malcolm Swan, I chose to build on something that already exists: I decided to apply the principles and layout that Malcolm frequently used in the Standards unit (Swan, 2005) to create my own task. Doing this increased my chances of successfully writing a good task, compared with attempting to come up with an original idea of my own. Much of the cognitive heavy lifting has already been done, in terms of how to make these tasks work. This section is an account of standing on the shoulders of one of the greatest task designers ever to live.

$$y = \frac{x^2 + 1}{3x + 2}$$

$$y = \frac{1}{x^2 - 3x - 4}$$

$$y = \frac{x^2}{x - 2}$$

$$y = -\frac{x^2}{x + 3}$$

$$y = \frac{6x}{3x + 2}$$

$$y = \frac{x}{x - 2}$$

$$y = -\frac{10x}{2x + 3}$$

$$y = -\frac{5x}{x + 3}$$

$$y = \frac{x^3}{x^2 - 3x - 4}$$

$$y = \frac{1}{x - 2}$$

$$y = \frac{x}{x^2 - 3x - 4}$$

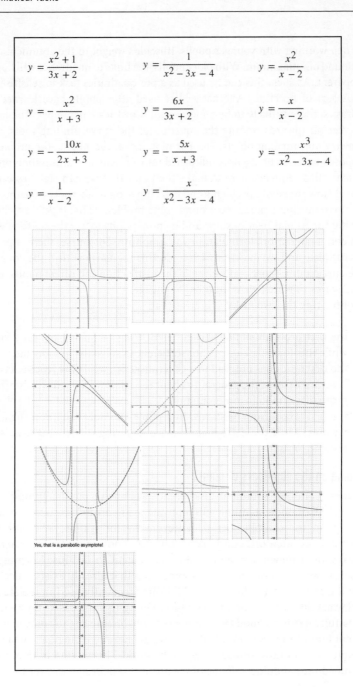

Yes, that is a parabolic asymptote!

I wrote the task above based on the assumption that there will have been some prior teaching, which has conveyed the following key facts:

- **Vertical asymptotes:** Occur when the denominator is equal to zero.
- **Horizontal asymptotes:** Division of coeffcients of terms with highest power, if the degrees are equal. This gives a horizontal asymptote. There is also the common case of $y = 0$ to consider.
- **Oblique asymptotes:** Long division is usually required, but we can get a rough sense of the asymptote by dividing terms of the highest power in the numerator and denominator.

At this level of mathematics, there is so much complexity and depth that it is hard for pupils to get a sense of ideas. Becoming procedurally fluent in all of the techniques at this level is a challenge in itself. Pupils may need to do a lot of lengthy practice to get a true sense of the principles underlying some topics. This rationale inspired me to write an asymptotes task. I didn't want pupils to have to do much (if any) written mathematics, until near the end of the task. Instead, I wanted them to encounter the key decision-making process repeatedly, in quick succession. This doesn't happen when working through full questions, since there are several steps in the 'normal' process:

- Establish the asymptote equation using algebra.
- Find the behaviour as the curve approaches the asymptote.
- Sketch the asymptote and function.

It can take pupils a significant amount of time to complete a single standard question and they may become bogged down in the technical details without developing a non-procedural appreciation of asymptotes. However, we can establish a great deal without doing any working at all. The intention with this task is to reduce the technical demand so pupils can focus on the key ideas instead. I decided to use a matching task so that most of the asymptotes and graphs are generated for pupils; this will enable them to focus on spotting patterns, connections and structure.

One of the things I learned from Malcolm Swan's work on the Standards unit (Swan, 2005) is always to leave a few cards blank. This means that the final matches cannot be made by a simple process of elimination. Here, there are two functions with no corresponding graph on a card, so pupils will have to generate possible graphs by themselves. It is not my intention for pupils to do this using algebra; instead, they simply need to sketch a rough but sensible graph based on what they have picked up from the rest of the task.

There is an assumption that the majority of pupils engaging with mathematics at this level are interested in the subject and might pursue their study of it as part of a mathematics or related degree at university. As such, I like to create opportunities for them to go slightly beyond the bounds of the curriculum and to think deeply and richly about ideas. These opportunities give them a chance to behave mathematically, while at the same time potentially strengthening their understanding of the principles that govern the topic they are working on. Anne Watson and John Mason refer to the 'example space' – that is to say, the range of examples pupils have encountered that relate to some idea. By extending this a little, I hope to provide some more insight – for example, there is a real challenge at the end of the asymptotes task. I have included a graph of a function with a parabolic asymptote. In Scotland, this is not assessed at school level; however, the thinking is accessible if pupils understand that the result of the long division is a quadratic, since all they then need to do is produce a polynomial of degree 4 in the numerator and with a quadratic in the denominator.

If this task had used thoughtlessly varied vertical asymptotes, the complexity would have been greatly reduced: it is easy to see vertical asymptotes and pupils would have matched using this. Instead, I chose to use some variation theory in the design of the task, so there were several rational functions with the same vertical asymptotes – for example:

$$y = \frac{1}{x-2} \qquad y = \frac{x}{x-2} \qquad y = \frac{x^2}{x-2}$$

This means pupils will have to focus on some other key features to refine their decisions. The final step before using this task is to randomise the cards: when I first write such a task, I create the cards in corresponding order, so the two grids match up with each other. This helps me keep track and also serves as an answer grid.

Principles for task design

One of the most challenging aspects of task design is that there is no set of instructions to build effective tasks. This is why teachers will benefit from using templates or learning about tactics for modifying existing tasks – just as I did with the asymptotes task, we can all draw on the thinking of others. It would be fantastic if we had a set of overarching principles for task design that we could break down as a flow chart, follow the steps and finish with something worthwhile, but alas. Even the question of what makes an effective task is controversial – there are those who outright dismiss problem-based approaches and others who would never advocate using a drill exercise with pupils. We all have different guiding principles, depending on our beliefs about what mathematics is and how it should be learned.

I asked Colin Foster for his thoughts on task design principles.

I'd love task design to be at the point where we have clear principles. It would be wonderful to choose to follow one set of defined principles or to follow an alternative set of principles, each of which would lead to different tasks. Even better would be if we could empirically see what the differences are when these tasks are used in the classroom. However, I don't think we are at that point yet.

Colin's experience of using task design principles has been reflective in nature. It has been about looking back at a task that has been written and thinking, 'well, I suppose you could describe what I've done like this.' Colin suggests that what made Malcolm Swan such an excellent task designer was his vast amount of experience, insight and a natural intuition for what a task could achieve.

In this section, I will discuss a range of different design principles, which can be used in a reflective manner as Colin suggests. For instance, Malcolm's own principles operate on a macro level, encompassing many types of task. In other cases, the principles could become part of a teacher's way of working. Dan Meyer's principles can be used to check whether a task meets the criteria but can also be used from the outset of design as they are specific to a certain style of task.

While there is some overlap in the principles, each set offers different ways of thinking about task design. As teachers, we need to consider our purposes in task design and whether we intend to work on procedural fluency, conceptual understanding, developing mathematical behaviours and problem solving or some combination of these.

Malcolm Swan

Writing in Collaborative learning in mathematics (Swan, 2006), Malcolm Swan makes a case for concept development lessons centred on a 'conflict and discussion' approach, rather than an expository or discovery approach. He provides evidence for the efficacy of such approaches, rooted in a connectionist orientation, and their advantages over other approaches when developing conceptual understanding. (It is noted, however, that the materials had differing outcomes when used by teachers with a more transmission or discovery orientation.)

Swan's principles are listed below. It is notable that they describe the activity arising from the task rather than the surface features of the task (such as the template used). What the pupil is thinking about is the fundamental concern, and the teacher is pivotal in supporting this activity.

Activities should be focused on particular conceptual obstacles

This allows conversations to converge, rather than facilitating diverging discussions, as might occur in discovery lessons. One should not pose too many questions in a lesson, as might happen in transmission lessons.

Activities should be designed to focus attention on general, structural features

That is, the focus should be on these structures rather than on task-specific features such as particular numbers. Tasks should not be open to superficial mechanical methods for tackling them. Some suitable types of activity are:

- Using intuition and then verifying using other methods:
  - Predict where the lines will fold. Now fold and check.
  - Complete the sequence 0.2, 0.4, 0.6… Repeat using a diagram approach.

- Question-generating tasks, where pupils create their own question using given constraints:
  - Make up two questions, with solutions, involving the following quantities: 20 miles, 20 mpg, 0.4 gallons, 8 miles, 8 mpg, 2.5 gallons.

- Interpreting a mathematical representation, or creating a corresponding representation:
  - Write a story to go with this graph.
  - Draw a bar model to go with this working.

- Evaluating errors made by others:
  - Spot the errors in a piece of work and explain the source of the error.

Activities should pose, or allow pupils to pose, questions that are challenging

Smoothing the path by gradually ramping questions in difficulty is useful in skill-acquisition activities but does not give results in conceptual lessons. These lessons should be social, with all pupils explaining, justifying, interpreting and proving.

Activities should encourage a variety of interpretations to emerge, become explicit and thus be compared and evaluated

Pupils should have opportunities to create and compare alternative explanations for mathematical ideas.

Questions or stimuli should be posed or juxtaposed in ways that create a tension that needs to be resolved

Inconsistencies which arise create an awareness in pupils that something needs to be learned. For instance, asking pupils to add one third to one quarter might result in answers such as two sevenths from pupils who have forgotten the 'process'. Asking pupils to verify using a calculator creates the tension.

Activities should provide multiple opportunities for meaningful feedback to the pupil on his or her interpretations

This traditionally comes from the teacher or from peer marking but is often superficial in nature, focusing on a number of marks. In the most successful lessons, pupils provided their own feedback through their interaction with tasks with the features listed above. Encountering a tension gave pupils a sense that 'something was wrong' and served as the basis for reflection. Group discussions may vary in depth and quality, but the teacher can encourage more precise articulation of thinking.

Activities should be followed by some form of whole-class discussion in which new ideas and concepts are made explicit and institutionalised

This requires an atmosphere of mutual respect where conflicting ideas are valued, points are not laboured and no one individual is allowed to dominate. There is no evidence to support the idea that pupils will remember 'incorrect explanations' (a concern among some teachers). Using a 'snowball' discussion strategy (having pupils pair up to discuss, then join with another pair, before reporting to the whole class) has the effect of 'disembodying' ideas from individual pupils and making them communal property.

Activities should provide opportunities to 'consolidate' what has been learned through the application of the newly-constructed concept

This can be done in many ways. For example, pupils could identify and correct mistakes in completed work, then explain these issues to the originator.

Malcolm noted that the 'conflict discussion' approach to teaching is much more demanding, in terms of the classroom management involved, than more conventional lessons. Taking this into account and thinking about how such lessons might work in classrooms where teachers have a transmission perspective were key considerations in coming up with tasks that use these principles.

Malcolm created the following sorts of task to embody these principles:

Comparing representations	As exemplified in the asymptotes task earlier.
Evaluating the validity of mathematical statements	Order doesn't matter for division: $a \div b = b \div a$
Diagnosing and correcting common mistakes	In a sale, there is 20% off the price of a shirt. A customer buys two shirts. He thinks he should get 40% off the total price.
Resolving problems that generate cognitive conflict	Ask pupils to predict the area of a square after all side lengths are doubled. The area, of course, does not double.
Creating problems and connections between concepts and representations	Two sorts of task: ■ Type 1: Give pupils a partially-completed concept map for a topic and ask them to modify and/or extend it, using the encouragement to 'write down all you know'. ■ Type 2: Generate a problem from a set of constraints (as in the example above, relating to miles, mpg and gallons).

(Swan, 2006)

A refined version of these activity types can be found in *Improving learning in mathematics: challenges and strategies* (Swan, 2005). This indispensable resource includes many excellent examples.

Dan Meyer

Dan likes to use three-act mathematics tasks to introduce new ideas, as in the example we explored in the previous chapter. He suggests that a key concern for task design is to consider how the task is pitched. Is it aimed at a pupil who has already bought into the idea that maths is valuable? Or does it try to expose what is beautiful about mathematics? He uses different media to put pupils in a place where they can experience the question, so they get a sense of why the idea matters.

When choosing a context to introduce an idea, Dan reflects on the following questions:

- What is the idea I want pupils to learn?
- What feels necessary about this mathematical idea?
- What led to the development of this mathematical idea? Was it a need for computation, communication, something else? How can I help pupils to experience that need?
- What is interesting about this context?

Dan argues that it is important to consider pupils' existing knowledge about the new ideas: he suggests it is unwise to assume pupils know nothing about a mathematical idea, just because we haven't talked about it with them. After all, every pupil brings with them their own mathematical knowledge. Dan doesn't think pupils should be required to discover ideas from scratch, but he does want to draw on their prior knowledge. He argues that connecting with their existing ideas makes his formal teaching easier. If we simply tell them new information, we might be interfering with old ideas – and this interference cannot be noted by the teacher in a 'telling' lesson. If pupils have previously encountered, and made some meaning of, the algorithms, symbolism, language or techniques that will arise in the new lesson, teachers should seek to establish what pupils already believe to be true.

Dan suggests that we need to consider the nature of the teacher–pupil dynamic carefully:

> When we communicate that we don't want to hear pupils' ideas, we communicate that their ideas are not valuable. By extension, we are communicating that they, as people, are not valuable. I am conveying that the person who is valuable is me.

As in the example from Fawn Nguyen, Dan doesn't like to pre-mathematise the contexts. An absence of numbers and formulae allows teacher and pupils to co-construct the mathematisation of the problem. This can lead to discussion around prompts such as:

- What might be helpful?
- What's your best guess?

It will then be possible to build a vibrant lesson around these ideas.

Dan argues that the role of the teacher, through pedagogy and knowledge of mathematics, is to bring pupil ideas together. How are they the same? How are they different? Once ideas have been shared and pulled together, the teacher should then focus pupils' attention on purposeful reflection, using the simple yet powerful prompt, 'what have we learned?'

While Dan is famous within the mathematics community for his approach, he emphasises that he values fluency and automaticity:

> *I think the people who say they don't value fluency can't be sincere – compare this to driving a car; it depends on the fluency and automaticity of bringing together lots of small actions which were once upon a time very difficult. Practice is important. My ability to think deeply about mathematics requires the automatic deployment of so many ideas.*

Dan's main concern is about how and when pupils experience practice. Are they told that how quickly they can perform the calculation is what matters? Is practice considered to be the main event in the lesson, or a supporting experience? Dan compares mathematics learning to sport. The practice in sports is often quite purposeful but is never as exciting as playing an actual game. In sports, pupils understand that practice supports their ability to play the game. In mathematics, for many pupils, practice is the game. I agree with Dan here: many pupils get to do all of the practice but never truly get to play the game.

Dan summarises his thinking on his blog dy/dan

1. Perplexity is the goal of engagement.
2. Concise questions are more engaging than lengthy ones.
3. Pure maths can be engaging. Applied maths can be boring.
4. Use photos and video to establish context, rather than words, whenever possible.
5. Use stock photography and stock illustrations sparingly.
6. Set a low floor for entry, a high ceiling for exit.
7. Use progressive disclosure to lower the extraneous load of your tasks.
8. Ask for guesses.
9. Make maths social.
10. Highlight the limits of a pupil's existing skills and knowledge.

(Meyer, 2012)

Laurinda Brown and Alf Coles

Over many years, Laurinda Brown and Alf Coles have developed a set of principles around a way of working, which focus on the utilisation of a task, the role of the teacher and the activity in which pupils will engage. In their paper, 'Task design for ways of working: making distinctions in teaching and learning mathematics' (Coles and Brown, 2016), Laurinda and Alf discuss these principles and some ideas for teaching. Here I outline the principles and take one example from the paper to highlight the thinking:

The seven principles

1. Start with a closed activity (which may involve teaching a new skill).
2. Consider at least two contrasting examples (where possible, images) and collect responses on a 'common board'.
3. Ask pupils to comment on what is the same or different about contrasting examples and/or to pose questions.
4. Have a challenge prepared in case no questions are forthcoming.
5. Introduce language and notation arising from pupil distinctions.
6. Have opportunities for pupils to spot patterns, make conjectures and work on proving them.
7. Have opportunities for the teacher to teach further new skills and for pupils to practise skills in different contexts.

An example task

The task below, 'Equable shapes', exemplifies these design principles. It begins with two shapes drawn on the board:

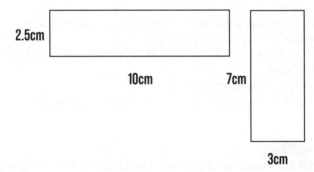

These shapes are two contrasting examples. With this image on the board, the teacher asks pupils, 'what is the same and what is different'. Pupils may or may not need support in remembering that ideas of area and perimeter can be used to judge the size of rectangles. This awareness leads the teacher to offer a closed task: to find the area and perimeter of each shape. The answers to this question are:

> 10 cm by 2.5 cm rectangle: area = 25 cm², perimeter = 25 cm
> 7 cm by 3 cm rectangle: area = 21 cm², perimeter = 20 cm

Pupils are asked to comment on anything they notice that is the same or different. A pupil will usually notice that, for the first rectangle, the values for area and perimeter are the same. At this point, the teacher introduces the label 'equable' as a name for the 10 × 2.5 cm rectangle. The teacher can then ask pupils what questions they could pose and gather ideas on the board.

Next, the teacher can present a prepared challenge, if these questions have not already arisen:

- What other equable rectangles can we find?
- Are there equable shapes that are not rectangles?

If the task continues to focus on rectangles, there will be opportunities for pattern spotting, generalising, algebra and conjecture. Depending on the direction in which the activity goes, skills may need to be taught to support pupils in solving linear equations, using Pythagoras' theorem or using trigonometry, all while focused on the idea of finding equable shapes.

Tom Francome and Dave Hewitt have worked closely with Laurinda and Alf. They offer five additional principles for the exploration of tasks:

1. Opportunities to gain further insights in related areas of maths.
2. Pupils to have an element of choice.
3. Opportunities to notice mathematical patterns and relationships and make conjectures.
4. Opportunities to justify and prove.
5. Mathematical situations that can be adapted and extended.

Better mathematics

The report *Better mathematics* (Ahmed, 1987) focused specifically on working with lower-attaining pupils and it is useful to review some of its key messages here.

In the paper, a college lecturer involved with the study contributed the idea of junk food versus junk mathematics:

Food for Thought	
Junk food	*Junk mathematics*
There is a lot of it about.	See most school textbooks.
All the preparation is done for you by someone else.	This is done by the author or teacher – all the nasties are removed.
The instructions for use are simple and laid out in steps.	See most textbook questions.
It is superficially attractive but turns out to lack flavour.	It looks well-structured and appears logical, but is dull and lacks substance.
It does you little good; it tends to pass through quickly.	Pupils are unable to retain or apply it in new contexts.
All the real nutrient is removed and substitutes have to be added.	It offers no real life situations but invents and contrives them.
DANGER: HEALTH WARNING **Junk mathematics can seriously damage your pupils.**	

The report also listed some common classroom actions which restrict pupils' mathematical development.

1.	The subject is broken down into 'easily digestible' topics.	Teachers often lament that pupils do not see and use links between different areas of the subject. When it is considered that, in the 'real world', mathematics does not come in the small fragmented packages that so frequently exist on our syllabuses (e.g. 'Perimeter' and 'Area'), it is not surprising that pupils are unable to get a useful overview, or see relationships.
2.	There is an over-concern to simplify, by breaking general ideas into seemingly unrelated stages.	The point of the overall task in hand is often obscured when step-by-step instructions are provided, for example, when a pupil neatly sets out a long multiplication sum to multiply by 100.
3.	Difficulties are smoothed out for pupils by, for example, ensuring that awkward cases do not occur or that the numbers cancel or that the answer is not a fraction.	This presents a false view of the subject and can lead to the situation where unusual extensions of these easier cases are not recognised. It also restricts opportunities for pupils' own interesting mathematical questions of the kind below: • What is infinity plus one? • Is 0 a number? • What's the square root of a minus number then? • What does this - mean on my calculator?

4.	It is often assumed that techniques must be learned and practised before problems are mentioned.	This can lead to a lack of motivation, as well as to a lack of understanding and meaning. When pupils complain that they 'don't see the point of doing all these', they are often given a remote justification – 'You'll need it when you buy a carpet.'
5.	An idea that arises naturally or that has a ready-made context is often unconsciously mystified by over-explanation/exposition.	For example, spending a great deal of time and effort arriving at a rule for rounding off money to the nearest pound. Once again, this can lead not only to confusion but also to a loss of purpose and motivation.

Some of this is at odds with much of the current narrative in mathematics education. The point about breaking ideas into stages is particularly in vogue. While this can be a useful strategy for technical proficiency, we need to ensure that pupils have opportunities to bring the small steps together, if we chose to use such an approach.

The report expressed some characteristics for a task to be considered 'rich'. Once more, the activity in which pupils are involved is central. It is not the written task that is rich, but rather the teacher's pedagogical choices that can make the task rich.

To be considered 'rich', a task:

- must be accessible to everyone at the start
- needs to allow further challenges and be extendable
- should invite children to make decisions
- should involve children in:
  - speculating
  - hypothesis making and testing
  - proving or explaining
  - reflecting
  - interpreting.

- should not restrict children from searching in other directions
- should promote discussion and communication
- should encourage originality/invention
- should encourage 'what if?' and 'what if not?' questions
- should have an element of surprise
- should be enjoyable.

The report then outlines some practical strategies for generating mathematical activity, based on the principles above. One nice prompt suggested is, 'how many different ways?' For example, we might ask pupils, 'how many different ways can you work out 21 × 13?' This can be used effectively in the connectionist classroom.

Colin Foster

Colin has a desire to 'produce materials that will provide some degree of challenge to a more traditional mathematics teacher, so as to inspire them to risk moving away from their habitual practice' (Foster, 2015 [2]). There is a risk of such resources being written off as 'impractical', so the tasks need to be accessible, at least to start with. Like teachers, pupils who are not used to working in more open-ended ways may be turned off by sudden requests to work in a creative and exploratory manner. It is important for such tasks to 'hook' pupils and be appropriately accessible. Colin states that tasks should possess the following qualities:

Enticing	The task should be immediately appealing to pupils. Perhaps what is posed is counterintuitive, paradoxical or provocative, so that a resolution or response needs to be actively sought. Whatever situation is chosen as the starting point for the task, it should raise mathematical questions, either explicitly or by provoking pupils to ask those questions. Little clarification should be required from the teacher on what the task is about. Ideally, the teacher should be able to speak for just a few minutes at the start of the lesson – or perhaps not at all – before asking, 'does the task make sense?'
Accessible yet challenging	Colin states, 'an effective task must possess depth and challenge without appearing totally out of reach'. That is, low threshold, high ceiling. The task should allow pupils to have something definite to do, such as exploring particular cases. Although the solution must not appear obvious to learners, the level of difficulty should not intimidate. Pupils should feel that the resolution to the problem is within reach, even if they do not yet know a path to get them there. Throughout, it is important that there are multiple possible ways to proceed, so that learners do not feel there is 'one right pathway'.
Naturally extendable	Colin states, 'the task must not lead to a dead end and resolve itself too neatly, too soon'. The task must possess sufficient depth and richness, so that it is naturally extendable. These extensions should come with the potential for significant challenge and pupil creativity. Colin observes that when pupils begin to get used to working in open-ended ways, they frequently do not feel they have really 'begun' until they have constructed an extension task for themselves, perhaps by asking, 'what if…?' The degree of extendability is perhaps a function of the classroom culture in which the task is deployed. If pupils work in a conjecturing atmosphere, they are more likely to post meaningful extension questions for themselves, without teacher prompting.

Colin captures his way of thinking about such tasks with the 'convergent–divergent model' (Foster, 2015 [2]), in which:

- a **convergent** task has a single, correct answer, which may be arrived at by a range of different methods
- a **divergent** task is more open-ended and provokes a more diverse range of outcomes.

A task that follows the pattern described above has a convergent phase followed by a divergent phase.

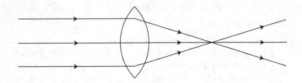

Colin adds:

> of course, learners' thinking (rays of light) is not influenced only by the task (lens) but by the whole social environment of the classroom in which the lesson takes place. I think of this as the medium (e.g. air) through which the rays travel, and which may also bend them – or even block them completely – according to its varying properties.

The way in which the teacher has established the mathematics classroom culture, the extent to which pupils are used to working in this way, and the range of knowledge and emotions that pupils bring with them all play a role in determining the effectiveness of a task.

Principles for traditional 'exercises'

I posted a question on Twitter asking: 'What are the characteristics of a 'good' textbook exercise for developing fluency in procedures?' Some people replied saying that such exercises have no place whatsoever. While it's fine to believe that, I think the reality for most classroom teachers is that there is a role for practice in the traditional sense, as part of a rich and varied diet of mathematical activities. The problem – as I have alluded to throughout this book – arises when practice exercises focused on procedure dominate at the expense of everything else. The selection of tweets below suggest principles we might use when creating a practice exercise.

Chris McGrane
@ChrisMcGrane84

I need your opinion.

What are the characteristics of a 'good' textbook exercise for developing fluency in procedures?

I'll start:

1. An appropriate ramping up of difficulty of questions

Gary Lamb @garyl82 · Apr 29
Replying to @ChrisMcGrane84 @mrbartonmaths and 14 others
Deliberate 'disrupters' to avoid mechanical auto-pilot?
Boundary style questions to exploit common mistakes or misunderstanding?
Not too many on a specific skill.
Qs with incorrect working for pupils to 'fix'.
Interleaved content from prior learning.
Deeper thinking tasks.

Sam Blatherwick @blatherwick_sam · Apr 29
Replying to @ChrisMcGrane84
Questions with similar procedures in different formats, questions with different procedures in similar formats. I'm thinking integration methods here.

Dave Taylor @taylorda01 · Apr 29
Replying to @ChrisMcGrane84
A starting point that gives students confidence and motivation to continue.

Emma McCrea @MccreaEmma · Apr 30
The best I came up with for trainees was this, but I'm not satisfied with it...

Clear, concise instructions
Focuses attention
Makes students think
Appropriate level of content
Steady progression

Tom Carson @offpistemaths · Apr 29
Replying to @ChrisMcGrane84 @mrbartonmaths and 14 others
Depends on what it's for. I like the exercises on mathshelper.co.uk for a couple of reasons. One is that the answers are right there beside each Q it becomes *about* something other than the answer. The other is, in my experience, they generate some energy to create more.

Mathematical themes

John Mason and Sue Johnston Wilder make a compelling argument for thinking about mathematics from the perspective of themes. Themes are recurrent throughout the subject and transcend topics. Instead of being ideas to be learned, they are awarenesses which pupils can become explicitly aware of. These themes are useful in the 'doing' of mathematics itself. They might act as techniques for the interrogation of some problem or phenomenon. They can also be used from the perspective of task design.

Freedom and constraint

This is where there is some element of choice in terms of the initial action, which is then constrained by the task, by the teacher redefining the problem, or by the mathematics itself. Consider the following chain of prompts.

- Create an addition with three numbers.
- Create another addition with three numbers where the total is less than 100 but greater than 50.
- Create another addition with three numbers where the total is less than 100 but greater than 50 and one of the numbers is greater than 100.

The degree of constraint is increased in each prompt, focusing pupils' thinking on some specific consideration each time.

Sometimes we are constrained by the mathematics itself. For example, when drawing a triangle, the first angle can have any value between 0 and 180°. The sum of angles in a triangle is 180°. Therefore, after the first angle, x, is drawn, the remaining angles are constrained as they must sum to 180 − x.

Invariance in the midst of change

Mathematics is full of relationships where some attribute varies as others remain invariant. For instance:

- Take any two odd numbers and add them together. The result will always be an even number. While there is variance in the numbers chosen, the results all share this invariant property.
- Consider the triangle drawing example mentioned above: we know that the sum of the angles is invariant regardless of the individual angle sizes.
- In quadratic theory, we know that for any parabola with a discriminant less than zero there will be no real roots. While the actual value of the discriminant may vary (it may be any number below zero), the geometric result will be invariant.

The idea of variation theory was popularised in Europe by the 2004 article from Lingyuan Gu *et al.* (Gu, Huang and Marton, 2004). This theory focuses on the intentionality of teaching. First, it is about directing pupils' attention towards structure and relationships. In addition, it can be used to establish the principles that govern those relationships. We aim for pupils to develop awareness of relationships and to discern principles through variations in their experience of some object of study.

Watson and Mason offer contrasting exercises in which pupils have to find gradients of straight lines (Watson and Mason, 2006). One of these exercises is shown below.

Find the gradient between each of the following pairs of points.			
(i)	(4, 3) and (8, 12)	(ii)	(−2, −3) and (4, 6)
(iii)	(5, 6) and (10, 2)	(iv)	(−3, 4) and (8, −6)
(v)	(−5, 3) and (2, 3)	(vi)	(2, 1) and (2, 9)
(vii)	(p, q) and (r, s)	(viii)	(0, a) and (a, 0)
(ix)	(0, 0) and (a, b)		

This is Watson and Mason... but adapted from
Backhouse & Houldsworth, 1957

In this case, from a procedural perspective, we can see that all technical variations of the question are encountered at least once. Pupils are asked to generalise a formula and to contend with two special cases that occur. The exercise moves attention towards the concept of a line, rather than gradient being a number without meaning.

The second task has less technical variation but focuses attention on the meaning of gradient specifically. On the face of it, the only variance here is that of the second x-coordinate in each pair.

Find the gradient between each of the following pairs of points.			
(i)	(4, 3) and (8, 12)	(ii)	(4, 3) and (4, 12)
(iii)	(4, 3) and (7, 12)	(iv)	(4, 3) and (3, 12)
(v)	(4, 3) and (6, 12)	(vi)	(4, 3) and (2, 12)
(vii)	(4, 3) and (5, 12)	(viii)	(4, 3) and (1, 12)

When the pair (4, 3) and (4, 12) is encountered, the technical practice falls down as pupils have to contend with division by zero! I have found this exercise to be particularly useful when I ask pupils to simultaneously plot the line segments as they find each gradient. As pupils progress through the exercise, the lines they draw change from sloping upwards, to vertical, to sloping downwards. Thus, excellent conversations around the relationship between the numerical gradient value and the properties of the lines can arise. For instance, the steeper the line, the larger the absolute value of the gradient.

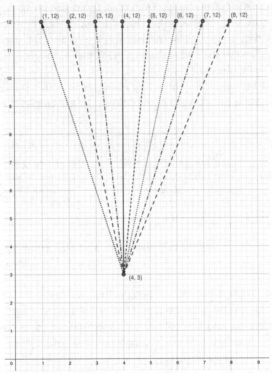

Extending and restricting meaning

This theme is evident in the history of the evolution of number and mathematics as an academic discipline.

Consider the natural numbers 1, 2, 3, 4 etc. The need for a placeholder and a representation of nothingness led to the idea of 0, which in turn led to the whole numbers 0, 1, 2, 3, 4 etc. Extending the meaning of number by posing the question, 'what comes before zero', we encounter the integers. The meaning of number is extended further as we consider the places between these whole numbers; thus, the rational numbers are introduced. Other types of number are later encountered, such as surds, and this leads to the irrational numbers. Meaning can be extended yet again by considering non-algebraic real numbers such as pi and e, which are called transcendental numbers. As the concept of number continues to expand, the ideas of imaginary numbers and complex numbers appear.

This idea of extending meaning also occurs when we consider the concept of powers. Once the idea of expressions such as 32 is well understood, this can be extended to consider 30, 3–1 , etc. Many teachers will use pattern spotting tasks to help pupils towards these new ideas. For instance:

$$5 + 4 =$$
$$5 + 3 =$$
$$5 + 2 =$$
$$5 + 1 =$$
$$5 + 0 =$$
$$5 + (-1) =$$
$$5 + (-2) =$$

By continuing the pattern, pupils will encounter the solutions of addition of a positive and negative integer, thus extending their understanding of what it means to add. (Note that this task also uses variance and invariance.)

We don't always extend the meaning of ideas; sometimes we restrict them instead, to create sub-classes of concepts. For instance, we can restrict triangles to have two equal angles, a sub-class we call the isosceles triangles. This sort of thinking is the basis of many classification tasks.

Doing and undoing

Whenever a question is asked, there is always a reverse problem waiting to be asked. 'What is 4 + 6?' is an example of a direct question. However, it is perhaps more interesting to ask the reverse question: 'Which two numbers can be added to give 10?' Often, reverse questions lead to a range of possibilities to be explored; in some cases, they give rise to new techniques to be learned.

Once pupils have mastered the techniques of applying the distributive law to a pair of algebraic binomial expressions, the obvious next step is to consider how this might be 'undone'. This gives rise to factorisation techniques. Similarly, on learning how to add algebraic fractions, pupils could be given the prompt, 'give some fractions that could have been added to give this answer'; this question is much more complex and gives rise to the more advanced skill of partial fractions.

It is often the case that the reverse problem is more 'interesting' and requires more sophisticated techniques. Consider calculus, for example, where it might be said that differentiation is 'brute force' technical strategy, whereas integration is an art form in the way in which we select and use strategies, identities and manipulations. In school, pupils are required to learn only a small range of simple strategies for differentiation. Integration, on the other hand, may require more challenging techniques such as integration by substitution or repeated integration by parts to undo what might have been a rather trivial product or chain rule question.

Final thoughts on themes

We now have four themes that can help us to make our teaching more impactful:

- Freedom and constraint.
- Invariance in the midst of change.
- Extending and restricting meaning.
- Doing and undoing.

It is important for teachers to be aware of these themes, as they can serve as the basis for the generation of tasks and rich questioning. They can be used to illustrate deep, rather than obvious, connections between topics and to highlight the nature of mathematics itself across topics.

So, questions such as:

- What is the undoing of this?
- How could we extend this?
- What is the variance here?
- What freedom and constraint exist here?

become part of the lexicon of mathematics classroom communities.

With repeated exposure and a developing awareness, pupils can begin to internalise these prompts for themselves. This is likely to be beneficial when undertaking an inquiry – the themes can serve as part of a framework for questioning and exploring.

For example, consider the prompt:

$$2^5 > 5^2$$

If this was presented to the class as the basis for some mathematical activity, which pupils were to lead, how might a pupil who is aware of these themes engage with it, compared with pupils who have not been educated in these awarenesses? What questions and lines of inquiry might arise? Which of the themes are applicable in this case? A pupil might suggest varying the values to test other cases. While considering freedom and constraints, the exploration could lead to investigation of negative or fractional values. Some pupils might look to the case that 'breaks' the prompt by considering the powers 0 and 1 (these are often powerful boundary examples).

Learner-generated examples

Anne Watson and John Mason offer a list of task strategies for pupils to generate their own examples (Watson and Mason, 2005). Learner generation requires pupils to exert significant energy in thinking about mathematical situations and the problems that may arise and is, therefore, a strategy that all teachers should be aware of and use.

I have selected and adapted some of these strategies for discussion here.

Make up an example

Asking pupils to give an example of a stated mathematical idea or scenario is a simple yet powerful teacher action. For example, teachers could say to a class:

- give me an equation of a quadratic
- draw an example of a pentagon.

A useful follow-up to these types of prompt is to add, '...and another, and another...' The discussions that arise will result in pupils gaining perceptions of what a mathematical object is and what the characteristics of a range of permissible changes involve. For instance, the first pentagon pupils produce is likely to be regular. Often, the second pentagon generated will also be regular but rotated somewhat. Some pupils will require prompting to consider irregular examples. Collating examples created by the class and then asking pupils to classify them, using whatever criteria they choose, brings to light what pupils see as the essential features of the idea at hand.

This type of task can be enhanced by adding constraint, for example, 'give me an equation of a quadratic with no real roots' or 'give me two fractions that add to $\frac{1}{10}$'. Again, the use of '...and another, and another...' as a follow-up can considerably enhance the task.

Make up a non-example

It is important to appreciate 'what is'. However, it is equally important to know the bounds of an object, so there is an appreciation of 'what is not'. For example, 'give me a pair of simultaneous equations that has no solution' or 'y = x passes through the origin. Give me the equation of a line that does not pass through the origin.'

Non-examples can also be used to expose the flaws in some articulation of mathematical ideas, with prompts such as, 'create an example where BODMAS doesn't work' or 'create a counter-example to prove that multiplying by 10 doesn't always mean adding on a zero'. Such prompts can be used to reveal the limitations of some commonly-expressed beliefs about mathematics.

Find

Each of the following prompts will trigger different expectations and generation.

- Find examples of...
- Find examples that...
- Find the example that...
- Find examples such that...
- Find all examples that...
- Find an example of... and another and another...
- Find an example that shows you understand how to use the technique for...
- Find the hardest / most complicated / simplest / easiest / strangest...

For instance:

- Find examples of regular polygons that tile the plane.
- Find examples of quadratics with zero as a coefficient of x, which you are able to factorise without using the quadratic formula.
- Find an example that shows you understand the technique for using the sine rule.

The nature of the thinking pupils must undertake is changed by the format of the prompt. That is to say, the outcome of a task varies depending on how the task is first considered.

Bury the bone

In Chapter 7, I related a story from Mike Askew: he described a task where teachers were asked to construct a story to go with a given calculation and struggled to do so. Watson and Mason call this idea 'bury the bone'. Other examples include:

- Tell me a story about a situation in which I would have to multiply 3 by 2.5
- The solution to a linear equation is $x = 5$. What could the equation be? Make easy, medium and hard equations.

Prompts such as those listed above can be written in advance and added to worksheets. However, it is often the case that these tasks are articulated verbally, in the moment, during lessons. If such prompts are internalised as available pedagogical actions, they can arise spontaneously during lessons as appropriate. You may wish to refer to the excellent booklet Questions and prompts for mathematical thinking (Watson and Mason, 1998), which provides many such examples for spontaneous tasks.

Spontaneous task design

Tasks are not necessarily written down. For instance, Tom Carson asked a class to create shapes with an area of 8 boxes. Some examples are shown below:

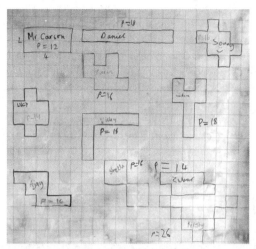

Tom had asked for these shapes at the end of a lesson and left them on the board. He started the next lesson by asking pupils to find the perimeter of each shape from the previous lesson. By doing this, he aimed to formatively assess their work on perimeter so he could then attend to pupils who were having difficulties; pupils often miss edges when finding the perimeter of composite shapes.

I asked Tom about writing tasks, to which he replied:

> At no point did I sit down and create a worksheet. It depends on what you mean by 'did I write this task?' Working to internalise Thinkers [Bills et al., 2018] and Questions and prompts [Watson and Mason, 1998] almost always allows me to create an appropriate task, at the appropriate time.

This is the crux of spontaneous task design.
Tom added some prompts to the images:

A. Zubair's shape is an octagon. Name everyone else's shape.
B. What is the biggest perimeter you can make with an area of 8 boxes?
C. What is the smallest perimeter you can make with an area of 8 boxes?
D. All the perimeters from yesterday were even numbers. Can you make a shape with an area of 8 boxes with an odd perimeter?

Prompt A is a result of Tom wanting to add some other layer of thinking to the lesson. The shapes are irregular, which initially causes pupils to rethink their ideas on polygons –most of the examples of polygons encountered in school, in architecture or in textbooks are regular. Pupils begin to ask themselves: 'What does it mean to be a polygon? Are any of these shapes not polygons?'

In undertaking this task, pupils had to make the distinction between perimeter and number of sides. Tom recalls that, 'it caused chaos – but in a good way! I had intended in getting through it all. But part A took 25 minutes.'

The lesson then took a spontaneous turn. Tom recalls:

> *I noticed one of the pupils creating the image below, in his book. The teacher part of me wanted to say, 'no, we are doing this.' But I managed to resist that urge.*

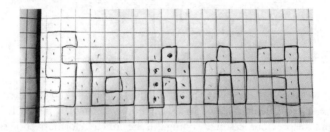

Tom realised this was a significant moment. The key focus of the learning was on perimeter and area. However, this context which had arisen was just as valid as what he had considered doing. So he wrote an alternative task, in the moment, for pupils to do:

Extra task

Sonny made his name out of shapes with an area of 8 boxes.
   a. What is the perimeter of each letter in his name?
   b. Make your name in the same way.
   c. What is the total perimeter of your name?
   d. Whose name would have the biggest and smallest perimeters in the class?

Tom then gave his pupils the option to do his task or move onto Sonny's task. Tom described the culture of this class, saying:

They adore owning the task. There is a culture of them coming out to the board and having them write their name next to their contribution on the board. A sense of pride. Kids who don't feel they are naturally very good at maths.

Tom explained that this same class regularly wouldn't talk to each other, but this task got them talking. Tom provided space for pupils to work on their own maths, just as Sonny had been doing. Why would you ever stop a pupil doing this? Natural engagement with the subject should be nurtured, encouraged and valued.

From a teacher's perspective, the key is to spotting opportunities for other tasks to arise in the moment. If we have internalised scaffolds for generating these spontaneous tasks, this way of working will be an available action during all lessons.

Tom's final thought is quite true of much task design: 'Designing tasks for other people or not for a specific class is so difficult. This task was related to my own pedagogy.' This is why, although we can use tasks off the shelf, we are likely to best meet the needs of our pupils if we are able to create and adapt tasks ourselves to complement these other resources.

Sequencing tasks

I have described tasks as being primarily about procedural fluency, conceptual understanding or problem-solving, while acknowledging that many tasks can serve multiple purposes. An important skill is being able to sequence tasks together. Dan Lewis and Gary Lamb are teachers who both write lovely task sequences.

Dan produced the tasks below.

Task 1
Are these sequences linear? Explain why/why not.
$5, 9, 13, 17, \dots$
$5, 8, 12, 17, 23, \dots$
$, , , , \dots$
$, , , , \dots$
$x, 5x, 9x, 13x, \dots$
$a, 2a, 4a, 8a, \dots$
$a, a^2, a^3, a^4, \dots$
$5\% \text{ of } 60, 15\% \text{ of } 60, 25\% \text{ of } 60, \dots$
$2a + b, 5a + 3b, 8a + 5b, 11a + 7b, \dots$

This task starts with some basic arithmetic sequences before proceeding to include fractions, algebra and percentages. Dan included these recently-encountered topics to provide some revision, in context, of these ideas.

Task 2

Sam represents her linear sequence as so:

Term 1   Term 2   Term 3

Without drawing any more patterns, what can you tell me about the linear sequence? What about pattern 4? Or pattern 10? Or pattern 100?

In this task, Dan connects with a visual representation. He explicitly asks pupils not to draw more patterns, so the focus is on the mathematical structure of the sequence.

He encourages pupils to discuss their thinking here and recalls that, when pupils were trying to express what the tenth term would look like, there was lots of arm waving and gesticulating as they expressed their thinking. Dan deliberately chose a simple picture as, in his experience, pupils struggle to pull out the mathematical structure if the picture is too 'busy'. With this layout, pupils made insightful comments such as, 'the number of dots at the top and the bottom is the same as the term number. So, we can just double the term number and add the spare dot in the middle.'

Task 3

Tom is generating the terms of a linear sequence. The sequence starts with 2. 135 is a term in the sequence. The term-to-term rule is '+7'. What is the position in the sequence of 135?

This task is an example of a classic working backwards task; in this case, the pupils have to establish the position of a given term in a sequence. Dan suggests that if he gave this to an older pupil, they might draw on algebra in finding the nth term, but he is equally happy for pupils to use simple arithmetic to calculate the answer here.

Task 4

Marie is generating the terms of a linear sequence. The sequence starts with 2. 79 is a term in the sequence. Her term-to-term rule involves an integer. How many different term-to-term rules could there be?

This is a richer task, which leads to the working backwards being more open in nature. Dan deliberately includes this as he is focused on shaping pupils' beliefs about mathematics. In this case, he aims to help pupils see that problems are not simply right or wrong; he achieves this by introducing an element of doubt through the use of the word 'could'.

Dan follows this sequence with the following task, which pupils work on in pairs. He asks them to complete the task on A3 paper.

On your sheet, in pairs, give an example of a **linear sequence** (including telling me the rule) where...

- the difference between terms is a decimal
- the difference between terms is a fraction
- the sequence is made of algebraic terms
- all terms are prime numbers
- the sequence is represented as a diagram
- all the terms are negative
- term 2 < term 3
- term 3 < term 2 < term 1.

How much detail can you give about these last two? What types of sequence must we always have for each question?

This task is more demanding than those typically found in textbooks, where pupils are given the first term and the rule and then asked to generate the sequence. In this task, there is an element of freedom for pupils to create their own sequences within the given constraints. As the constraints change, pupils need to think carefully about the related content. For the algebra prompt, Dan recalls how some pupils chose something 'safe' like x, 3x, 5x etc. while other pupils were more adventurous and wanted to show off what they knew. It is useful to draw these responses together and to challenge pupils to create 'another example', 'a harder example', 'an example nobody else will have' and so on. Again, Dan communicates the nature of mathematics to pupils through this task. Maths is, after all, a creative subject and this task leads pupils to create their own mathematics.

Gary Lamb often uses a three-part task structure as shown in the following examples. He usually uses such tasks after some initial work on a basic procedure, often through example-problem pairs and a short practice exercise.

In the fractions sequence below, Gary has written a series of tasks where pupils continue to practise the procedure, while beginning to develop more appreciation of the meaning of their calculations.

- In the first exercise, pupils have to realise that the resulting fraction needs to be improper to be greater than one.
- The second exercise demands more of pupils, forcing them to think about the relationships between fractions of different denominators.
- The final exercise is open-ended and allows pupils to pose (and solve) their own problems, which is a useful formative assessment strategy – it provides immediate insight into what the pupil considers to be straightforward and interesting examples. That is, it gives us an insight into the 'example space' pupils perceive. Gary likes to collect the questions generated by pupils and share them on the board so the whole class can work on them together. There are often some very creative questions posed by pupils!

EXERCISE **ONE**

1. Find a pair of fractions that **add** to give an answer **greater** than **1**.

2. Find a pair of fractions that **subtract** to give an answer **less** than **1**.

EXERCISE **TWO**

Using the whole numbers 1 - 10, at most **one time each**, fill in the boxes so that the sum is equal to 1.

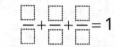

$$\frac{\square}{\square} + \frac{\square}{\square} + \frac{\square}{\square} = 1$$

EXERCISE **THREE**

Create a **straightforward question** and a **more interesting** question using fraction **addition** and **subtraction**.

In the expressions task below, various demands are made on pupils' thinking. This helps to develop flexible knowledge.

- In the first exercise, pupils are asked to suggest the missing coefficients. This focuses their attention on the role of positive and negative coefficients.
- The second exercise is a multi-step process where pupils need to draw on knowledge of perimeter and realise that collecting like terms is involved even though the question doesn't directly ask for this.
- The third exercise uses the same principles as in the fractions task.

EXERCISE **ONE**

What could the **missing** numbers be?

$$\square x + 5y - 6x + \square y = 7x + 6y$$

$$\square x - 5 + 2x + \square = -8x + 4$$

$$\square y + 5z + \square - 7y + \square z + 4 + 2z = 3y + z + 4$$

$$-x + \square x - 4x - 8x = 2x$$

EXERCISE **TWO**

If both shapes have the **same** perimeter, what expressions could the rectangle have for its **length** and **width**?

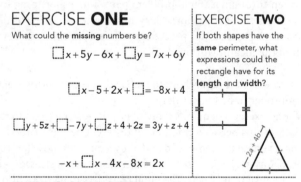

EXERCISE **THREE**

Create a **straightforward question** and a **more interesting** question that can be simplified by collecting like terms.

What struck me about the tasks Gary and Dan have written is that they arose in work designed for lower-attaining groups. A tragedy of many mathematics classrooms is that the tasks issued to lower-attaining pupils are almost entirely routine with low levels of demand. Not only does this give those pupils a false sense of what mathematics is, it also fails to provide the rich diet of tasks required for effective learning. All pupils need to engage with tasks from all three of the categories I have discussed. Routine practice is important but inadequate on its own – this is equally (especially) true for lower-attaining pupils.

Another excellent example of task sequencing comes from Luke Pearce. The following sequence on the area of triangles starts with pupils considering the triangle as the area of half a rectangle.

Areas of Triangles

Section A

1. a) Find the area of the rectangle to the right by counting squares.
b) What fraction of the rectangle is the triangle?
c) What is the area of the triangle?

Normally, in the UK, pupils would now go on to practise finding areas of right-angled triangles. However, the next two questions focus instead on parallelograms. According to Luke, the rationale for this came from something he heard about the Japanese curriculum. Every triangle is half of a parallelogram, but few are half of a rectangle. Indeed, the majority of triangles are not right-angled.

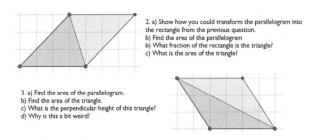

2. a) Show how you could transform the parallelogram into the rectangle from the previous question.
b) Find the area of the parallelogram
b) What fraction of the rectangle is the triangle?
c) What is the area of the triangle?

3. a) Find the area of the parallelogram.
b) Find the area of the triangle.
c) What is the perpendicular height of this triangle?
d) Why is this a bit weird?

As pupils continue to work through the task, it becomes clear that the focus is not on 'half base times height'. Instead, it is about perpendicular measurements.

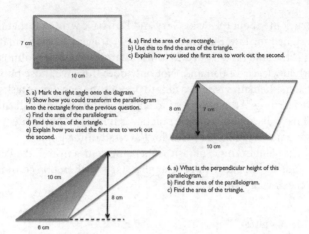

4. a) Find the area of the rectangle.
b) Use this to find the area of the triangle.
c) Explain how you used the first area to work out the second.

5. a) Mark the right angle onto the diagram.
b) Show how you could transform the parallelogram into the rectangle from the previous question.
c) Find the area of the parallelogram.
d) Find the area of the triangle.
e) Explain how you used the first area to work out the second.

6. a) What is the perpendicular height of this parallelogram.
b) Find the area of the parallelogram.
c) Find the area of the triangle.

Pupils working through Luke's task sequence have to engage with all forms of triangle – not just right-angled – from the beginning. This means their understanding of finding areas of triangles is potentially more resilient, because it can be applied to any triangle.

The task sequence progresses to questions that are much harder than those pupils would typically encounter in the first part of a UK textbook exercise on the area of a triangle. By making the initial task harder, Luke has ensured the resulting learning is generalisable to all triangles, instead of being an approach that works in only one situation. This enables Luke to include problems which pupils will need to address in a much more interesting way, as shown below.

Section B

For each triangle
a) Mark on any right angles.
b) Draw a rectangle or parallelogram around it.
c) Find the area of the rectangle or parallelogram
d) Hence find the area of the triangle.

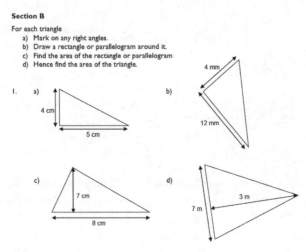

Section C

For each triangle:
   a) Mark on any right angles.
   b) Work out the area of these triangles using the formula $\frac{1}{2}$ base × perpendicular height

1.

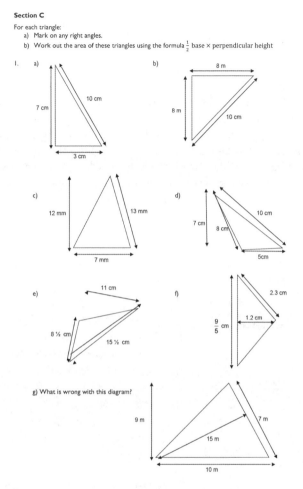

g) What is wrong with this diagram?

Don Steward

Over the past few years, the task writer I have turned to most often for resources and for inspiration has been Don Steward. Sadly, during the period of writing this book, Don passed away. He is certainly somebody I would have liked to speak to when writing the book. I recall sending Don some tasks a couple of years ago to discuss and he was kind in his response. It is a real regret that I never got to see one of his renowned CPD sessions.

The person who introduced me to Don's incredible work was Jo Morgan, via her Resourceaholic website. Jo has a multitude of links to Don's work on her website and shared some lovely anecdotes of both meeting and corresponding with Don over the years. She kindly agreed to select and discuss three tasks to showcase some of Don's work. The words around the following tasks are entirely from Jo.

Procedural fluency task

When my students had developed a reasonable degree of fluency in expanding single brackets, I added a step of complexity by asking them to expand and simplify expressions containing more than one set of single brackets. This is a common 'next step' in teaching this topic. I chose the Don Steward task below mainly because I like the direction in which it goes. The first part of the exercise is all about procedural fluency – lots of practice means ample opportunity for me to circulate around the room and look over my students' shoulders, identifying those who need help and addressing common mistakes. The second part of the exercise is different – it presents the opportunity for a bit more thinking.

simplification

a) expand the brackets and then simplify the expressions

1) $5(b + 5) + 7(b + 2) + 2(b + 1)$

2) $3(2a + 1) + 6(a + 3)$

3) $3(2m + 15) + 10(m + 1) + 4(5m + 2)$

4) $5(2n + 3) + 3(10n + 3) + ½ (6n + 20)$

5) $4(2t + 3) + 5(t + 6) + ½ (4t + 18)$

6) $15(3k + 1) + 2(17k + 1) + ½ (4k + 2)$

7) $6(5d + 8) + 3(4d - 5) + d + 1$

8) $8(p + 5) + 6(7p - 3) + 2(p + 1.5)$

9) $2(4h + 21) + 5(4h - 1) - 5(h + 1)$

b) six expressions:

$2(9b - 13a)$
$3(2b - 11a)$
$4(3a - 5b)$
$5(2a - 3b)$
$6(3a - b)$
$7(3a + 2b)$

1) which two sum to $4(3b - 2a)$?

2) which two add to $7(4a - 3b)$?

3) which three sum to zero?

4) which three add to $4(a - 2b)$?

So my students set off completing the first exercise. Being a busy time-stretched teacher, I hadn't prepared the answers in advance, so after circulating the room for a few minutes, I started working them out on the whiteboard. I had written down three answers when I noticed something lovely... there was a pattern.

$$14B + 41$$
$$12a + 21$$
$$36m + 63$$

The interesting – or perhaps worrying – thing was that even though some students were ahead of me in the exercise, not one of them had spotted this pattern. Perhaps it was more obvious to me because of the way I'd listed the answers on the board. Or perhaps I'm just well-practised at spotting patterns. I stopped the class and excitedly asked if they'd noticed anything in the answers. They looked at my list on the board. Slowly, a few students cottoned on. But only a few. This is quite revealing: I don't do enough pattern spotting with my students. They hadn't noticed something that was incredibly obvious to me. We have a long way to go!

Of course the pattern in the answers is delightful, and not only because I no longer had to work out the answers. When one student finished all nine questions in the first exercise, a quick glance at his page showed me that he'd made one mistake – I could tell immediately, because his answer didn't follow the pattern. What a clever marking mechanism Don built into this exercise! In hindsight, I could have asked my students to make up their own question that followed the pattern. That would have been a worthwhile task, I think.

He was clever, was Don Steward. Nowhere does he tell us that there's a pattern in the answers to this exercise. He left hidden Easter eggs in his tasks for teachers and students to discover and be delighted by. What a hero.

Conceptual understanding task

Back when I was a newly qualified teacher, I helped my students to understand negative indices using the division law. I would present them with two equivalent expressions and hope they would make sense of that equivalence. Something like this:

$$\frac{y \times y}{y \times y \times y \times y \times y} = \frac{1}{y^3}$$

And equivalently,

$$y^2 \div y^5 = y^{-3}$$

Hence,

$$y^{-3} = \frac{1}{y^3}$$

To me this seems crystal clear (that pesky curse of knowledge!) and it was only after a few years of teaching it this way that, inspired by an old SMILE resource, I realised that my students might understand the meaning of negative indices better by exploring patterns:

10^4	10 000
10^3	1000
10^2	100
10^1	10
10^0	?
10^{-1}	?
10^{-2}	?
?	?

Some students got it, but still I found that many students would later struggle with negative indices, because they were trying to remember a rule rather than actually understanding the concept.

At the same time, I struggled with my explanation of fractional indices. Again, I expected all of my students to understand an equivalence that seemed totally clear to me, but I was often left facing a room full of confused faces.

$$\sqrt{9} \times \sqrt{9} = 9$$
$$9^{\frac{1}{2}} \times 9^{\frac{1}{2}} = 9^1$$
$$\text{Hence, } 9^{\frac{1}{2}} = \sqrt{9}$$

Both fractional and negative indices are a bit tricky conceptually because pupils are often introduced to powers with a definition that later breaks. They are told that an index represents the number of times 'we multiply a number by itself'. But not in $25^{-0.5}$. This is complex.

Don Steward's 'Shifting bases' task, below, has a few different elements. However, I feel that what Don calls 'power lines' are the most interesting parts of this task. These power lines bring together ideas around fractional and negative indices, plus index laws and changing bases, in an accessible pattern-spotting exercise. Through this task and the ensuing class discussion, students can start trying to make sense of these fundamental and complex ideas.

comparing power lines (i)

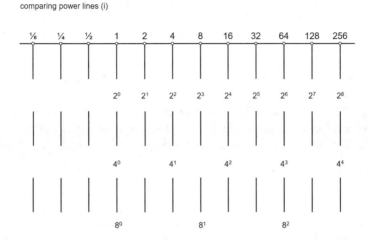

fill in the missing powers

Problem-solving task

Area mazes were not invented by Don Steward, but I came to know them through his blog. A teacher on Twitter asked how this question could be done without using fractions, and at first I was utterly confused.

find the missing lengths or areas
you should not need to use any fractions

(1)

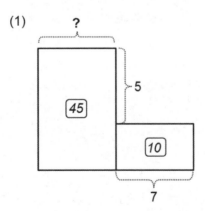

My 'usual' procedure took me to a fraction, so I assumed there must be some mistake. I tried to think differently – something I don't do often enough – and eventually spotted the wonderfully elegant approach that was intended. And that was it – area mazes became my new favourite thing!

These tasks move us away from 'area by formula' and take us down a route in which reasoning is king. They are delightfully satisfying, and lead to rich discussion and deep thinking.

Don Steward was incredibly creative and full of amazing ideas. He also worked hard to share the work of other great mathematicians, ensuring that puzzles like these made their way into our classrooms.

Conclusion

In this chapter, I have attempted to offer a range of principles, strategies and ideas for thinking about task design and modification. As in the rest of education, there is no simple answer. There is a lot of expert experience we can learn from and many excellent tasks we can use, but the most effective lessons will always come from teachers who understand how to react to their pupils on a day-to-day and moment-to-moment basis.

10 Conclusion

I offer some final thoughts on the nature of mathematics teaching and, in particular, tasks.

Tasks should focus attention beyond surface features

Tasks should provide opportunities for pupils to interact with the mathematics beyond the surface level features. Many procedural tasks keep pupil thinking rooted in the manipulation of abstract symbols, but mathematics has meaning and, as such, pupils should encounter and interact with this meaning. The nature of pupil activity has a significant effect on what pupils attend to and what they learn.

Connectionist perspective

It is important for pupils to make connections both within and across mathematical ideas. Teaching should draw on what pupils bring with them, but guide their attention towards new ideas. A blend of teaching approaches and tasks is required to help pupils make sense of mathematics. Telling is not entirely effective for conceptual teaching, while fluency is unlikely to result from an overly discovery-biased approach.

It is possible to start with a problem

As we have learned from several sources, it is perfectly valid to present a problem at the start of a lesson. The Japanese approach to problem-solving lessons, and the work of Dan Meyer, illustrate how new learning can emerge from a combination of collaborative whole-class discussion, individual productive struggle and appropriate exposition by the teacher. However, the selection of the problem matters – it needs to be within touching distance of pupils' current understanding.

Teachers play a key role in the 'success' of a task

Even a dry textbook exercise can result in a rich mathematics lesson if the teacher is sufficiently skilled. Teaching between the desks is essential. Responsive teaching, which takes account of the whole class and individuals, can ensure high levels of cognitive activity for every pupil. Engagement with tasks provides a shared mathematical activity from which discussion and reflection can follow. The orchestration of whole-class discussion and the focused reflection on tasks undertaken are features of effective mathematics classrooms.

A succession of experiences is not the same as an experience of succession

We need layers of tasks, over time, to fully develop each strand of mathematical understanding. Teaching that is rooted in working through procedural textbook tasks will fail to provide this. Specific tasks are required to bring things together. Mixed exercises are useful for discriminating ideas, but not for establishing connections between them.

Tasks need not be written down

A task is any invitation to engage in mathematical thought or action. Teachers regularly engage in spontaneous task design, mid-lesson, every time they pose a question. Having awareness of task design principles and being sensitised to pupil thinking allows us to create new tasks 'off the cuff' in order to be responsive.

The impact of tasks

It is not easy to measure the impact of a task. There are far too many variables at play in a classroom. Teachers, classroom culture and pupils' existing attitudes and understanding complicate the picture. However, the evidence supports connectionist approaches and collaborative learning focused on cognitively demanding activity. We must not be fooled by short-term, instantaneous performance. Regurgitation is not learning. Learning is deep and stands the test of time.

Tasks support professional learning

I advise heads of department to spend some collegiate time focused on tasks. Working together on tasks helps us to gain insight into the nature of doing mathematics. It is sometimes nice to work on tasks with which we are not totally comfortable – to develop sensitivity to what pupils feel. Working together on curriculum tasks can bring to light the thinking processes and cognitive demand that will be required of pupils. Discussion of these tasks, and reflection on how they could be or have been used in lessons, can open up the pedagogical choices which exist for all teachers. Practising task design helps teachers to become aware of opportunities for spontaneous task design, but also to become aware of the shortcomings of many commercially-produced resources in fulfilling the requirements of a rich mathematical diet.

Final thoughts

In this book, I have offered a range of perspectives and examples from which I hope you can draw some insight to take into your own practice. Learning and teaching are complicated, so I have resisted any urge to take a reductionist approach. Instead, I have aimed to share various insights and awarenesses around teaching and tasks. I have also tried to avoid ideas from cognitive science and popular phrases such as 'variation theory', hoping to offer some alternative perspectives for busy classroom teachers. There is no unified theory of learning and teaching. Teaching is personal – it is rooted in our own experiences, values and beliefs. I hope the awareness and insights I have shared will help you to develop and refine your own theories and practice.

Similarly, task design has no unified approach. There are many ideas and practical reflections throughout this book which may serve as a basis for your own task design. Most importantly, I encourage you to start writing tasks: the best way to learn the craft is to engage in it. Set yourself a challenge. Choose some idea that is coming up in the next few weeks and try to write three tasks related to it – one procedural, one conceptual and one problem-solving. You might not be impressed with your initial attempts, but remember Malcolm Swan's message: iteration is the key to successful task design. Stick those first attempts in a folder and try again.

Tasks are, as the title of this book states, the bridge between teaching and learning. Teaching needs to take place somehow – it requires a medium, and the most effective medium is mathematical tasks. By engaging with tasks, pupils are able to behave mathematically and to get to grips with mathematical ideas and the connections between them. By communicating through tasks, teachers are able to take an idea which is well-known and understood to them, and transform it into a series of actions; the hope is that these actions will allow someone (the pupil) who does not already know the ideas at hand to make sense of novel information, concepts and techniques. Through designing or refining tasks, teachers are able to experience for themselves (to role play, if you like) what the pupil will go through and, by doing so, to plan pedagogic choices for key moments. By working through mathematical tasks designed by others, teachers keep their own mathematical dispositions honed and maintain a true interest in a subject that they hope to interest young people in. Tasks transform the necessary and important instruction phase, that teachers must supply, into meaning and purpose.

Instruction is not sufficient to be called teaching, because teaching has only occurred if learning has occurred. Tasks bridge this difficult challenge to ensure that a mathematical education educates rather than simply informs.

My own journey now takes me back to school, where I will continue to test out ideas and theorise about my own practice. I hope that reading this book has provoked you, in some way, such that there is a benefit for the pupils you teach.

Bibliography

ACME: Advisory Committee on Mathematics Education (2015) *Beginning teaching: best in class?* Retrieved from ACME: http://www.acme-uk.org/media/33228/beginningteachingbestinclass2015.pdf

Ahmed, A. A. (1987) *Better mathematics: a curriculum development study based on the Low Attainers in Mathematics Project.* London: Her Majesty's Stationery Office.

Anderson, L. M. (1989) Classroom instruction. In Reynolds, M. *Knowledge base for the beginning teacher.* Oxford: Pergamon Press, pp. 1010–1115.

Askew, M. (2015) *Transforming primary mathematics: understanding classroom tasks, tools and talk.* Abingdon: Routledge.

Askew, M., Hodgen, J., Hossain, S. and Bretscher, N. (2010) *Values and variables: mathematics education in high-performing countries.* London: King's College London.

Askew, M., Rhodes, V., Brown, M., Wiliam, D. and David Johnson, D. (1997) *Effective teachers of numeracy: report of a study carried out for the Teacher Training Agency.* London: King's College, University of London.

Askew M. and Wiliam D. (1995) *Recent research in mathematics education 5–16.* London: Her Majesty's Stationery Office.

Back, J., Foster, C., Tomalin, J., Mason, J., Swan, M. and Watson, A. (2012) Tasks and their place in mathematics teaching and learning, part 1. *Mathematics Teaching* 231 pp. 6–8.

Backhouse, J., & Houldsworth, S. (1957). *Pure mathematics: A first course.* London: Longmans.

Banwell, C., Saunders, K. D. and Tahta, D. (1972) *Starting points for teaching mathematics in middle and secondary schools.* Oxford: Oxford University Press.

Barton, C. (2018) *How I wish I'd taught maths.* London: John Catt.

Bills, C., Bills, L., Mason, J. and Watson, A. (2004) *Thinkers: a collection of activities to provoke mathematical thinking.* Derby: Association of Teachers of Mathematics.

Bjork, R. A. (1994) Institutional impediments to effective training. In Druckman, D. D. and Bjork, R. A. (eds.) *Learning, remembering, believing: enhancing human performance.* Washington, DC: National Academy Press, pp. 295–306.

Black P. and Wiliam D. (1998) *Inside the black box: raising standards through classroom assessment.* London: King's College, University of London School of Education.

Blair, A. (date unknown) *Creating a prompt*. Retrieved from Inquiry Maths: http://www.inquirymaths.org/home/creating-prompts

Blair, A. (2020, June 22) *Right-angled triangles inquiry*. Retrieved from Inquiry Maths: http://www.inquirymaths.org/home/geometry-prompts/right-angled-triangles

Brown, A. (1987) Metacognition, executive control, self-regulation, and other more mysterious mechanisms. In Weinert, F. E. and Kluwe, R. H. *Metacognition, motivation, and understanding*. Hillsdale, NJ: Lawrence Erlbaum, pp. 65–116.

Brown, L. and Waddingham, J. (1982) *An addendum to Cockcroft: a response by Avon teachers to the Cockcroft report 'Mathematics Counts'*. County of Avon Resources for Learning Development Unit.

Brown, S. I. and Walter, M. I. (2005) *The art of problem posing*. New York: Psychology Press.

Burkhardt, H. (1990) Specifying a National Curriculum: reflections on the English experience. In Wirszup, I. and Streit, R. *Developments in school mathematics education around the world: Volume 2*. Virginia: National Council of Teachers of Mathematics, pp. 98–108.

Burkhardt, H. (2009) On strategic design. *Educational Designer* 1 (3). Retrieved from http://www.educationaldesigner.org/ed/volume1/issue3 /article9

Burkhardt, H. and Swan, M. (2013) Task design for systemic improvement: principles and frameworks. *Task Design in Mathematics Education*, Proceedings of ICM Study 22, pp. 431–439.

Cardone, T. (2015) *Nix the tricks: a guide to avoiding shortcuts that cut out math concept development*. CreateSpace Independent Publishing Platform.

Carey, S. (1985) *Conceptual change in childhood*. London: The MIT Press.

Christiansen, B. and Walther, G. (1986) Task and activity. In Christiansen B. Howson, A. G. and Otte, M. (eds.) *Perspectives on mathematics education*. Dordrecht: Springer.

Christodoulou, D. (2016) *Making good progress? The future of assessment for learning*. Oxford: Oxford University Press.

Cockcroft, W. H. (1982) *Mathematics counts*. London: Her Majesty's Stationery Office.

Coles, A. and Brown, L. (2016) Task design for ways of working: making distinctions in teaching and learning mathematics. *Journal of Mathematics Teacher Education* 19 pp. 149–168.

Crabbe, D. (2007) Learning opportunities: adding learning value to tasks. *ELT Journal* 61 (2) pp. 117–125.

Cuban, L. (1993) The lure of curricular reform and its pitiful history. *The Phi Delta Kappan* 75 (2) pp. 182–185.

DiMaggio, P. (1997) Culture and cognition. *Annual Review of Sociology* 23 pp. 263–287.

Doyle, W. (1985) *Managing academic tasks in high school science and English classes: background and methods*. Austin, Texas: Research and Development Center for Teacher Education, University of Texas at Austin.

Doyle, W. (1988) Work in mathematics classes: the context of students' thinking during instruction. *Educational Psychologist* 23 (2) pp. 167–180.

Ferreras, A., Kessel, C. and Kim, M. (2015) Mathematics curriculum in Korea. In *Mathematics Curriculum, Teacher Professionalism, and Supporting Policies in Korea and the United States. Summary of a Workshop*. Washington, DC: National Academies Press, pp. 9–22.

Foster, C. (2015 [1]) Expression polygons. *Mathematics Teacher* 109 (1) pp. 62–65.

Foster, C. (2015 [2]) The convergent–divergent model: an opportunity for teacher–learner development through principled task design. *Educational Designer* 2 (8) pp. 1–25.

Foster, C. (2018) Developing mathematical fluency: comparing exercises and rich tasks. *Educational Studies in Mathematics* 97 pp. 121–141.

Foster, C. (2019) The fundamental problem with teaching problem solving. *Mathematics Teaching* 265, pp. 8–10.

Fullan, M. (1997) *Leading in a culture of change*. New Jersey, Jossey-Bass.

Gagné, R. M. (1965) *The conditions of learning and theory of instruction*. New York: Holt, Rinehart & Winston.

Gardiner, T., (2016) *Teaching Mathematics at Secondary Level*. Cambridge, Open Book Publishers. https://www.openbookpublishers.com/product/340

Garon-Carrier, G., Boivin, M., Guay, F., Kovas, Y., Dionne, G., Lemelin, J.-P. and Tremblay, R. E. (2016) Intrinsic motivation and achievement in mathematics in elementary school: a longitudinal investigation of their association. *Child Development* 87 pp. 165–175.

Gauss, C. F. (tr. Clarke, A.) (2009) *Disquisitiones Arithmeticae*. New Haven: Yale University Press.

Gu, L., Huang, R. and Marton, F. (2004) Teaching with variation: a Chinese way of promoting effective mathematics learning. In Lianghuo, F., Ngai-Ying, W., Jinfa, C. and Shiqi, L. (eds.) *How Chinese learn mathematics: perspectives from insiders*. London: World Scientific Publishing Co, pp. 309–347.

Gulikers, J. T., Bastiaens, J. T. and Kirschner, P. A. (2004) A five-dimensional framework for authentic assessment. *Educational Technology Research and Development* 52 (3) pp. 67–86.

Haggarty, L. and Pepin, B. (2002) An investigation of mathematics textbooks and their use in English, French and German classrooms: who gets an opportunity to learn what? *British Educational Research Journal* 28 (4) pp. 567–590.

Hausman, H. and Kornell, N. (2014) Mixing topics while studying does not enhance learning. *Journal of Applied Research in Memory and Cognition* 3 pp. 153–160.

Henningsen, M. and Stein, M. K. (1997) Mathematical tasks and student cognition: classroom-based factors that support and inhibit high-level mathematical thinking and reasoning. *Journal for Research in Mathematics Education* 28 (5) pp. 524–549.

Hewitt, D. (1998) Approaching arithmetic algebraically. *Mathematics Teaching* 163 pp. 19–29.

Hewitt, D. and Francome, T. (2017) *Practising Mathematics*. ATM.

Hiebert, J. C. (1997) Making mathematics problematic: a rejoinder to Prawat and Smith. *Educational Researcher* 26 (2) pp. 24–26.

Hiebert, J. and Carpenter, T. P. (1992) Learning and teaching with understanding. In Grouws, D. (ed.) *Handbook of research on mathematics teaching and learning.* New York: Macmillan, pp. 65–97.

Hodgen, J. and Wiliam, D. (2006) *Mathematics inside the black box: assessment for learning in the mathematics classroom.* London: GL Assessment.

Jacobs, V., Lamb, L. and Philipp, R. (2010) Professional noticing of children's mathematical thinking. *Journal for Research in Mathematics Education* 41 (2) pp. 169–202

Johnston-Wilder, S. and Mason, J. (2004) *Fundamental constructs in mathematics education.* Abingdon: Routledge.

Kalyuga, S. (2005) Implications of levels of learner expertise for instructional methods. *ICLEPS.*

Kalyuga, S. (2007) Expertise reversal effect and its implications for learner-tailored instruction. *Educational Psychology Review* 19 pp. 509–539.

Kaur, B., Wong, L. F. and Chew, C. K. (2018) Mathematical tasks enacted by two competent teachers to facilitate the learning of vectors by grade ten students. In Toh, P. C. and Chua, B. L. *Mathematics instruction: goals, tasks and activities.* Singapore: Association of Mathematics Educators, pp. 49–66.

Kimani, P., Olanoff, D. and Masingila, J. (2016) The locker problem: an open and shut case. *Mathematics Teaching in the Middle School* 22 (3) pp. 144–151.

Komoski, P. K. (1979) How can the evaluation of instructional materials help improve classroom instruction received by handicapped learners? In Heinich, R. *Educating all handicapped children.* New Jersey: Educational Technology Publications, pp. 187–225.

Komoski, P. K. (1985) Instructional materials will not improve until we change the system. *Educational Leadership* 42 (7) pp. 31–37.

La Salle Education. (2020) *Complete mathematics.* Retrieved from Complete Mathematics: https://completemaths.com/

Lappan, G. and Briars, D. (1995) How should mathematics be taught? In Carl, I. M. (ed.) *Seventy-five years of progress: prospects for school mathematics.* Reston, Virginia: National Council of Teachers of Mathematics, pp. 115–156.

Lockhart, P. (2009) *A mathematician's lament: how school cheats us out of our most fascinating and imaginative art form.* New York: Bellevue Literary Press.

Mason, J. (2001) *Researching your own practice: the discipline of noticing.* Abingdon: Routledge.

Mason, J. (2015) Perimeters and areas. *ATM London Branch Meeting.* London: ATM.

Mason, J. and Johnston-Wilder, S. (2006) *Designing and using mathematical tasks.* St Albans: Tarquin.

McCourt, M. (2019) *Teaching for mastery.* London: John Catt.

Mercer N. (2000) *Words and minds: how we use language to think together.* Abingon: Routledge.

Meyer, D. (2012, April 17) *Ten design principles for engaging math tasks.* Retrieved from dy/dan: https://blog.mrmeyer.com/2012/ten-design-principles-for-engaging-math-tasks/

Michaels, S., O'Connor, C. and Resnick, L. B. (2008) Deliberative discourse idealized and realized: accountable talk in the classroom and in civic life. *Studies in Philosophy and Education* 27 pp. 283–297.

Morris, P. (2016, December 20) *Closest to one.* Retrieved from Open Middle: https://www.openmiddle.com/closest-to-one/

NCETM (2016) It stands to reason. *Secondary Magazine 131.*

NCTM (2014) *Students need procedural fluency in mathematics.* Retrieved from NCTM: https://www.nctm.org/News-and-Calendar/News/NCTM-News-Releases/Students-Need-Procedural-Fluency-in-Mathematics/

Neubrand, J. (2006) The TIMSS 1995 and 1999 video studies. In Leung, F. K., Graf, K. D. and Lopez-Real, F. J. *Mathematics education in different cultural traditions: a comparative study of east Asia and the West.* New York: Springer, pp. 290–318.

Nguyen, F. (2013, May 8) *When I let them own the problem.* Retrieved from Finding Ways: http://fawnnguyen.com/let-problem/

Nolin, R. (2006, April 16) *Pennies.* Retrieved from Orlando Sentinel: https://www.orlandosentinel.com/news/os-xpm-2006-04-16-pennies16-story.html

Nunes, T., Bryant, P., Sylva, K. and Rossana Barros, R. (2009) *Development of maths capabilities and confidence in primary school.* Oxford: University of Oxford.

Ollerton, M., Stratton, J. and Watson, A. (2020) Inquisitive about inquiry? Loaded with cognitive load? Part 1. *Mathematics Teaching* 270 pp. 32-36.

Pólya, G. (1957) *How to solve it: a new aspect of mathematical method.* Princeton, NJ: Princeton University Press.

Pólya, G. (1962) *Mathematical discovery: on understanding, learning, and teaching problem solving, Volume I.* London: Wiley.

Pólya, G. (1990) *How to solve it: a new aspect of mathematical method. 2nd edition.* London: Penguin.

Remillard, J. and Heck, D. (2014) Conceptualizing the curriculum enactment process in mathematics education. *ZDM Mathematics Education* 46 pp. 705–718.

Remillard, J. and Taton, J. (2013) Design arcs and in-the-momentdesign decisions. *Research Presession of the Annual Meeting of the National Council of Teachers of Mathematics.* Denver, CO: NCTM.

Renkl, A. and Atkinson, R. K. (2003) Structuring the transition from example study to problem solving in cognitive skill acquisition: a cognitive load perspective. *Educational Psychologist* 38 pp. 15–22.

Resourceaholic website. https://www.resourceaholic.com

Rittle-Johnson, B., Siegler, R. and Alibali, M. (2001) Developing conceptual understanding and procedural skill in mathematics: an iterative process. *Journal of Educational Psychology* 93 (2) pp. 346–362.

Rohrer, D. (2012) Interleaving helps students distinguish among similar concepts. *Educational Psychology Review* 24 pp. 355–367.

Rohrer, D. and Taylor, K. (2006) The effects of overlearning and distributed practise on the retention of mathematics knowledge. *Applied Cognitive Psychology* 20 pp. 1209–1224.

Rohrer, D., Dedrick, R. F. and Stershic, S. (2015) Interleaved practice improves mathematics learning. *Journal of Educational Psychology* 107 pp. 900–908.

Romberg, T. A. and Carpenter, T. P. (1986) Research on teaching and learning mathematics: two disciplines of scientific inquiry. In Wittrock, M. C. (ed.) *Handbook of research on teaching (third edition)*. New York: Macmillan.

Ruthven, K. (1994) Better judgement: rethinking assessment in mathematics education. *Educational Studies in Mathematics* 27 pp. 433–450.

Schoenfeld, A. H. (1985) *Mathematical problem solving*. New York: Academic Press.

Schoenfeld, A. H. (1987) *Cognitive science and mathematics education*. New Jersey: Lawrence Erlbaum Associates.

Schoenfeld, A. H. (1992) Learning to think mathematically: problem solving, metacognition, and sense-making in mathematics. In Grouws, D. *Handbook for research on mathematics teaching and learning*. New York: Macmillan, pp. 334–370.

Schoenfeld, A. H. (2013) Classroom observations in theory and practice. *ZDM Mathematics Education* 45 (4) pp.607–621.

Schoenfeld, A. H. (2014) What makes for powerful classrooms, and how can we support teachers in creating them? A story of research and practice, productively intertwined. *Educational Researcher* 43 (8) pp. 404–412.

Schoenfeld, A. H. (2016) *The teaching for robust understanding (TRU) observation guide for mathematics: a tool for teachers, coaches, administrators, and professional learning communities*. Retrieved from The Teaching for Robust Understanding Project: http://TRUframework.org.

Scottish Government (2016 [1]) *Experiences and outcomes*. Retrieved from Education Scotland: https://education.gov.scot/Documents/numeracy-maths-eo.pdf

Scottish Government. (2016 [2]) *Curriculum for excellence benchmarks*. Retrieved from Education Scotland: https://education.gov.scot/improvement/learning-resources/curriculum-for-excellence-benchmarks/

Scottish Government. (2018) *National numeracy and mathematics progression framework (NNMPF)*. Retrieved from Education Scotland: https://education.gov.scot/improvement/research/national-numeracy-and-mathematics-progression-framework-nnmpf/

Senk, S. L. and Thompson, D. R. (2003) *Standards-based school mathematics curricula: What are they? What do students learn?* London: Routledge.

Shell Centre (1984) *Problems with patterns and numbers*. Nottingham: University of Nottingham.

Shimizu, Y. (1999) Aspects of mathematics teacher education in Japan: focusing on teachers' roles. *Journal of Mathematics Teacher Education* 2 (1) pp. 107–116.

Sugiyama, Y. (2008) *Introduction to elementary mathematics education*. Tokyo: Toyokan Publishing Co.

Silver, E., Behr, M., Post, T. and Lesh, R. (1983) Rational number concepts. In Lesh, R. and Landau, M. (eds.) *Acquisition of mathematics concepts and processes*. New York: Academic Press, pp. 91–125.

Simon, M. A. (1995) Reconstructing mathematics pedagogy from a constructivist perspective. *Journal for Research in Mathematics Education* 26 (2) pp. 114–145.

Singapore Ministry of Education (2012) *Mathematics Syllabus: Primary One to Six.* Curriculum Planning and Development Division.

Skemp, R. R. (1976) Relational understanding and instrumental understanding. *Mathematics Teaching* 77 pp. 20–26.

Skinner, B. F. (1958) Teaching machines. *Science* 128 (3330) pp. 969–977.

Snapper, E. (1979) The three crises in mathematics: logicism, intuitionism and formalism. *Mathematics Magazine* 52 (4) pp. 207–216.

Sowder, L. (1980) Concept and principle learning. In Shumway, R. *Research in mathematics education.* Reston, VA: National Council of Teachers of Mathematics, pp. 244–285.

Stein, M. and Smith, M. (2011) *5 practices for orchestrating productive mathematics discussions.* Reston, Virginia: NCTM

Stein, M., Smith, M., Henningsen, M. and Silver, E. (2009) *Implementing standards-based mathematics instruction: a casebook for professional development, second edition.* New York: Teachers College Press.

Stephens, W. M. and Romberg, T. A. (1982) *Mathematical knowledge and school work: a case study of the teaching of developing mathematical processes (DMP).* Wisconsin: Wisconsin Center for Education Research, University of Wisconsin.

Steward, D. (2011, March 19) *Directed number arithmetic sped up.* Retrieved from Median: https://donsteward.blogspot.com/2011/03/addingsubtracting-directed-numbers.html

Steward, D. (2014, March 25) *Percent Spiders.* Retrieved from Median: https://donsteward.blogspot.com/2014/03/percent-spiders.html

Swan, M. (2005) *Standards unit. Improving learning in mathematics: challenges and strategies.* Nottingham: University of Nottingham.

Swan, M. (2006) *Collaborative learning in mathematics.* Leicester: National Institute of Adult Continuing Education.

Swan, M. and Burkhardt, H. (2012). A designer speaks: designing assessment of performance in mathematics. *Educational Designer* 2 (5) pp. 1–41.

Tahta, D. (1981). Some thoughts arising from the new Nicolet films. *Mathematics Teaching* 94 pp. 25–29.

Takahashi, A. (2016) Recent trends in Japanese mathematics textbooks for elementary grades: supporting teachers to teach mathematics through problem solving. *Universal Journal of Educational Research* 4 (2) pp. 313–319.

Terrace, H. S. (1963) Errorless transfer of a discrimination across two continua. *Journal of the Experimental Analysis of Behaviour* 6 (2) pp. 223–232.

Thomas, J., Jong, C., Fisher, M. and Schack, E. O. (2017) Noticing and knowledge: exploring theoretical connections between professional noticing and mathematical knowledge for teaching. *The Mathematics Educator* 26 (2) pp. 3–25.

Thomsen, B. M. (2017) *Strength in numbers: how computational estimation impacts mathematics achievement of high school students with and without disabilities.* Retrieved from Open Access Dissertations: https://digitalcommons.uri.edu/oa_diss/669

Thorndike, E. (1905) *Elements of psychology.* New York: A. G. Seiler.

van den Kieboom, L. A. (2013) Examining the mathematical knowledge for teaching involved in pre-service teachers' reflections. *Teaching and Teacher Education* 35 pp. 146–156.

Verhulst, F. (2012) Mathematics is the art of giving the same name to different things: an interview with Henri Poincaré. *Nieuw Archief Voor Wiskunde Serie 5* 13 (3) pp. 154–158

Vygotsky, L. S. (1978) *Mind in society: the development of higher psychological processes.* Boston, MA: Harvard University Press.

Wake, G., Swan, M. and Foster, C. (2015) Professional learning through the collaborative design of problem-solving lessons. *Journal of Mathematics Teacher Education* 19 pp. 243–260.

Watson, A. and Mason, J. (1998) *Questions and prompts for mathematical thinking.* Derby: Association of Teachers of Mathematics.

Watson, A. and Mason, J. (2005) *Mathematics as a constructive activity: learners generating examples.* London: Routledge.

Watson, A. and Mason, J. (2006) Seeing an exercise as a single mathematical object: using variation to structure sense-making. *Mathematics thinking and learning* 8 (2) pp. 91–111.

Watson, A. and Ohtani, M. (2015) *Task design in mathematics education.* Switzerland: Springer.

Wertheimer, M. (1959) *Productive thinking.* New York: Harper.

Wikipedia (2020, July 6) *Expertise reversal effect.* Retrieved from Wikipedia: https://en.wikipedia.org/wiki/Expertise_reversal_effect

Yeo, J. B. and Yeap, B. H. (2010) Characterising the cognitive processes in mathematical investigation. *International Journal for Mathematics Teaching and Learning.*

Zhou, Z., Peverly, S. T. and Xin, T. (2006) Knowing and teaching fractions: a cross-cultural study of American and Chinese mathematics teachers. *Contemporary Educational Psychology* 31 (4) pp. 438–457.